NO-CODE AI AGENTS

Build Smart Systems Without Writing a Line of Code

Hayden Van Der Post

Reactive Publishing

CONTENTS

PREFACE

I magine a world where building advanced systems is not limited to expert coders or tech giants—but available at your fingertips, regardless of your technical background. Welcome to No-Code AI Agents: Build Smart Systems Without Writing a Line of Code. This book is your invitation to harness the transformative power of artificial intelligence without the daunting complexities of traditional programming. Whether you're a business leader eager to optimize operations, an innovator excited by emerging technology, or an individual passionate about creating smarter digital solutions, you're about to embark on a journey that will redefine what you thought possible.

Over the past few years, no-code platforms have revolutionized how we approach problem-solving in technology. As barriers to innovation lower, creativity and efficiency flourish, paving the way for a future driven by democratized software development. Here, you'll explore not just the "how," but the "why" behind this sweeping change. From understanding the fundamentals of AI agents, with their reactive, proactive, and hybrid models, to witnessing real-world successes that have redefined industries, this book encapsulates a vibrant ecosystem at the frontier of digital transformation.

Each chapter has been meticulously crafted to build your

expertise step-by-step. We begin by diving into the no-code revolution—where accessibility meets opportunity—and then we demystify the exciting world of AI agents with practical insights into how they work, what they can achieve, and how to overcome common misconceptions. You'll discover how to choose the right platform tailored to your needs, set up your environment, and even build your very first AI agent using intuitive drag-and-drop tools. Advanced features such as natural language processing, image recognition, and predictive analytics are demystified, enabling you to craft personalized and efficient systems.

Yet, our journey is more than technical mastery; it's about fostering a mindset of innovation, ethical responsibility, and continuous learning. We not only cover the nuts and bolts —like robust data management, seamless integrations with existing systems, and maintenance best practices—but also explore how to guard against biases and build trustworthy, sustainable AI solutions. Through real-world case studies and success stories, you'll gain insights into how leaders from various industries have embraced these tools to solve complex challenges and drive significant results.

This book is structured to empower you from day one, offering practical checklists, design templates, and a community-oriented approach for ongoing support. As you turn each page, you'll be walking alongside fellow pioneers who are passionate about making AI accessible to all. Our call to action is simple: dare to innovate, experiment fearlessly, and join the conversation shaping the future of no-code AI agents.

In a time when technology evolves faster than ever, your ability to adapt and innovate is the key to remaining ahead of the curve. With this book as your guide, you're not just learning about artificial intelligence—the world you create with it is only limited by your imagination. Let this be the catalyst that transforms your ideas into intelligent, automated realities without a single line of code.

Welcome to a new era of creation. Welcome to your future.

INTRODUCTION

In today's fast-paced technological landscape, the combination of artificial intelligence and no-code platforms has transformed our approach to problem-solving. This shift enables individuals to create complex systems without traditional programming knowledge, marking a significant democratization of technology. Now, entrepreneurs, marketers, educators, and hobbyists can design AI-driven solutions tailored to their unique needs, leading to profound and far-reaching implications.

Take, for example, a small business owner who once relied on costly developers for simple automation tasks. Now that we have no-code tools, they can now easily craft personalized customer interactions or automate repetitive processes with minimal effort. This newfound accessibility not only encourages experimentation and innovation but also fosters an environment where ideas can flourish—ideas that may have previously been stifled by technical barriers.

The rise of no-code platforms has also unleashed creativity in ways we could hardly imagine. Artists and designers are now using these tools to create interactive installations that respond dynamically to audience engagement. Such projects beautifully blend technology with artistic expression, showcasing how AI can enhance creativity rather than overshadow it. This intersection has given rise to a vibrant community of creators who share insights and collaborate across various disciplines.

Education plays a vital role in this transformation as well. Learning environments are increasingly integrating no-code platforms into their curricula, enabling students from diverse backgrounds to engage with AI concepts early on. By equipping the next generation with these skills, we are nurturing a workforce capable of navigating the complexities of future technological landscapes—where understanding AI will be as fundamental as literacy is today.

However, as we embrace these advancements, it's essential to remain mindful of the ethical considerations they bring. Throughout this book, we will explore the capabilities of no-code AI agents while addressing critical themes around responsible use. How can we ensure fairness and transparency? What measures should be taken to protect data privacy? Tackling these questions will be integral as we venture into uncharted territories.

This introduction sets the stage for our exploration of no-code AI agents—a realm where innovation knows no bounds and every idea can flourish without extensive coding expertise. The pages ahead will equip you with the knowledge and practical tools needed to embark on your own projects. By engaging with this revolution, you will enhance your capabilities while contributing to a future where technology meets everyone's needs—an exciting prospect indeed!

The Rise of No-Code Platforms

The rise of no-code platforms marks a significant milestone in the evolution of technology, transforming the way we create digital solutions. This movement is not just a passing trend; it represents a fundamental shift in how individuals and organizations utilize technology to solve problems and drive innovation. By enabling users from various backgrounds to engage with complex tools, no-code platforms empower individuals who previously felt limited by a lack of programming expertise.

Consider the entrepreneur faced with the daunting task of automating routine processes. In the past, they would have had to navigate the intricate landscape of software development. Now, with no-code solutions, they can effortlessly drag and drop elements to create workflows that streamline operations—all without writing a single line of code. This transition is about more than just efficiency; it's about liberation—the ability to realize ideas without traditional barriers. As these platforms become more widespread, they democratize access to technology, allowing anyone with a vision to turn their concepts into functional systems.

And, the emergence of no-code tools fosters an unprecedented level of creativity and collaboration. Artists, for instance, are leveraging these platforms not only for practical purposes but also as mediums for artistic expression. Through interactive installations or AI-generated art, creators can engage audiences in innovative ways, transforming passive viewers into active participants. This intersection of technology and artistry opens new avenues for innovation where cross-disciplinary projects thrive, bringing together diverse skill sets.

The influence of no-code platforms extends into education as well. Schools and universities are incorporating these tools into their curricula, allowing students to experiment with AI concepts from an early age. This hands-on experience equips them with essential skills that are increasingly vital in a technology-driven workforce. Students learn not just how to use these tools but also how to think critically about the problems they can address—an invaluable combination that prepares them for future challenges.

As we delve deeper into this landscape, it becomes clear that the implications of no-code platforms reach beyond mere convenience or creativity. We must also consider the ethical dimensions surrounding their use. How can we ensure these powerful tools are employed responsibly? With greater access to AI capabilities comes heightened awareness of issues like data privacy and algorithmic bias. It is crucial to not only create effective solutions but also promote equitable practices within these innovations.

Understanding the rise of no-code platforms provides valuable insights into our collective technological future—a future where anyone can contribute solutions tailored to their unique contexts and needs. By demystifying technology and making it accessible, we foster a culture of experimentation that encourages groundbreaking ideas to emerge from unexpected sources.

The growing popularity of no-code tools suggests we are on the brink of a revolution in how we create and interact with technology. It invites us to reimagine what is possible when barriers dissolve and innovation becomes inclusive rather than exclusive. Embracing this change means stepping into a world where creativity knows no bounds—an exhilarating prospect awaiting us all as we navigate this new era together.

Understanding Artificial Intelligence at a High Level

Artificial intelligence (AI) is more than just a trendy term; it represents a transformative force that is reshaping industries and changing the technology landscape. At its essence, AI involves creating systems capable of performing tasks that typically require human intelligence, ranging from simple pattern recognition to complex decision-making. By understanding AI at a fundamental level, we can better appreciate its potential impact on our daily lives and work environments.

To grasp the significance of AI, it is essential to consider its foundational elements: data, algorithms, and computing power. Data acts as the fuel for AI systems; the more data these systems can access, the more effectively they can learn and make predictions. Algorithms, which are sets of rules or instructions, dictate how this data is processed. They guide the system in interpreting information, recognizing patterns, and making decisions. However, even the most advanced algorithms require sufficient computing power to function efficiently. Recent advancements in hardware have significantly enhanced our ability to process vast amounts of data in real time.

A prime example of AI in action is machine learning—a subset where systems learn from data rather than relying solely on explicit programming. Consider recommendation engines used by streaming services like Netflix or Spotify. These engines analyze user behavior—tracking what shows you watch or what songs you listen to—to suggest new content you might enjoy. This personalization relies on algorithms that detect patterns in your habits, ultimately enhancing your experience.

While machine learning stands out as a key aspect of AI, there are other important forms as well. Natural language processing (NLP) enables machines to understand and engage with human language. Applications such as virtual assistants like Siri or Alexa exemplify NLP's capabilities, as they use extensive datasets and sophisticated algorithms to interpret spoken commands and respond appropriately while continuously learning from user interactions.

AI's reach extends into automation as well, optimizing processes across various sectors—from manufacturing to healthcare. Robotic process automation (RPA), for instance, employs AI to handle repetitive tasks such as data entry or invoice processing. By incorporating these intelligent agents into workflows, organizations can boost efficiency and minimize human error, freeing employees to concentrate on higher-value tasks.

However, with great capabilities comes significant responsibility. As we harness the power of AI, it's vital to address ethical considerations surrounding its use. Issues like algorithmic bias and privacy concerns deserve careful attention. For example, an AI trained on biased historical hiring patterns may perpetuate those biases in future hiring decisions. Tackling these challenges necessitates transparency in how AI systems are developed and deployed.

Where X meets Y AI and no-code platforms illustrates how democratization can change technology usage. No-code tools empower users without technical backgrounds to harness AI capabilities effectively. This shift opens new avenues for problem-solving across diverse fields; entrepreneurs can now create chatbots for customer service or develop predictive models for sales forecasts without requiring extensive programming expertise.

As we delve deeper into these possibilities, it's crucial to remain aware of emerging trends that will shape the future landscape of artificial intelligence. Future innovations may include greater integration between AI and Internet of Things (IoT) devices or advancements in deep learning techniques that allow machines to learn from unstructured data—such as images or videos—more adeptly.

By viewing artificial intelligence from this broader perspective, we establish a framework for understanding its potential societal impact—an influence that continues to evolve rapidly with technological advancements and new applications emerging daily. This exploration into the world of AI not only equips us with knowledge but also encourages us to engage thoughtfully with the tools that will shape our interactions with technology and one another in the future.

The Power of AI Agents for Businesses and Individuals

AI agents are more than just a trend; they signify a fundamental shift in how individuals and businesses operate.

These intelligent systems can automate tasks, analyze extensive datasets, and make informed decisions—all while working tirelessly without the limitations faced by human workers. As we delve into the capabilities of AI agents, it's crucial to understand their diverse roles across various sectors and the transformative benefits they bring.

In the business realm, AI agents act as catalysts for both efficiency and innovation. For example, a retail company might employ AI-driven chatbots to enhance customer service. These bots can manage inquiries around the clock, providing instant answers to questions about product availability or order status. This not only boosts customer satisfaction but also allows human employees to concentrate on more complex issues that require personal attention. The integration of AI in customer service illustrates how automation can improve operational effectiveness while ensuring meaningful engagement with customers.

On a larger scale, businesses harness AI agents for data-driven decision-making. Many organizations struggle with vast datasets that traditional analysis methods find overwhelming. Equipped with machine learning algorithms, AI agents can navigate through this information, uncover trends, and offer actionable insights. Take this example, an e-commerce platform may utilize an AI agent to analyze customer purchasing patterns, enabling the business to optimize its inventory and marketing strategies accordingly. This adaptability allows companies to respond swiftly to market demands, giving them a competitive edge.

Individuals also benefit significantly from AI agents in their daily lives. Personal finance management applications use AI to examine spending habits and propose budgeting strategies tailored to each user's needs. By tracking transactions in real time, these apps can notify users of overspending or highlight saving opportunities—empowering people to take charge of their financial health without requiring advanced financial knowledge.

The educational landscape is also experiencing a transformation due to AI agents that personalize learning experiences for students. Intelligent tutoring systems can adjust content delivery based on individual learning speeds and styles. For example, a student struggling with algebra may receive additional practice problems, while those mastering the concepts are presented with more advanced challenges. This personalized approach not only enhances engagement but also fosters a deeper understanding by catering to diverse learning needs.

The potential applications for AI agents extend even further when integrated into smart home environments. Devices like smart thermostats learn user preferences over time and adjust heating or cooling settings accordingly—creating comfort while optimizing energy use. Similarly, smart speakers can streamline household management through voice commands, enabling users to control everything from music playlists to grocery lists effortlessly.

However, reaping these benefits requires careful consideration of the ethical implications surrounding AI deployment. Businesses must proactively address issues such as data privacy and algorithmic bias—ensuring their AI systems operate transparently and fairly. This is especially critical when developing systems that influence significant life decisions such as hiring practices or loan approvals; biased algorithms could exacerbate existing inequalities rather than alleviate them.

As technology rapidly advances and no-code platforms become more accessible, the barrier for entry into creating effective AI solutions continues to diminish. Individuals without extensive programming backgrounds can now build sophisticated applications using intuitive interfaces that leverage powerful machine learning models. Take this example, an entrepreneur might create an app designed to recommend local events based on user preferences using drag-and-drop tools available on no-code platforms—no coding required.

By embracing this democratization of technology, both businesses and individuals can unlock unprecedented opportunities for innovation across various domains—from healthcare delivery systems powered by predictive analytics to streamlined supply chain management facilitated by intelligent automation tools.

Exploring what makes AI agents so powerful reveals a world full of possibilities that transcend traditional boundaries of work and daily life. Whether you're looking to improve efficiency within your organization or seeking ways to simplify personal tasks, these intelligent systems provide key solutions without necessitating extensive technical expertise or resources.

In this evolving landscape where artificial intelligence meets no-code solutions, adopting these tools becomes not just beneficial but essential for future success—creating an empowering reality where anyone can become an innovator equipped with the resources necessary for meaningful change.

Overview of Book Structure and Objectives

To fully appreciate the framework and objectives of this book, it's important to understand your journey into the realm of no-code AI agents. Each chapter has been thoughtfully designed to build upon your knowledge, guiding you from fundamental concepts to more advanced applications. Our goal extends beyond simply informing you; we aim to inspire action, empowering you to create intelligent systems without the need for traditional coding skills.

We begin with a thorough introduction to no-code platforms, examining their rise in the tech landscape and their potential to democratize software development. This foundational understanding prepares you for a deeper exploration of how these platforms function and why they are crucial in today's digital age. As we delve into key features and advantages, you'll see how these tools can empower individuals and organizations by lowering barriers to entry in technology.

The following chapters explore AI agents in detail. We'll define what they are, categorize their types, and investigate their diverse applications across various industries. Each section will include real-world examples that illustrate how organizations utilize AI agents to enhance efficiency, streamline operations, and drive innovation. Through case studies, you'll gain insight not only into the potential benefits but also into the challenges that may arise without careful implementation and ethical considerations.

Once you've gained a solid understanding of AI agents' capabilities, we'll shift our focus to practical guidance on selecting a no-code platform tailored to your specific goals. You'll discover important factors such as cost, ease of use, integration with existing systems, and community support —each accompanied by examples from popular platforms currently shaping this landscape.

As you move into hands-on applications, you'll identify specific use cases for AI agents that resonate with your context. Whether your goal is enhancing customer engagement or automating repetitive tasks, we'll outline practical strategies alongside detailed walkthroughs utilizing the drag-and-drop tools provided by no-code platforms.

Our exploration continues with advanced features that enhance AI agent capabilities—such as automated decision-making processes and natural language processing functionalities. Real-world examples will help you visualize how these sophisticated components integrate seamlessly across various domains.

Effective data management becomes essential as we address

the preparation of datasets for training purposes. You'll gain insights into cleaning techniques and managing large datasets while receiving recommendations for tools that support data organization—critical elements ensuring your AI agent performs optimally.

A significant focus will also be on customizing agent behavior through personalized rules and algorithms aimed at creating engaging user experiences. You'll explore methods for incorporating personality traits or adapting agents based on real-time interactions—vital aspects that contribute to user satisfaction.

Integration with existing systems is another crucial area we'll cover, revealing strategies for maximizing synergy between your AI solutions and pre-existing infrastructures. Through clear explanations of API integrations and cross-platform data sharing techniques, you'll see how seamless interactions enhance overall functionality.

Next, we'll turn our attention to monitoring systems; here you'll learn how to set up dashboards for tracking performance metrics while quickly diagnosing potential issues when they arise. Effective monitoring frameworks facilitate continuous improvement of your intelligent systems—a necessity for achieving long-term success.

We'll conclude our exploration by addressing user experience enhancements through personalization techniques and UI/UX best practices essential for creating appealing interfaces that resonate with users across diverse demographics. Engaging interfaces directly impact retention rates; improving interaction quality ultimately leads to increased technology adoption.

The ethical implications of AI implementation are equally important; discussions around bias mitigation strategies and transparency emphasize responsible practices when developing technologies that can significantly impact lives—

from hiring decisions to personal finance management apps.

Looking ahead is vital as well; we'll examine scaling opportunities within both individual projects and broader organizational contexts. Navigating challenges while planning strategically ensures future-proofing against the rapidly evolving demands of the tech landscape is achievable.

This overview encapsulates not just the structure but also embodies an actionable mission aimed at empowering you with the tools necessary to transform ideas into reality without extensive technical skills or resources. Throughout this journey lies an invitation—to think creatively about possibilities while remaining grounded in the ethical responsibilities essential for harnessing artificial intelligence's true potential within society today.

Getting Started with No-Code Tools

Navigating the world of no-code tools opens a realm where anyone, regardless of their technical background, can harness the power of artificial intelligence to create intelligent systems. These platforms prioritize user-friendliness, allowing you to focus on your ideas rather than getting bogged down in complex coding languages. Your journey doesn't begin with exhaustive tutorials or intricate scripts; instead, it starts with understanding the landscape and selecting the right tools that meet your specific needs.

Start by exploring the leading no-code platforms available today. Tools like Bubble and Airtable have transformed how individuals approach web and app development, removing barriers that once made these endeavors feel daunting. For example, Bubble allows users to build fully functional web applications without writing a single line of code. You can simply drag and drop elements like buttons, text boxes, and images onto a canvas, configuring their properties through intuitive menus. This approach shifts your focus from development logistics to creating an engaging user experience from day one.

When choosing a no-code platform, consider your specific functionalities. If your primary goal is to automate tasks and workflows within your organization, tools like Zapier might be more beneficial than a comprehensive web development platform. With Zapier, you can set up automated actions between different applications by defining triggers and actions in a straightforward manner. Take this example, if you want to save email attachments directly into cloud storage, Zapier's simple interface makes this an effortless task that enhances efficiency.

Once you've selected the right tool for your needs, configuring your no-code environment becomes essential for maximizing productivity. Begin with initial settings, such as establishing user roles or adjusting security permissions based on who will access the application or system you're building. If you're developing an internal tool for your team while ensuring sensitive data remains protected, granting specific permissions can safeguard that information effectively.

Customization is also crucial in tailoring your project to meet unique requirements. Utilizing features such as user interface design options allows you to enhance functionality while aligning aesthetics with branding guidelines or personal preferences. This level of personalization fosters user engagement and encourages interaction.

API integrations further expand what you can achieve within these platforms. For example, suppose you've built a customer relationship management (CRM) tool using a no-code platform but want it to sync seamlessly with your existing email marketing service. Most leading no-code platforms offer APIs or integrations for popular services like Mailchimp or Salesforce, enabling data flow between systems without manual entry. Many integrations come with guided walkthroughs to help you set them up quickly.

Data management is another critical aspect; preparing datasets for AI agents requires precision and care. Take the time to clean and preprocess any information before inputting it into your systems; this step ensures accurate outputs from your AI models later on. Utilizing built-in tools within platforms can simplify this process significantly —for instance, using Airtable's filtering features allows you to eliminate duplicates before feeding data into an agent's training environment.

Creating feedback loops can enhance agent performance over time; setting up mechanisms for users to share insights directly impacts how agents evolve based on real-world applications rather than hypothetical scenarios envisioned during the initial design phase.

Monitoring performance is also vital; implementing dashboards that visualize metrics enables continuous improvement while allowing for quick diagnosis of any issues that may arise. This reassurance ensures that everything runs smoothly behind the scenes.

Think of all these components as part of a larger ecosystem working harmoniously together—each piece contributes to an overall vision aimed at delivering compelling results without requiring extensive programming knowledge.

diving into no-code tools isn't just about bypassing traditional coding barriers; it's about fostering creativity and innovation through accessible technology solutions that can transform ideas into actionable outcomes swiftly and efficiently. By leveraging these tools effectively alongside sound strategies rooted in best practices—including ethical considerations— you position yourself at the forefront of a revolution reshaping our technological landscape today and beyond.

CHAPTER 1: THE NO-CODE REVOLUTION

Emergence of No-Code in Tech

T he rise of no-code platforms represents a significant evolution in technology, democratizing the application development process. Just a few years ago, creating applications often required navigating complex programming languages, investing countless hours debugging code, and depending on teams of developers. Today, however, individuals from various backgrounds—such as marketers, entrepreneurs, and educators—can craft digital solutions without writing a single line of code.

This transformation reflects a growing belief that innovation should not be limited to those with technical expertise. Companies like Webflow and Glide have led the charge by offering intuitive interfaces that simplify the app-building process. Take this example, Webflow employs a design-first approach that allows users to visually construct websites while ensuring responsiveness across devices. By removing the complexities of coding, these platforms enable users to focus on creativity and user experience—areas where they truly excel.

Businesses have already begun harnessing these tools to enhance workflows and improve customer engagement. Take an educational institution that uses Glide to develop a mobile app connecting students with campus resources and events. In just a few hours, the school can launch an interactive tool tailored specifically for its community —without overburdening IT departments or incurring high development costs.

As no-code tools become more prevalent, understanding their capabilities is essential for maximizing impact. Features like templates offer starting points for various applications —from e-commerce sites to project management tools— allowing users to build on established frameworks rather than starting from scratch. This approach can significantly reduce development time and facilitate quicker iterations based on user feedback.

Another notable advantage of many no-code platforms is their ability to integrate functionalities seamlessly. For example, integrating payment processing through tools like Stripe allows creators to monetize their applications effortlessly. Imagine launching a subscription-based service that grants users access to premium content without worrying about backend complexities; these integrations manage transactions smoothly in the background.

However, ease of use is just one aspect; performance metrics are also crucial in guiding ongoing development efforts. Incorporating analytics into projects helps track user interactions and behaviors, which is essential for optimizing applications for better engagement. Tools like Google Analytics can be embedded within no-code environments, providing valuable insights into how users navigate apps and which features resonate most.

While this accessibility opens up opportunities, it also introduces challenges related to data management and security. As you leverage these platforms for your projects, understanding best practices around data privacy becomes paramount. Many leading no-code solutions offer robust security measures, but it's vital to remain vigilant about how user information is handled within your applications.

The journey into the world of no-code extends beyond building apps; it encompasses continuous improvement driven by feedback loops and user insights. Companies like Zapier exemplify this iterative approach by enabling automation between different apps based on real-time data triggers—an excellent way to enhance efficiency while freeing up time for creative pursuits.

To wrap things up, the emergence of no-code tools has revolutionized technology by opening doors for anyone willing to embrace innovation without being constrained by technical barriers. Each platform offers unique strengths that cater to specific needs—from design flexibility to integration capabilities—creating an ecosystem ripe for exploration and creativity. By leveraging these resources wisely, you position yourself not only as a builder but also as an innovator ready to make meaningful contributions in this rapidly evolving digital landscape.

Democratising Software Development

The rise of no-code platforms has dramatically reshaped the software development landscape, allowing a wider range of individuals to engage in application creation and process automation. This shift democratizes technology access, empowering those without coding skills to transform their ideas into reality. As barriers created by programming languages and technical jargon diminish, innovation becomes more inclusive and accessible.

Platforms like Airtable and Bubble exemplify this transformation in project management and app development. With their intuitive interfaces, these tools enable users to visually manipulate data and build complex workflows with ease. Take this example, a small business owner can develop a customized customer relationship management (CRM) system tailored to their specific needs in less time than it would take to arrange a meeting with a developer. This capability allows individuals not only to conceptualize solutions but also to implement them independently.

Also, this democratization fuels creativity across various sectors. Non-technical professionals are now equipped to tackle unique challenges relevant to their industries. For example, a nonprofit organization can quickly design surveys and gather community feedback using no-code tools like Typeform or Jotform, refining their programs based on real insights without relying on IT support. In this manner, the ability to create applications directly enhances organizational agility.

A key advantage of no-code platforms is their seamless integration with existing tools and services, further streamlining operations. Take Zapier, for example; it empowers users to create automated workflows that link multiple applications without the need for coding. A marketer can easily set up a process that automatically transfers new leads from a web form into their email marketing platform while simultaneously notifying the sales team via Slack—all triggered by straightforward actions that anyone can manage.

This interconnectedness also promotes collaboration within teams. When everyone in an organization—from marketing managers to product designers—can contribute ideas through accessible platforms, innovative solutions often emerge organically. Imagine a product team utilizing Figma alongside Bubble; they can prototype designs while developing functional elements simultaneously, reducing the back-and-forth communication that typically hinders traditional development processes.

However, as we celebrate these advancements, it's important to acknowledge the challenges that accompany them. The simplicity of application creation can lead individuals and organizations into complex issues related to data governance and compliance. Users must remain vigilant in adhering to best practices surrounding security and privacy—particularly when dealing with sensitive information such as customer data or financial transactions.

To navigate these challenges effectively, users should take advantage of available educational resources on responsible no-code technology use. Many platforms offer comprehensive tutorials and community forums where learners can ask questions and share experiences, fostering an environment of collective growth rather than individual struggle.

An inspiring illustration of no-code's potential can be seen in how local governments have adopted these solutions during emergencies such as natural disasters or public health crises. They have swiftly developed apps that inform citizens about evacuation routes or provide updates on health regulations —all without the lengthy bureaucratic delays associated with conventional software development methods.

the democratization facilitated by no-code tools represents a profound shift in our approach to technological problem-solving. It encourages innovation by transforming everyday users into active creators who leverage technology according to their unique visions instead of relying solely on expert developers confined within traditional frameworks.

The possibilities are vast; new ways of thinking arise when everyone has access not only to technology but also to the empowerment that comes with the ability to create meaningful solutions from scratch—without requiring extensive technical expertise. As you contemplate how these tools might fit into your own context, consider not just application building but also how you might drive change within your organization or community by effectively harnessing the power of no-code solutions.

Advantages of No-Code Solutions

No-code solutions are transforming not only the software development landscape but also who can engage in that process. Their true power lies in enabling individuals from diverse backgrounds, even those without coding experience, to bring their ideas to life. This transition goes beyond mere technical advancements; it signifies a fundamental shift in how we approach problem-solving and innovation.

One of the primary benefits of no-code platforms is the significant reduction in time and resources required to develop applications. Traditional software development typically involves extensive planning, coding, testing, and revisions, which can take weeks or months. In contrast, no-code tools like Webflow and Adalo empower users to create fully functional applications in just hours or days. For example, a local restaurant can swiftly launch an online ordering system using a no-code tool rather than waiting for a developer to craft a custom solution. This rapid development not only enhances operational efficiency but also enables businesses to adapt quickly to market changes.

Also, no-code tools cultivate a culture of experimentation. With reduced financial risk associated with development mistakes, organizations can rapidly test new ideas. Take, for instance, a marketing team using Unbounce to experiment with various landing page designs; they can fine-tune their strategies based on real-time data without incurring substantial costs. This environment encourages creativity and innovation—crucial elements for remaining competitive in today's fast-paced marketplace.

In addition to fostering creativity, no-code platforms enhance cross-functional collaboration. When team members from various backgrounds contribute directly to the development process, the resulting solutions tend to be more comprehensive and varied. For example, a healthcare provider could unite doctors, nurses, and administrative staff to create an app tailored to specific patient needs; each participant's perspective enriches the design and functionality, ultimately leading to a product that truly serves its users.

Another significant advantage of no-code solutions is their integration capabilities. Many platforms facilitate seamless connections with existing services, streamlining workflow automation across departments. With tools like Integromat (now Make), users can easily set up intricate automations that link CRM systems with email marketing or social media platforms. Take this example, a sales team can automatically update customer records while triggering follow-up emails based on user actions—all without writing any code.

While these advantages are compelling, it's essential to recognize that the ease of use associated with no-code platforms comes with challenges. As users assume roles traditionally held by developers, there is potential for mismanagement of data and security risks if proper protocols are not observed. Organizations must prioritize training and establish clear guidelines for using these tools—especially when handling sensitive information like client records or financial data.

Educating users about best practices in security and compliance can help mitigate many potential issues. Many platforms offer resources such as webinars and community support forums where users can share knowledge and strategies for responsible tool usage. By fostering an informed user base, organizations can minimize risks while maximizing the innovative potential that no-code solutions provide.

Consider a non-profit organization that harnessed no-code tools during the COVID-19 pandemic to swiftly set up contact tracing applications. This adaptability allowed them to respond effectively to the evolving situation, prioritizing public health without being hindered by bureaucratic delays.

The empowerment offered by no-code platforms marks a paradigm shift in who gets to be a creator and how we collectively address challenges. When individuals possess the tools necessary to turn their visions into reality, barriers dissolve, allowing for new perspectives and solutions once thought unattainable.

As you reflect on your own journey into the world of no-code solutions, think about how these advantages could apply within your organization or personal projects. Consider not only how you might build applications but also how you could cultivate an environment where innovation thrives—one where anyone can engage in meaningful technology creation, regardless of their technical background. The transition from user to creator represents not just an evolution in technology but also a profound shift in our collective mindset toward problem-solving—a move toward democratization that benefits us all.

Common Misconceptions

Misconceptions about no-code platforms are widespread, often arising from a misunderstanding of their true capabilities. One common myth is that no-code equates to limited functionality or an inability to manage complex tasks. In reality, no-code solutions prioritize ease of use while also offering remarkable versatility, capable of supporting intricate workflows and sophisticated applications. For example, a financial institution might utilize a no-code platform like Bubble to develop a robust customer relationship management (CRM) system that integrates complex data analytics—all without the traditional coding requirements.

Another prevalent misunderstanding is the belief that no-code development is only suitable for small projects or startups. This notion overlooks the scalability potential of these tools. Large organizations are increasingly embracing no-code platforms to enhance their operational agility. Companies like GE have effectively employed no-code solutions to streamline internal processes, illustrating that businesses of any size can harness these tools. A notable instance is GE's use of no-code to automate their supply chain management, demonstrating that significant scale and complexity can be managed efficiently without extensive coding.

Additionally, some individuals assume that opting for no-code tools means sacrificing quality for speed, which can deter organizations from adopting this technology. In contrast, many no-code platforms come equipped with templates and best practices designed to ensure high-quality outputs while accelerating the development process. Take this example, Shopify enables e-commerce businesses to quickly launch fully functional online stores without compromising design or user experience. This rapid production capability empowers users to test ideas and iterate on their designs in real-time.

Security is another area fraught with misconceptions. Some may believe that by abstracting away coding, these platforms compromise on security features. However, reputable no-code solutions prioritize user data protection through robust security measures such as encryption and compliance with regulations like GDPR. For example, Airtable offers built-in permission settings and data encryption features, allowing businesses to manage sensitive information securely within a user-friendly interface.

There is also a prevailing notion that adopting no-code solutions will eliminate the need for professional developers entirely. In reality, while no-code empowers non-technical users to create and manage applications, it does not replace developers; rather, it enhances their capabilities. Developers can concentrate on more strategic initiatives while less technical team members handle day-to-day projects using no-code tools. This collaboration creates an environment where technical expertise and creative solutions work together seamlessly.

Educating stakeholders about these misconceptions is vital as organizations consider adopting no-code solutions. By addressing misunderstandings, organizations can foster an informed atmosphere where users feel empowered rather than constrained by perceived limitations. Sharing success stories —such as how the healthcare sector rapidly scaled telehealth services using no-code solutions during the pandemic—can further illustrate the vast potential these tools offer across various industries.

dispelling these myths paves the way for broader acceptance and utilization of no-code platforms. As awareness grows regarding their capabilities and strengths, individuals and organizations can better harness technology's potential to innovate without being hindered by technical barriers.

As you contemplate integrating no-code tools into your workflow or project management strategies, take a moment to reflect on your perceptions of these platforms. Consider how challenging common misconceptions can unlock new avenues for creativity and innovation within your organization— transforming not only how you develop solutions but also who participates in the creation process itself.

Real-World Impact and Case Studies

The transformative power of no-code platforms is increasingly evident across various industries, reshaping not only internal processes but also redefining customer experiences. A notable example can be found in the education sector, where a mid-sized university faced challenges in efficiently managing student applications and enrollment. In response, the institution adopted Airtable, a no-code solution, to develop a comprehensive student management system tailored to its specific needs. By utilizing pre-built templates and customization features, the university streamlined application tracking and automated communications with prospective students. This approach significantly reduced administrative bottlenecks, improved operational efficiency, and enhanced student engagement by providing timely updates throughout the application process.

Similarly, in retail, no-code platforms have revolutionized inventory management systems. A local clothing store leveraged Zoho Creator to create an inventory tracking app that seamlessly integrated with their existing e-commerce platform. This innovation allowed the store's team to monitor stock levels in real time and receive automatic alerts for low inventory. So, the business experienced a significant reduction in stockouts and overstock situations, enabling it to respond more agilely to market demands and seasonal trends without needing an entire tech team for custom development.

Healthcare has also seen a profound impact from no-code tools. During the COVID-19 pandemic, many healthcare providers quickly adopted platforms like Glide to facilitate telehealth services. One prominent telemedicine provider utilized Glide to develop a patient intake app that enabled users to book virtual consultations effortlessly. This implementation took mere days instead of the weeks or months typically associated with software development cycles. By harnessing this tool, they met urgent needs while ensuring compliance with health regulations—showcasing how no-code solutions can effectively bridge gaps during crises.

The nonprofit sector has embraced these platforms as vehicles for empowerment and community engagement as well. Take this example, a nonprofit dedicated to environmental conservation used Bubble to create an interactive platform where community members could report local pollution incidents and track improvement initiatives. Volunteers with minimal technical knowledge could easily submit reports through an intuitive interface while management visualized data trends via dashboards created within Bubble—all without writing any code.

These examples illustrate broader trends where organizations leverage no-code solutions to foster innovation and adapt more flexibly to evolving demands. Often regarded as a strategic advantage in competitive environments, businesses find themselves not just keeping pace but leading initiatives driven by user-centered design approaches and rapid iterations.

As we explore these impactful case studies, it becomes clear that success hinges on understanding specific organizational needs before selecting a platform or tool. Each instance serves as a reminder of the importance of engaging stakeholders during the initial phases of project design—collectively identifying pain points, setting clear objectives, and aligning goals around shared visions of success.

As industries continue navigating this landscape rich with potential, companies are encouraged not only to adopt no-code tools but also to cultivate cultures of experimentation that empower individuals at all levels within their organizations. Encouraging team members—from marketing professionals designing campaigns using simple workflow builders like Zapier—to analysts creating dashboards through Tableau—fosters collective creativity and insight-driven decisions that can accelerate growth trajectories.

The road ahead will undoubtedly feature further advancements in technology designed with accessibility at their core—enabling even those without programming backgrounds to contribute meaningfully while enhancing existing systems across domains. Through real-world examples of innovation driven by no-code solutions combined with proactive stakeholder engagement strategies, organizations stand poised at the forefront of transforming challenges into opportunities for growth—the essence of intelligent adaptation in today's dynamic environment.

No-Code vs. Low-Code vs. Traditional Coding

The landscape of software development has evolved into a broad spectrum, encompassing everything from traditional coding practices to innovative no-code and low-code solutions. Each of these approaches offers distinct advantages, limitations, and use cases that cater to diverse needs across various industries. For organizations aiming to leverage technology effectively, understanding the differences among these methodologies is essential, particularly as they navigate the steep learning curves and resource constraints often associated with traditional programming.

Traditional coding relies on languages such as Java, Python, or C++, requiring developers to have significant technical expertise. This method provides unparalleled flexibility and control over software design, enabling the creation of highly customized solutions tailored to specific organizational needs. However, it can also be time-consuming and resource-intensive; projects may stretch for months or even years before deployment. The high barrier to entry means that only those with programming skills can fully engage in the development process, often sidelining non-technical stakeholders who could contribute valuable insights.

Conversely, no-code development democratizes access to technology by allowing users with little to no programming knowledge to create applications. Platforms like Webflow or Bubble enable individuals to drag and drop elements to quickly build functional applications. This approach significantly reduces time-to-market, facilitating rapid prototyping and iteration based on user feedback. Take this example, a small business could develop a customer relationship management system in just days using a no-code platform, rather than waiting months for a custom-built solution. The accessibility of these tools fosters creativity and innovation across all levels of an organization, creating an environment where ideas can thrive without being stifled by technical constraints.

Low-code platforms serve as a middle ground between traditional coding and no-code solutions. They offer more customization options than no-code counterparts while simplifying many coding processes through visual interfaces. Tools like OutSystems or Mendix allow developers to create applications faster than traditional methods but still require some coding knowledge for more complex functionalities. This approach is particularly beneficial for organizations with existing technical teams looking to enhance productivity while maintaining control over their projects.

Each approach has its role within an organization's strategy. For example, a tech startup may initially rely on traditional coding to establish core product functionalities that require fine-tuning. As the company grows, it might transition towards low-code tools for rapid feature deployment—enabling quick market feedback without overwhelming its engineering team.

Integration capabilities further differentiate these methodologies. Traditional coding facilitates deep integration with legacy systems but often requires extensive custom workarounds that can be costly and time-consuming. In contrast, no-code platforms typically come equipped with built-in integrations for popular services like Google Sheets or Slack, making them appealing for teams seeking to streamline workflows without significant overhead.

However, this ease of use raises concerns regarding scalability and security. Organizations must carefully evaluate whether a no-code or low-code solution can adequately support their growth trajectory in terms of performance and compliance standards. For example, while small businesses might find no-code tools invaluable for managing daily operations, larger enterprises may encounter limitations that hinder their ability to scale effectively across multiple departments.

Real-world scenarios illustrate how various sectors successfully leverage these approaches. In financial services —where regulations are stringent and security is critical —organizations may favor low-code platforms that strike a balance between flexibility and oversight mechanisms, allowing for rapid development without compromising compliance standards. In contrast, creative agencies often excel using no-code solutions for project management tools that require constant updates based on client feedback.

choosing between no-code, low-code, or traditional coding necessitates aligning technology decisions with organizational goals and capabilities. This process involves engaging a diverse group of stakeholders—those familiar with technical intricacies as well as those from operational backgrounds—to cultivate a shared understanding of project objectives and constraints.

Future Trends and Predictions

The future of no-code and low-code platforms is exceptionally bright, fueled by technological advancements and an increasing demand for agile solutions. As businesses recognize the potential of these platforms to democratize technology, emerging trends are set to redefine how organizations develop software and integrate artificial intelligence into their operations. With advancements in AI and machine learning, we can anticipate that no-code tools will become even more sophisticated, allowing users to create complex applications with minimal effort.

One significant trend is the direct incorporation of artificial intelligence features into no-code platforms. This integration empowers users to not only build applications but also enhance them with intelligent functionalities such as predictive analytics, natural language processing, and image recognition—all without requiring a deep understanding of AI technologies. Take this example, consider a small business owner who can easily create a chatbot for their customer service application. By simply dragging and dropping components within a no-code tool equipped with AI capabilities, they can develop a solution that learns from user interactions over time. This accessibility encourages more non-technical users to experiment with AI-driven applications, creating a ripple effect across various industries.

At the same time, we are seeing a growing emphasis on collaboration between technical and non-technical teams. As organizations adopt no-code solutions, the traditional barriers between developers and end-users begin to dissolve. Cross-functional teams become the standard, bringing together diverse perspectives in the application development process. Companies will increasingly seek tools that facilitate this collaborative approach—platforms with intuitive interfaces that allow marketers, designers, and business analysts to contribute directly to development initiatives. For example, marketing teams might leverage no-code tools for campaign automation while IT manages data integration strategies; this synergy fosters innovation that could otherwise be stifled in siloed environments.

Additionally, the rise of cloud-based no-code platforms enhances accessibility for remote teams. As remote work cements its place in various industries, businesses are turning to cloud solutions that can be accessed from anywhere. This trend aligns seamlessly with the principles of no-code development: speed, flexibility, and user empowerment. Remote product teams can collaborate on application design in real time, iterating based on feedback without enduring lengthy development cycles.

However, as companies embrace these new methodologies, concerns about security and compliance remain critical—especially as data privacy regulations tighten globally. The challenge lies in ensuring that no-code solutions maintain robust security frameworks while remaining user-friendly. We can expect emerging platforms to prioritize features such as automated compliance checks or built-in data governance tools designed specifically for non-technical users who may lack security expertise but need assurance that their applications meet regulatory standards.

Another noteworthy trend is the shift toward community-driven innovation within no-code ecosystems. Platforms are increasingly cultivating communities where users can share templates, components, and best practices—creating a rich repository of resources that accelerates learning across diverse skill levels. Users can easily access pre-built elements to expedite their projects or customize solutions based on shared experiences from peers. In this interconnected landscape, knowledge-sharing becomes essential for driving continuous improvement.

Looking ahead, there's a clear trajectory toward integrating emerging technologies like blockchain into no-code development platforms. As businesses seek greater transparency and traceability—especially in supply chain management or financial transactions—the ability to create decentralized applications without extensive coding knowledge will be invaluable. No-code platforms that integrate blockchain functionalities could emerge as game-changers in sectors where trust is paramount.

In summary, the future of no-code tools holds immense potential as they evolve alongside other technological advancements. The seamless integration of AI capabilities will empower users across all skill levels while fostering collaborative environments among diverse teams— a paradigm shift that enhances creativity and innovation. Organizations navigating this landscape must remain vigilant about security challenges while leveraging community-driven insights in their pursuit of operational excellence.

these trends signify a shift toward greater inclusivity in technology development—a democratization that invites everyone into the fold of innovation, regardless of their technical background or available resources. By proactively embracing these changes and aligning with market demands and user needs, organizations can position themselves favorably in an ever-evolving digital landscape.

CHAPTER 2:
UNDERSTANDING
AI AGENTS

What are AI Agents?

AI agents are at the forefront of innovation, serving as automated systems capable of performing tasks autonomously while adapting to user inputs and environmental changes. Imagine an AI agent as a digital assistant that not only comprehends your commands but also learns from each interaction to enhance its performance over time. These agents operate across a wide range of domains, from managing your calendar and providing customer service responses to assisting in complex decision-making processes.

To grasp the essence of AI agents, it's crucial to understand their core components. At the heart of any AI agent is a set of algorithms designed to process data and generate responses. Machine learning techniques enable these agents to analyze patterns within large datasets, allowing them to improve their accuracy and effectiveness with every interaction. For example, a chatbot assisting customers on an e-commerce site learns from past conversations, becoming increasingly skilled at understanding queries and delivering appropriate solutions. This evolution not only reduces response times but also enhances overall user satisfaction.

The operational structure of an AI agent typically comprises three key stages: perception, reasoning, and action. Perception involves gathering information from the environment—this may include user inputs, sensor readings, or other relevant data sources. The reasoning stage evaluates this information to determine possible actions based on established criteria or learned experiences. Finally, during the action phase, the agent interacts with its environment—whether by sending a message, making a recommendation, or executing a task. This three-step framework illustrates how AI agents perform tasks intelligently by leveraging data-driven insights.

Take this example, consider a virtual health assistant designed to help users track their fitness goals. It begins by perceiving data inputs such as daily activity levels and dietary habits through integration with wearables or manual entries. Using this information, it generates personalized suggestions —like adjusting calorie intake or recommending specific workouts tailored to the user's progress. Through continuous interactions, the health assistant evolves, becoming increasingly effective at promoting healthier lifestyles.

However, what makes an AI agent truly effective extends beyond task execution; it also involves adaptability and the quality of user interaction. A successful AI agent must navigate unexpected scenarios—such as ambiguous queries or rare edge cases—while still delivering relevant responses. This adaptability often hinges on natural language processing (NLP) capabilities that allow the agent to grasp context and nuances in human language.

Take customer service AI agents as an example; they are utilized across various industries to provide round-the-clock support. A well-designed customer service agent not only resolves queries but also identifies when a conversation needs to be escalated to a human representative seamlessly. Such functionality is rooted in thorough training on diverse interaction scenarios combined with ongoing learning mechanisms that refine their performance based on feedback.

As we delve deeper into the realm of AI agents, it becomes evident that their applications extend beyond simple tasks; they can evolve into valuable team members within organizations by streamlining workflows and enhancing operational efficiency. In sectors ranging from healthcare to finance, businesses are beginning to implement these systems not only for automation but also for strategic decision-making assistance.

In summary, AI agents represent a shift toward intelligent automation where machines are not just tools but collaborative partners that adapt over time through learning and experience. Their ability to perceive environments, reason through information, and take action opens up new opportunities for enhancing productivity while transforming our interactions with technology in everyday life. Understanding AI agents lays the groundwork for recognizing their immense potential across various sectors—a potential that can be harnessed without requiring deep technical expertise from users themselves.

Types of AI Agents: Reactive, Proactive, and Hybrid

AI agents can be classified into three main types based on their operational characteristics: reactive, proactive, and hybrid agents. Each type offers unique functionalities and applications, enabling organizations to choose the most appropriate agent for their needs. Understanding these categories enhances our grasp of how AI agents operate and underscores their diverse applications across various sectors.

Reactive agents represent the most basic form of AI. They respond to specific stimuli or inputs from their environment without retaining memory or learning from past interactions. A simple example is a chatbot designed to answer frequently asked questions; it analyzes user queries and provides responses based solely on pre-defined rules. This type of agent excels in straightforward tasks where complex reasoning is not required. Take this example, a reactive customer service agent can efficiently address basic inquiries, such as store hours or return policies, delivering accurate information swiftly. While reactive agents may lack adaptability, they thrive in environments where consistent and predictable outputs are crucial.

In contrast, proactive agents can initiate actions based on anticipated user needs or environmental conditions. These agents analyze trends and patterns over time, enabling them to make recommendations or decisions before being explicitly prompted. Take, for example, a virtual shopping assistant that not only helps customers find products but also suggests items based on their past purchases and browsing behaviors. If a customer frequently buys fitness gear, the assistant might proactively recommend new workout apparel or relevant accessories the next time the user logs in. This capability fosters a personalized experience and can significantly enhance customer satisfaction and loyalty.

Hybrid agents combine the strengths of both reactive and proactive capabilities, resulting in a more versatile system. By integrating rule-based responses with learning algorithms, hybrid agents can adapt to user preferences while accurately addressing immediate requests. A prime example is advanced virtual assistants like Siri or Alexa, which not only respond to direct questions but also learn from user interactions to improve future responses. Take this example, if you often ask your assistant for morning weather updates, it may eventually start providing forecasts before you even ask—keeping you informed proactively based on your habits.

The implications of these different agent types are profound for businesses looking to implement AI solutions. Reactive agents may suffice for basic customer support functions where speed and accuracy are paramount. In contrast, proactive agents can elevate user engagement by anticipating needs, potentially leading to higher conversion rates in sales contexts. Hybrid agents exemplify the future of intelligent automation, offering the flexibility and adaptability necessary to meet diverse user requirements across various situations.

Each type of AI agent presents distinct advantages and challenges. Reactive agents deliver simplicity and reliability but may struggle in complex interactions that require nuance and personalization. Proactive agents enhance engagement but rely on more sophisticated algorithms and data management practices for effective operation. Hybrid models strike a balance—offering straightforward task execution while also exhibiting adaptive capabilities.

Choosing the right type of AI agent should align with an organization's goals and customer expectations. As businesses increasingly integrate AI solutions into their operations, comprehending these distinctions becomes essential for maximizing the potential of AI technologies.

By leveraging insights into these agent types, organizations can strategically deploy AI solutions tailored to their specific needs, enhancing efficiency and user satisfaction. This targeted approach not only optimizes operational workflows but also fosters deeper connections with users, driving innovation across industries. the future of AI agents lies not only in their task performance but also in their ability to seamlessly understand and adapt to human behaviors and preferences.

Applications of AI Agents in Various Industries

AI agents have moved beyond theoretical concepts and are now making significant impacts across various industries, fundamentally transforming how businesses operate, engage with customers, and innovate. The applications of these intelligent systems are diverse, each designed to address specific needs and challenges within different sectors. By examining real-world implementations, we can gain a deeper understanding of the substantial influence AI agents have on contemporary business practices.

In healthcare, for example, AI agents are reshaping patient care and streamlining administrative workflows. Virtual health assistants serve as an excellent illustration; they provide preliminary assessments based on patients' reported symptoms. These agents guide users through a series of questions to identify potential health issues before directing them to appropriate healthcare professionals. This approach not only enhances the patient intake process but also reduces the workload for medical staff, enabling them to concentrate on more critical cases. A notable example is the AI platform Ada Health, which employs intelligent algorithms to analyze user inputs and recommend subsequent steps in their healthcare journey. This not only boosts patient engagement but also ensures timely medical assistance.

The education sector is also undergoing significant transformation thanks to AI integration. Adaptive learning platforms utilize intelligent agents to customize educational content to meet individual student needs, adjusting the difficulty based on performance analytics. Take this example, Carnegie Learning's AI-driven tool analyzes students' interactions with math problems and adapts future assignments accordingly. This creates a personalized learning experience that maximizes comprehension and retention while empowering educators with insights into student performance trends, which facilitates more effective instructional strategies.

Similarly, the finance industry has experienced a surge in AI applications designed to enhance customer experiences and streamline decision-making processes. Robo-advisors exemplify this trend by leveraging sophisticated algorithms to offer personalized investment advice tailored to user profiles and market conditions. Wealthfront is one such platform that automates portfolio management and rebalancing, allowing users with limited investment knowledge to benefit from professional financial strategies without needing direct intervention from advisors. This democratization of investment advice reflects a broader movement towards making sophisticated financial services more accessible.

Retail has also embraced this evolution, with AI agents playing a crucial role in enhancing customer experiences and driving sales through personalized recommendations. Companies like Amazon employ recommendation engines powered by machine learning algorithms that analyze browsing history and purchase behavior to suggest products aligned with individual preferences. By anticipating customer needs before they are expressed, retailers can create highly engaging shopping experiences that foster loyalty and encourage repeat business.

In manufacturing, companies are leveraging AI agents for predictive maintenance—a proactive strategy that identifies potential equipment failures before they happen. By integrating sensors with intelligent monitoring systems, organizations can track machine performance in real-time and schedule maintenance only when necessary. This approach not only cuts costs associated with unnecessary repairs but also minimizes production downtime, ultimately boosting efficiency and output.

In logistics, AI agents optimize supply chain management through real-time tracking and predictive analytics. For example, firms like DHL use smart logistics platforms that analyze transport routes and inventory levels driven by AI insights to streamline operations—ensuring timely deliveries while reducing operational costs. Such systems enable businesses to adapt quickly to fluctuating demand patterns or unexpected disruptions.

What ties these diverse applications together is the ability of AI agents to enhance efficiency while personalizing user interactions. However, the deployment of these technologies is not without challenges; data privacy concerns remain a top priority as organizations strive to balance personalization with robust security measures protecting user information.

As industries continue to harness the power of AI agents, it becomes essential for businesses to assess their unique contexts and objectives when integrating these solutions. Understanding how these intelligent systems can specifically address pain points allows organizations not merely to adopt technology but to transform it into a strategic advantage.

This exploration demonstrates that the impact of AI goes well beyond mere automation; it signifies an ongoing transformation in how businesses engage with their customers and optimize their operations. The future promises even more innovative uses as technology advances—each breakthrough paving the way for more efficient processes while fostering deeper connections between organizations and their stakeholders. The potential is limitless; all it requires is a willingness to embrace change and invest in the capabilities that will drive tomorrow's advancements today.

Basic Concepts and Terminologies

To fully understand AI agents, it's essential to grasp the fundamental concepts and terminology that define their operations, applications, and implications. At the heart of this discussion is the AI agent itself—a software system capable of autonomously perceiving its environment and taking actions to achieve specific goals. This autonomy sets AI agents apart from basic automated scripts or systems that require constant human oversight. Their true essence lies in their ability to learn from data and adapt their behaviors over time.

Central to the functionality of AI agents is machine

learning, a key subset of artificial intelligence focused on developing systems that learn from data rather than relying solely on predefined instructions. Within this realm, various approaches exist, notably supervised learning, unsupervised learning, and reinforcement learning.

In supervised learning, algorithms are trained on labeled datasets where the relationships between inputs and outputs are known. This allows them to make predictions or classify new data based on learned patterns. Take this example, email filtering systems utilize supervised learning models to distinguish between spam and legitimate messages by recognizing their common characteristics.

Conversely, unsupervised learning operates on unlabeled data, seeking to identify patterns or groupings without explicit guidance. This approach is essential for clustering similar items; e-commerce platforms often use it to segment customers based on purchasing behavior, facilitating targeted marketing strategies. Lastly, reinforcement learning teaches agents to make decisions through trial and error in dynamic environments. A prime example of this is seen in gaming AI, where agents learn optimal strategies to maximize rewards.

Another vital area within AI is Natural Language Processing (NLP), which enables machines to understand and interact using human language. NLP powers chatbots and virtual assistants like Siri and Alexa, allowing users to communicate naturally without needing technical jargon. These systems analyze text inputs, derive meaning, and generate appropriate responses, making them invaluable for customer service applications.

The effectiveness of AI agents heavily relies on data—the quality and quantity of input data directly influence their performance. Understanding concepts like data preprocessing —the steps taken to clean and format data for analysis— is crucial. This phase may involve addressing missing values, normalizing data scales, or converting categorical variables into numerical formats.

As organizations increasingly integrate AI agents into their operations, ethical considerations become paramount. Issues related to bias in algorithms can lead to unfair outcomes if not properly addressed. For example, facial recognition technologies have faced criticism due to higher misidentification rates among certain demographic groups, underscoring the need for fairness and accountability in AI implementations.

Additionally, the concept of feedback loops is critical when discussing AI agents. These loops facilitate continuous improvement as agents learn from their experiences over time. Practically, this might involve adjusting an agent's parameters based on user interactions or incorporating new datasets for retraining models—ensuring they remain relevant and effective in evolving contexts.

It is also important to distinguish between different types of AI agents: reactive agents respond solely to current situations without memory; proactive agents consider past experiences when making decisions; hybrid agents combine both approaches to enhance adaptability across various environments. Each type offers unique advantages depending on the use case, making it essential for organizations to select the most suitable technology for their needs.

In summary, familiarizing yourself with these foundational concepts lays the groundwork for understanding how AI agents function across diverse industries. Each term intricately connects with real-world applications; as we delve deeper into implementation strategies and tools for building no-code AI solutions, this foundational knowledge will empower you to leverage these powerful technologies effectively. Whether navigating ethical dilemmas or managing data complexities, a solid grasp of these terminologies equips you with the insights necessary for successfully integrating AI into everyday processes.

Capabilities and Limitations

AI agents are equipped with a remarkable array of capabilities that enable them to engage with their environments and perform tasks with increasing sophistication. One of their most significant strengths is the ability to learn and adapt over time. This learning process is powered by various machine learning techniques, which allow agents to identify patterns in data and enhance their performance as they encounter new information.

A key feature of AI agents is automated decision-making. For example, in a customer service context, an AI agent can analyze incoming queries, assess the context, and provide relevant responses without the need for human intervention. Picture an online retail platform utilizing an AI agent to handle customer inquiries about order status or product details. The agent can efficiently navigate large volumes of data, drawing on past interactions to personalize responses and swiftly resolve issues.

The integration of Natural Language Processing (NLP) further amplifies these capabilities by enabling agents to communicate effectively with users. A well-trained NLP model can interpret user inputs—whether spoken or typed—and respond in a way that feels natural. Take this example, in a healthcare application where patients interact with a virtual assistant for symptom checking, the AI agent can comprehend nuanced language, ask clarifying questions, and suggest potential next steps based on the flow of conversation.

Despite these impressive capabilities, AI agents are not without limitations that merit careful consideration. A major challenge lies in their reliance on data quality. If an agent is trained on biased or incomplete datasets, it may produce skewed results that lead to poor decision-making outcomes.

Take this example, hiring algorithms trained on biased historical data can perpetuate systemic discrimination against certain groups.

Additionally, AI agents often struggle with contextual understanding. While they excel at recognizing patterns within structured data, they may falter in ambiguous situations or when confronted with unstructured inputs that lack clear guidelines. For example, if an AI-driven chatbot encounters slang or idiomatic expressions that are outside its training set, it might misinterpret the user's intent, resulting in frustrating interactions.

Another challenge involves generalization, which refers to an agent's ability to apply learned knowledge across different scenarios. Many models perform exceptionally well in controlled environments but encounter difficulties when faced with real-world variability. An autonomous vehicle trained primarily in urban settings may struggle when navigating rural areas or adverse weather conditions—factors not adequately represented in its training data.

Ethical considerations around transparency and explainability also present hurdles for AI deployment. Stakeholders often seek insights into how decisions are made by AI agents, particularly in high-stakes domains like finance or healthcare. If an agent cannot clearly explain its reasoning process, trust may wane among users who are hesitant to rely on automated systems for critical decisions.

To address some of these limitations, integrating feedback mechanisms into AI systems can facilitate continuous learning and improvement. When users provide feedback on the accuracy of responses or recommendations made by an agent, this input becomes invaluable for refining algorithms and enhancing overall performance. Such mechanisms ensure that AI agents remain relevant and capable of adapting to evolving user needs.

understanding both the capabilities and limitations of AI agents equips organizations with the knowledge necessary for effective implementation. This dual perspective fosters realistic expectations regarding what these systems can achieve while highlighting areas that require caution during deployment.

Recognizing these dynamics enables businesses to leverage AI agents strategically—maximizing their benefits while navigating challenges responsibly. As organizations increasingly incorporate these intelligent systems into their everyday operations, maintaining a balanced view of what AI can deliver versus its constraints will be pivotal for achieving successful outcomes across diverse applications.

Data Requirements and Management

AI agents rely heavily on data, which serves as the foundation for their functionality. To fully leverage their capabilities, it's crucial to understand their specific data requirements. The quality and structure of the data significantly impact an AI agent's ability to learn, adapt, and execute tasks effectively. This interplay between data quality and AI performance underscores the importance of implementing strong data management practices.

At the heart of successful AI deployment lies the necessity for clean, high-quality data. Before training an AI agent, organizations must ensure that their datasets are devoid of errors, inconsistencies, and biases. For example, a retail business using an AI agent for sales forecasting could face significant challenges if historical sales data contains inaccuracies—such as incorrect product codes or mislabeled categories. Such errors could lead to misguided inventory decisions and affect overall business performance. Therefore, meticulous attention to data cleaning and validation is essential.

Another vital consideration is data formatting. AI agents

generally perform best with structured data—numerical values organized in rows and columns—because this format facilitates straightforward analysis through algorithms. However, many real-world scenarios involve unstructured data, such as customer feedback in text or images from social media. Converting this unstructured information into a usable format often requires additional preprocessing steps, like applying natural language processing (NLP) techniques for text or image recognition methods for visual content. Take this example, a company might use NLP to analyze sentiment in customer reviews before incorporating these insights into its AI system for trend analysis.

The volume of data also plays a critical role in the training process. Larger datasets usually lead to more effective models since they provide a broader range of examples for the AI agent to learn from. However, managing large volumes of data can pose challenges related to storage and processing power. Organizations need to assess their infrastructure capabilities; cloud-based solutions can offer scalable storage options while delivering the necessary computational resources. Utilizing platforms like Google Cloud or AWS allows businesses to handle extensive amounts of data efficiently without incurring the high costs associated with on-premise systems.

Additionally, effective data management must include robust security measures to protect sensitive information. In regulated sectors such as healthcare or finance, where personal data handling is subject to laws like HIPAA or GDPR, ensuring compliance is vital. Organizations should implement encryption protocols and access controls to safeguard user information against breaches while enabling AI agents to function within legal frameworks.

A clear strategy for ongoing data collection and maintenance is another essential consideration. As environments change and new data emerges, regularly updating datasets ensures that AI agents remain relevant and capable of making informed decisions based on current trends. For example, a travel booking platform may need to continuously refresh its flight availability data to provide accurate recommendations for users seeking optimal travel options.

And, feedback loops are instrumental in refining AI agents over time. User interactions with these systems —whether through customer service inquiries or product recommendations—yield valuable insights that can enhance model accuracy. By systematically collecting user feedback and integrating it into the training process, organizations can improve their agents' learning capabilities while building user trust through visible advancements.

As businesses navigate the complexities surrounding data requirements and management for AI agents, they should adopt a mindset of continuous improvement. Understanding how various types of data interact with different algorithms not only optimizes performance but also fosters innovation in developing smarter systems tailored to specific use cases.

By prioritizing effective data management strategies— ensuring cleanliness and structure while maintaining compliance—organizations position themselves to maximize the benefits of deploying AI agents across diverse applications. Striking a balance between robust practices and innovative solutions cultivates an environment where intelligent systems can flourish in an ever-evolving landscape, ultimately leading to smarter decision-making processes that drive business success.

AI Ethics and Responsible AI Use

The discussion around AI ethics and responsible use has gained significant momentum as technology becomes increasingly integrated into our everyday lives. With AI agents now playing pivotal roles in business operations and daily routines, it is crucial to understand the ethical implications of their deployment. The stakes are high; how we choose to implement these intelligent systems can profoundly impact privacy, fairness, accountability, and societal norms.

At the heart of ethical considerations is transparency—users must grasp how AI agents make decisions. This understanding is especially critical in sectors like finance and healthcare, where automated decisions can have life-altering consequences. For example, an AI system used for credit scoring might inadvertently perpetuate biases inherent in historical data, resulting in unfair lending practices. Therefore, organizations must ensure that their AI models are not only effective but also understandable. By clarifying the reasoning behind an AI agent's recommendations, trust can be built, enabling users to feel secure in its application.

Addressing bias in AI systems is equally essential. Bias can infiltrate AI models through various means; for instance, training data may reflect historical prejudices or exclude certain demographic groups altogether. A notable example is facial recognition technology, which has faced scrutiny for exhibiting higher error rates among minority groups due to inadequate representation in training datasets. Organizations should actively identify and rectify potential biases by diversifying training data and employing algorithms designed to mitigate these issues. Regular audits of AI systems can reveal hidden biases and prompt necessary adjustments.

Privacy concerns are also paramount in the realm of AI ethics. As AI capabilities expand, so does the potential for increased surveillance; thus, establishing clear guidelines on data collection practices becomes vital. Users need reassurance that their personal information will be handled with care and security. Implementing privacy-by-design principles ensures that systems prioritize user consent and confidentiality from the beginning. And, adhering to regulations like GDPR requires meticulous attention to user data management.

As organizations deploy AI agents across various applications

—from customer service chatbots to predictive analytics tools —the need for accountability becomes increasingly clear. When an AI agent malfunctions or produces harmful outcomes, it is essential to establish a clear line of responsibility within the organization. Creating frameworks for accountability fosters a culture of responsible AI usage, where all stakeholders—from developers to executives—are held accountable for their contributions throughout the deployment process.

Beyond internal governance, fostering dialogue about ethical standards among industry peers can help cultivate a broader culture of responsibility. Collaborating with external organizations dedicated to ethical technology can inform best practices while providing insights into emerging trends in responsible AI use.

The landscape of responsible AI is constantly evolving as society confronts these complex challenges. A forward-thinking approach involves not only adhering to current ethical standards but also anticipating future implications as technology rapidly advances. This foresight can drive innovations that align technological progress with societal values.

Establishing feedback loops between users and developers is another effective strategy for maintaining ethical integrity within AI systems. Encouraging user input on their experiences enables organizations to continually refine models while addressing any emerging ethical concerns promptly.

While the journey toward ethically sound AI implementation presents its challenges, prioritizing ethics and responsibility paves a sustainable path forward for leveraging intelligent systems effectively and equitably. By embedding these principles into their operations, organizations can harness the transformative power of AI agents while ensuring they contribute positively to society.

Navigating this intricate landscape requires diligence but offers substantial rewards—trust from users, compliance with legal frameworks, and ultimately a positive impact on the communities served by these technologies. As you explore no-code AI solutions, keeping ethical considerations at the forefront will empower you not only to create smarter systems but also to foster a more equitable future shaped by your innovations.

Success Stories and Failure Lessons

As the landscape of AI continues to evolve, stories of both triumph and setbacks provide invaluable lessons for those venturing into the realm of no-code AI agents. By examining real-world implementations, we can uncover insights that not only highlight best practices but also illuminate potential pitfalls to avoid.

One notable success story comes from a healthcare startup that developed a no-code AI agent to streamline patient appointment scheduling. Their primary goal was to reduce wait times and enhance patient satisfaction. Utilizing a no-code platform, they quickly built an intuitive chatbot that facilitated seamless interactions between patients and clinic staff. The results were impressive: within months, patient no-shows decreased by 30%, and feedback indicated a significant improvement in satisfaction scores. This success was largely attributed to their ability to iterate rapidly based on user feedback—an agile approach made possible by the no-code framework.

However, not all narratives end on a positive note. A contrasting example arises from a retail company that launched an AI-driven recommendation engine using a popular no-code tool. In their haste to bring the product to market, the team overlooked crucial testing and failed to address customer data privacy concerns. When customers learned that their purchase histories were being used to tailor ads without explicit consent, backlash ensued. This incident resulted in significant reputational damage, forcing the company to invest considerable resources in rebuilding trust and rectifying the situation. This case highlights the critical importance of transparency and ethical considerations when deploying AI solutions.

Another instructive example comes from the financial services sector, where an AI agent designed to predict loan defaults encountered a significant flaw due to biased training data. Initially, the model performed well; however, over time it began generating disproportionately high denial rates among certain demographics, leading to public outcry and regulatory scrutiny. This incident underscored that while the no-code approach allows for rapid deployment, it often lacks rigorous checks for data quality and bias mitigation strategies —reinforcing the necessity of thorough data management processes.

The contrast between these stories reveals essential lessons regarding success and failure in implementing no-code AI agents. First and foremost, comprehensive testing is non-negotiable; rushing into deployment without validating functionality can lead to serious consequences. Additionally, actively seeking user feedback throughout the development process—rather than solely after launch—is vital for ensuring alignment with expectations and needs. Lastly, understanding data ethics is not merely advisable; it is essential for sustainable practices.

Reflecting on these experiences reveals common threads: successful projects prioritize stakeholder engagement and iterative design processes while embedding robust ethical standards into their operational fabric. Organizations that foster an environment where learning from failures is valued tend to be better equipped for future endeavors.

Also, establishing metrics for success early in a project can guide teams in effectively measuring performance post-launch. Take this example, if the objective is improved customer engagement through a chatbot interface, tracking metrics such as response times, user satisfaction ratings, and engagement levels will help identify areas needing refinement.

As we analyze these narratives—both positive and negative—it becomes clear that building successful AI agents is not solely about technology; it hinges on understanding users' needs and maintaining a commitment to ethical principles throughout development cycles. Embracing this holistic perspective fosters resilience against challenges while amplifying the potential for success in deploying intelligent systems.

learning from real-world examples enhances our ability to navigate the complexities of no-code AI deployment effectively. By internalizing these lessons—whether through triumphs or missteps—we can better position ourselves as creators of meaningful technology that positively impacts our communities while remaining responsive to ethical imperatives.

Key Components and Architecture

At the heart of any no-code AI platform is its user interface (UI). An intuitive UI accommodates users of varying technical backgrounds, facilitating easy navigation and allowing for effortless visualization of workflows. For example, many platforms feature drag-and-drop functionality, which enables users to organize components logically without requiring programming skills. Imagine creating a customer support chatbot; a straightforward interface lets you arrange elements like message prompts, user inputs, and decision trees in a way that mirrors the natural flow of conversation.

Data management is another crucial aspect of no-code platforms. Since data serves as the lifeblood of any AI system, effective management is vital for optimal agent performance.

Users should be able to seamlessly connect various data sources, whether they are databases, APIs, or spreadsheets. Take this example, integrating a Google Sheets database with your no-code tool provides real-time access to customer information without needing advanced technical expertise. This integration can lay the groundwork for training your AI agent based on historical user interactions.

The architecture of no-code platforms often includes pre-built templates or modules tailored for specific applications. These templates simplify development by offering foundational structures that can be customized to meet your needs. For example, if you are developing an e-commerce recommendation system, starting with a template designed for product suggestions saves both time and effort while ensuring adherence to best practices in design.

Workflow automation is another fundamental feature that enables users to define sequences of actions triggered by specific events. Consider creating an AI agent that automatically sends welcome emails when new customers sign up. Many no-code platforms offer visual workflow editors that make it easy to set conditions—such as "If User signs up, then send Email." This capability not only streamlines processes but also enhances user engagement through timely interactions.

Integrations with third-party services play an equally important role in many successful no-code projects, allowing users to expand functionality without complex coding efforts. Services like Zapier or Integromat enable seamless connections between different applications; for instance, if you want your chatbot not only to respond to queries but also to log interactions automatically in a CRM system like HubSpot, this integration makes it possible without additional coding.

A comprehensive understanding of the architectural

framework also involves recognizing how backend processes operate within these systems. While front-end experiences are crucial for user interaction, back-end processing—where much of the heavy lifting occurs—is equally important for performance optimization. No-code platforms often simplify backend complexities through user-friendly configuration settings while still offering options for custom logic when necessary.

Finally, integrated monitoring and analytics tools empower users to actively track performance metrics after launch. Implementing key performance indicators (KPIs) from the outset clarifies what success looks like—whether that's measuring user engagement levels with chatbots or tracking conversion rates from automated email campaigns.

As we bring together these components—user interfaces, data management strategies, pre-built templates, automation capabilities, third-party integrations, backend processing insights, and monitoring tools—it becomes evident that constructing effective no-code AI agents relies not just on selecting individual features but on understanding how they interconnect within a cohesive framework.

This holistic perspective enables creators not only to deploy functional systems but also encourages continuous improvement based on real-world feedback and performance data—a critical element that fosters growth and enhances overall effectiveness in leveraging no-code solutions for AI development.

Problem-Solving with AI Agents

Problem-solving with AI agents goes beyond understanding their individual capabilities; it involves recognizing how these capabilities can effectively address real-world challenges. At the heart of an AI agent's functionality is its ability to analyze data, learn from patterns, and respond adeptly to various situations. As we delve into the ways these agents can tackle problems, it's important to focus on designing systems that are both adaptable and efficient.

One area where AI agents truly shine is in automating routine tasks. Take this example, consider customer service: an AI-driven chatbot can manage common inquiries—like order tracking or refund requests—without needing human intervention. Imagine a retail business inundated with hundreds of queries daily. By implementing an AI agent capable of handling these repetitive questions, the company can free its human staff to concentrate on more complex issues that require nuanced understanding and empathy. This not only boosts operational efficiency but also enhances customer satisfaction through faster response times.

Data analysis represents another powerful application of AI agents in solving problems. Businesses generate vast amounts of data, making it difficult to extract actionable insights manually. Here, an AI agent equipped with machine learning capabilities can analyze this data, uncovering trends and anomalies that might otherwise go unnoticed. For example, a health organization collecting patient data across diverse demographics could leverage an AI agent to identify health trends, enabling proactive measures to address potential public health issues before they escalate.

Predictive analytics further exemplifies how AI agents can influence decision-making processes. By analyzing historical data to forecast future outcomes, these agents empower organizations to make informed choices. In finance, for instance, an AI agent might assess market trends and economic indicators to predict stock movements. A financial advisor utilizing such technology can offer clients tailored investment advice based on predictive insights, ultimately enhancing portfolio performance.

The adaptability of AI agents also allows businesses to customize solutions to meet their unique challenges. For example, if a company aims to boost its lead conversion rates, it can design an AI agent that qualifies leads based on predefined criteria while learning from interactions over time. This flexibility ensures the agent improves its understanding of customer behavior and preferences, leading to more effective engagements.

Integrating feedback mechanisms further strengthens the problem-solving capabilities of AI agents. Continuous learning enables these systems to refine their approaches based on user interactions and outcomes. Take a travel booking assistant powered by AI: it could adjust its accommodation suggestions based on past customer preferences, analyzing which features led to higher bookings or positive reviews. This iterative learning process keeps the system relevant and effective as user expectations evolve.

Collaboration among different AI agents can also yield innovative solutions for complex problems. Envision a scenario where separate agents manage various aspects of a supply chain—from inventory management to delivery tracking—communicating seamlessly to optimize operations. This interconnectedness allows businesses to streamline processes and respond dynamically to shifting market conditions or logistical challenges.

We must also consider the ethical implications surrounding the use of AI in problem-solving. As organizations increasingly depend on automated systems for decision-making, ensuring transparency and fairness in these technologies is crucial. Establishing guidelines for ethical use promotes accountability and builds trust with stakeholders who may have concerns about automation's impact on employment or data privacy.

When we integrate these elements—automation of routine tasks, robust data analysis capabilities, predictive analytics, customization options, feedback integration, collaborative frameworks among agents, and ethical considerations—we can see how no-code AI agents significantly enhance problem-solving across various domains.

Each application highlights not only the versatility of these systems but also their potential to drive innovation while effectively addressing real-world challenges. The landscape is ripe for experimentation; as users creatively engage with these tools, they will discover new ways to leverage AI agents in tackling problems once considered too complex or resource-intensive to resolve. This paves the way for a future where intelligent systems are not merely supportive tools but key players in the ongoing evolution of industries worldwide.

CHAPTER 3:
CHOOSING THE
RIGHT NO-CODE
PLATFORM

Key Features to Look for

C hoosing the right no-code platform can have a profound impact on your success in building AI agents. With so many options available, it's crucial to understand the key features that set these platforms apart. Not all no-code solutions are created equal, and knowing what to prioritize can save you time while enhancing your project's effectiveness.

Start by evaluating ease of use. A user-friendly interface is essential, especially if you're new to no-code development. Look for platforms that offer intuitive design elements, such as drag-and-drop functionality, which allow you to create workflows with ease. Take this example, platforms like Bubble and Adalo stand out for providing a seamless experience that enables users to visually construct applications without wrestling with complex coding syntax.

Next, take a closer look at integration capabilities. Your chosen platform should easily connect with various data sources and services, including APIs, databases, and other tools necessary for your AI agents to operate effectively. Opt for platforms that support extensive integrations with popular services like Google Sheets or Zapier, enabling you to leverage existing data while ensuring your AI agent fits into a broader ecosystem.

Another essential aspect to consider is scalability. As your projects evolve, so will your needs. It's vital to select a platform that can grow alongside you—whether in terms of user capacity or additional functionalities. For example, if you start with a simple chatbot but later want to incorporate advanced machine learning capabilities, your platform should accommodate this growth without necessitating a complete overhaul of your existing setup.

Security features also deserve careful attention. In light of growing concerns over data privacy and compliance regulations, ensure the platform adheres to industry standards such as GDPR or CCPA. Robust security measures—including encryption and user authentication—are crucial for protecting sensitive information and maintaining user trust in your AI systems.

Additionally, look into the community and support options each platform offers. An active community can provide invaluable resources such as tutorials, forums, and user-generated content that enhance your learning experience. For example, platforms like Airtable have vibrant communities where users share templates and workflows, making it easier to get started and troubleshoot common issues.

Cost is another important factor to consider. Different platforms come with varying pricing models—some may charge monthly subscriptions while others operate on a pay-per-use basis. Evaluating potential costs against your budget ensures you select a solution that meets your needs without compromising sustainability over time.

Finally, think about the customization options available on the platform. While no-code solutions aim for simplicity, having the ability to tweak settings or add custom logic can significantly enhance flexibility. This is particularly important when developing AI agents tailored to specific use cases or industries.

For example, consider using a platform like Voiceflow to create an interactive voice assistant designed for customer service in a niche market like eco-friendly products. The ability to customize dialogue flows while integrating with existing customer relationship management systems (CRMs) can greatly enhance the relevance and effectiveness of the solution you create.

In summary, selecting the right no-code platform requires careful consideration of several key features: ease of use, integration capabilities, scalability, security measures, community support, cost implications, and customization options. By prioritizing these aspects in your decision-making process, you position yourself not only to build effective AI agents but also to drive innovation within your organization or personal projects. As the landscape continues to evolve rapidly, staying informed about these criteria will empower you to make choices that align with both your current needs and future aspirations in no-code AI development.

Cost Considerations

Cost considerations are crucial in the decision-making process when selecting a no-code platform. Understanding the financial implications of your investment can significantly influence your overall strategy and determine how effectively you can utilize these tools to develop AI agents. With a plethora of platforms available, each featuring distinct pricing structures, being well-informed will help you make a choice that aligns with both your budget and project objectives.

To begin evaluating costs, assess the pricing models various platforms offer. Some adopt a subscription-based approach, charging a fixed monthly or annual fee for access to their features and functionalities. Others utilize a pay-as-you-go model, where fees are based on usage metrics such as API calls or active users. Take this example, platforms like Bubble provide tiered subscriptions that unlock additional capabilities as your needs expand. Familiarizing yourself with these models will enable you to predict expenses according to your anticipated usage patterns.

It's also important to uncover any hidden costs that may accompany platform usage. A low upfront price might initially seem appealing, but extra fees for integrations, premium features, or customer support can quickly add up and strain your budget. To avoid surprises, thoroughly review each platform's pricing page and terms of service for any costs that may not be immediately visible. For example, some platforms impose additional charges for advanced data storage options or for exceeding certain usage thresholds.

Another critical aspect to consider is scalability. While initial expenses may fit within your budget constraints, it's essential to think about how those costs will evolve as your project grows. A platform that appears economical at first glance could become prohibitively expensive if scaling up requires higher-tier plans or add-ons. If you're planning to launch an AI agent that gains traction and attracts thousands of users, ensure the pricing structure can accommodate this growth without causing significant financial strain.

Integration capabilities also indirectly affect costs. If a no-code platform lacks seamless integration with essential tools you currently use—such as CRM systems or data management applications—you may face additional expenses in custom development or third-party services. Selecting a platform with robust integration support from the outset, such as those offering Zapier integrations, can help you minimize potential hurdles and hidden costs down the line.

Evaluating long-term value is equally important in this analysis. Some no-code platforms may require higher upfront investments due to their comprehensive features or exceptional scalability potential; however, their ability to streamline processes and reduce development time can lead to substantial cost savings over time. For example, investing in a comprehensive solution like Airtable could facilitate quicker deployment of AI agents and ultimately lower operational costs by allowing teams to manage workflows more efficiently.

Don't overlook community support when assessing costs either. Platforms with active user communities can provide access to free resources—such as templates, workflows, and troubleshooting forums—that reduce reliance on paid support options. Engaging with these communities can save both time and money while enhancing your skill set through shared knowledge.

While examining cost considerations is vital for making informed choices about no-code platforms, aligning these factors with your project's specific needs will lead to better outcomes. Striking the right balance between affordability and functionality ensures that you choose a platform based on its overall value proposition rather than just its price tag.

To wrap things up, approaching cost considerations with an analytical mindset allows you to navigate the myriad options available in no-code platforms effectively. By focusing on pricing models, hidden costs, scalability potential, integration capabilities, long-term value propositions, and community resources, you'll be well-equipped to make decisions that align with both immediate requirements and future aspirations for your AI projects. Prioritizing these financial aspects not only leads to smarter investments but also positions you to innovate confidently within the evolving landscape of no-code

AI development.

Ease of Use and Learning Curve

Navigating the world of no-code platforms often hinges on user-friendliness and the learning curve associated with each tool. When selecting a no-code platform, ease of use significantly influences how quickly you can develop AI agents and integrate them into your workflows. Thus, understanding a platform's intuitiveness is crucial for maximizing productivity and minimizing frustration.

An important part of user-friendliness is the user interface (UI) design. An intuitive UI enables users of all technical backgrounds to quickly grasp functionalities and start creating without extensive training. Take this example, platforms like Glide and Adalo feature visually appealing drag-and-drop interfaces that simplify application building. Users can see real-time changes to their app as they work, which boosts confidence and accelerates the learning process.

However, an effective UI is just one piece of the puzzle; clear documentation and support are equally important. Comprehensive tutorials, video guides, and well-organized help sections enhance the overall learning experience. Look for platforms that not only offer these resources but also create an environment where users can seek assistance from support teams and community forums. For example, Zapier provides extensive documentation along with a vibrant community where users share tips and workflows. This supportive ecosystem helps learners overcome challenges more quickly than if they were navigating a tool in isolation.

Beyond initial setup, the learning curve tied to mastering a platform is essential for long-term usability. While some tools appear straightforward at first glance, deeper functionalities may require additional skills or knowledge. Consider whether you prefer to gradually scale your capabilities or dive into advanced features from the outset. Platforms that promote incremental learning encourage exploration without overwhelming new users with complexity right away. Take Integromat (now Make), for instance; it offers basic automation options while allowing users to explore more complex scenarios as they become comfortable with the interface.

Customization options also significantly impact ease of use. A flexible platform should adapt to your specific needs without necessitating extensive modifications or complicated workarounds. For example, if you're developing an AI agent for customer service, customizable templates tailored for chatbots can streamline setup considerably. Tools like Tars provide pre-built templates designed for various industries, enabling users to get started quickly rather than starting from scratch.

Additionally, consider how well platforms integrate with your existing tools—seamless interoperability is invaluable. A no-code tool that connects effortlessly with your current systems reduces barriers to implementation and lessens the need for extensive retraining on new processes. Take this example, platforms like Airtable serve not only as powerful databases but also integrate smoothly with services like Slack and Google Drive, facilitating fluid workflows across different applications.

As you evaluate ease of use, take time for hands-on experimentation before making a commitment. Many platforms offer free trials or demo versions that allow potential users to explore functionalities without financial risk. This approach helps you assess how intuitive the interface is and whether it aligns with your preferred working style.

Also consider your learning style when reviewing a platform's educational resources. Some individuals may prefer video demonstrations for specific tasks, while others might benefit more from written documentation. Platforms that cater to diverse learning preferences foster an empowering environment rather than one that feels overwhelming.

prioritizing ease of use goes beyond finding a user-friendly interface; it involves ensuring access to essential resources while fostering an environment conducive to continuous learning and adaptation. This mindset cultivates resilience against challenges encountered while developing sophisticated AI agents.

As you thoughtfully weigh these factors, remember that choosing a no-code platform is an investment of both time and effort. Selecting one that aligns with your skills and expectations will pave the way for successful projects moving forward. Embracing an approachable tool not only enhances creativity but also allows you to bring ideas to life more effectively—an essential aspect in today's rapidly evolving technological landscape.

Integration with Existing Systems

Integrating no-code AI agents with existing systems is a vital step in their deployment journey. For businesses aiming to leverage the capabilities of these intelligent systems, establishing seamless connections with current software and data infrastructures is essential. This integration not only enhances operational efficiency and reduces redundancy but also fosters innovation.

Begin by identifying the existing systems your no-code AI agent will interact with. This could include customer relationship management (CRM) tools, enterprise resource planning (ERP) software, databases, or social media platforms. Each system has its unique data structures and protocols, making it crucial to understand these intricacies. Take this example, when integrating with a CRM like Salesforce, familiarizing yourself with its API documentation can guide you on how to retrieve customer data or update records in real time.

Next, focus on mapping out workflows. Take a moment to analyze how data flows between these systems and where your AI agent fits into this landscape. Creating a visual diagram that outlines key interactions can be immensely helpful. Tools such as Lucidchart or Miro can assist you in designing this flow visually, clarifying integration points while identifying potential bottlenecks early in the process.

Once your workflows are mapped, turn your attention to utilizing APIs and webhooks for integration. Many no-code platforms provide built-in connectors that simplify this task. For example, platforms like Zapier enable you to create automated workflows between applications without writing any code. You can establish triggers based on specific events —like adding a new lead in your CRM—and automate related tasks, such as sending welcome emails or updating records elsewhere.

Imagine your AI agent is designed to manage customer inquiries via chatbots integrated into your website and social media channels. By leveraging APIs from these platforms, your agent can access relevant information from databases while responding contextually based on previous interactions logged in your CRM. This interconnectedness enhances the user experience and improves customer satisfaction.

Data synchronization is another critical aspect to consider. Keeping information accurate and up-to-date across multiple platforms is essential for the effectiveness of any intelligent system. Investigate solutions that provide real-time synchronization capabilities to ensure that updates in one system are reflected across all others instantly. Many modern tools offer this feature natively; however, if custom solutions are necessary, consider using middleware to bridge different software applications.

Security must also be a priority during integration. Ensure

that all data transmitted between systems is encrypted and that robust access controls are in place. Regular audits of your integration points can help identify vulnerabilities before they are exploited. This proactive approach not only protects sensitive information but also builds trust among users interacting with your AI agents.

Finally, it's important to regularly evaluate the performance of your integrated systems. Use analytics tools available within many no-code platforms to monitor the effectiveness of integrations and pinpoint areas for improvement. By keeping an eye on response times and error rates, you can ensure that users enjoy seamless interactions with your AI agents.

By implementing effective integration strategies, businesses can unlock the full potential of their no-code AI agents, transforming them from isolated tools into integral components of an interconnected digital ecosystem that drives growth and innovation forward.

Community and Support

Building a vibrant community around your no-code AI agents is not just advantageous; it's crucial for ongoing support, collaboration, and innovation. As users navigate the development and deployment of intelligent systems, they often encounter challenges that can be alleviated through shared experiences and resources. By establishing a strong support network, you can enhance problem-solving capabilities and inspire creativity in using these powerful tools.

To get started, delve into online forums and social media groups focused on no-code development and AI. Platforms like Reddit, Discord, and LinkedIn host lively communities where individuals exchange tips, pose questions, and showcase their projects. Engaging in these spaces provides access to a wealth of knowledge while also facilitating networking with like-minded individuals. You may discover potential collaborators who can offer fresh perspectives or insights based on their own experiences.

In addition to online communities, participating in webinars or online workshops centered on no-code AI tools is highly beneficial. Many providers offer educational sessions covering everything from basic functionalities to advanced integrations. These events frequently feature industry experts who share best practices, emerging trends, and real-world case studies. Take this example, a workshop might illustrate how a specific tool seamlessly integrates with popular CRM platforms, providing actionable strategies you can implement right away.

Documentation plays a pivotal role in community support as well. While many no-code platforms offer extensive help resources, contributing to or creating user-generated documentation can significantly enhance understanding within the community. Writing tutorials or how-to guides based on your own experiences not only reinforces your knowledge but also assists others in navigating challenges more effectively. Tools like Notion or GitBook are excellent for compiling resources in an organized manner that is easily accessible.

When you encounter specific technical hurdles while building your AI agent, don't hesitate to reach out directly to the platform's customer support team. Most reputable no-code solutions provide multiple support channels—such as live chat, email, or dedicated help centers—to address inquiries ranging from basic usage questions to more complex integration issues. Your proactive engagement can lead to quick resolutions and valuable insights that may not be readily available in community forums.

Fostering camaraderie within your user group can also create an environment ripe for innovation. Organizing local meetups or virtual gatherings allows users to share their projects face-to-face or via video conference, encouraging collaboration on ideas that push the boundaries of what's possible with no-code AI agents. These interactions create opportunities for mentorship; experienced users often find fulfillment in guiding newcomers through their initial learning curves.

As your projects evolve and grow more complex, consider documenting your journey through blogs or video content. Sharing success stories alongside lessons learned from failures resonates with others facing similar challenges. This transparency not only builds trust within the community but also encourages newcomers to take risks, knowing they are supported by shared experiences.

Networking at events such as hackathons focused on no-code solutions can ignite innovative ideas while providing hands-on experience in a collaborative setting. These competitions challenge participants to create functional prototypes under time constraints—stimulating creative thinking and honing skills that might otherwise remain dormant.

Finally, nurturing a culture of feedback is vital for growth within any development-focused community. Regularly seek input on your projects from peers—whether through formal reviews or casual discussions during meetups—and remain open to constructive criticism. This exchange of ideas not only strengthens relationships but also drives individual and collective progress.

By embracing these community-building strategies, you empower yourself not only as a developer but also as part of a larger movement harnessing the potential of no-code AI agents—a collaborative force dedicated to democratizing technology for all involved.

Popular Platforms Overview: Features and Pros/Cons

The landscape of no-code platforms is vast and varied, offering a wide array of options designed to cater to different needs and preferences. Gaining an understanding of the features, advantages, and limitations of popular platforms can significantly enhance your ability to choose the right tool for your projects.

Let's start with Bubble, a highly regarded platform that empowers users to build web applications without any coding knowledge. Its powerful visual editor allows for the design of user interfaces through intuitive drag-and-drop functionality. One of Bubble's standout features is its flexibility; users can create anything from simple websites to complex applications with integrated databases and API connectivity. However, beginners may find the learning curve steep due to the platform's extensive feature set, leading to initial frustration as they strive to grasp its full capabilities.

Next up is Zapier, which automates workflows by connecting various applications through triggers and actions. If your goal is to streamline repetitive tasks across multiple platforms, Zapier excels with its user-friendly interface and thousands of available integrations. Its ease of use and quick setup times make it particularly appealing for those new to no-code solutions. That said, Zapier's automation capabilities can become limited when faced with more intricate scenarios that require conditional logic or advanced data manipulation.

Moving on, Adalo presents another attractive option, especially for mobile app development. Users can craft fully functional apps featuring user authentication and real-time data updates without writing a single line of code. Its intuitive layout encourages creativity while offering customization options through components like lists and forms. However, while Adalo is great for creating minimum viable products (MVPs), some users have reported performance issues when attempting to scale applications beyond basic functionalities.

For those interested in building chatbots or conversational AI agents, Chatbot.com emerges as an accessible choice. This platform enables users to design chat experiences effortlessly using templates and a visual editor specifically tailored for dialogue flows. With built-in AI capabilities supporting natural language processing, interactions feel seamless and intuitive. Nevertheless, users may encounter limitations regarding advanced customization options when compared to more developer-centric frameworks.

Another strong contender is Airtable, often described as a blend between a spreadsheet and a database. Its versatility makes it ideal for organizing data in visually appealing formats while facilitating easy integration with other tools via APIs or automation platforms like Zapier or Make (formerly Integromat). While Airtable simplifies project management tasks, it may not offer the depth required for complex relational database needs that traditional coding could better address.

As you explore these platforms, consider their specific strengths in relation to your own goals and technical comfort level. Each tool presents unique benefits but also comes with trade-offs that could influence your project's outcomes.

In evaluating these popular solutions, pay attention to community engagement surrounding each platform—active communities can provide invaluable resources such as tutorials and troubleshooting advice that enhance your learning experience. Take this example, forums dedicated to Bubble users often contain extensive documentation shared by experienced developers who have navigated similar challenges.

Additionally, consider the support structures offered by each platform. A responsive customer service team can make a significant difference when you encounter obstacles during development phases. Platforms like Adalo have received praise for their dedicated support channels that assist users swiftly with their inquiries.

selecting the right no-code platform involves aligning

your project requirements with each tool's strengths while remaining mindful of potential limitations related to scaling or customization efforts. By thoughtfully considering features against your personal or team capabilities, you will be well-equipped to embark on your no-code journey—transforming ideas into functioning systems smoothly and efficiently.

Comparing Platform Scalability

When considering the scalability of no-code platforms, it's crucial to recognize the subtleties of each option, as these can profoundly influence the success of your project. Scalability extends beyond simply accommodating more users; it involves the ability to adapt to evolving needs in functionality, performance, and integrations. Each no-code platform has its unique approach to scalability, and understanding these differences can significantly inform your decision-making process.

Take Bubble, for instance. Renowned for its capacity to support complex web applications, Bubble offers scalable database management and customizable user interfaces. Users can develop applications that grow in tandem with their user base by tweaking workflows and database structures without needing extensive overhauls. However, navigating these adjustments can be challenging as projects scale up, largely due to Bubble's extensive feature set. While powerful, it often requires a solid grasp of its architecture to optimize performance under increased load.

In contrast, Zapier excels at automating processes across various applications but does come with its own scalability challenges. It allows for seamless integration with thousands of apps via simple triggers and actions; however, a heavy dependence on Zapier for intricate workflows may lead to bottlenecks as your operations expand. For example, if you find yourself chaining multiple Zaps to complete a task, you could encounter delays or limits on task executions within specified timeframes. Thus, while Zapier is excellent for smaller-scale automations, it may become cumbersome as processes grow in complexity.

Adalo**, on the other hand, shines in mobile app development but has raised scalability concerns among users seeking to exceed its foundational functionalities. Creating a minimum viable product (MVP) with Adalo is straightforward and effective; however, developers may face challenges when incorporating advanced features that require enhanced performance or customization. In instances where user engagement surges unexpectedly—such as during promotional events—the platform's limitations in handling increased traffic can become evident.

Similarly, Chatbot.com provides user-friendly tools for building chat interfaces but may struggle to scale efficiently when managing large volumes of interactions simultaneously. Although its templates facilitate quick setup and deployment of conversational bots, ensuring that the underlying infrastructure can handle high traffic without compromising service quality is essential. Users aiming for more extensive bot functionalities might need to balance ease of use with considerations regarding server capacities and load management.

Airtable is another versatile tool for data management that requires careful consideration regarding scalability. As projects increase in complexity—particularly those involving intricate relationships between datasets—Airtable's linear data structure may encounter limitations that traditional relational databases navigate more effectively. Users transitioning from smaller projects to larger initiatives often discover that while Airtable is user-friendly, it may not meet the demands of more sophisticated data manipulation needs.

Understanding these distinctions is vital not only for immediate project success but also for long-term growth potential. If you foresee rapid growth or significant feature expansions in the future, opting for a platform like Bubble, which offers greater scalability features, could be advantageous compared to others that cater primarily to simpler applications.

Engagement within each platform's community often plays a pivotal role in overcoming scalability challenges. Active forums and resource sharing among users provide valuable insights and support during critical moments when scaling becomes necessary or when unexpected issues arise during growth phases.

Support structures are equally important; reliable customer service can accelerate resolutions when scaling challenges occur. Platforms with responsive support teams generally enhance user experience by ensuring assistance is available precisely when it's needed.

selecting a no-code platform based on its scalability involves aligning your anticipated growth trajectory with each tool's capabilities while carefully weighing their individual strengths against potential limitations during expansion efforts. Armed with this knowledge, you'll be better prepared to launch and sustain innovative projects that can adapt seamlessly as demands shift over time.

Security and Compliance

Security and compliance are essential pillars in the deployment of no-code AI solutions. As these tools democratize access to technology, it becomes increasingly important for businesses to understand their security frameworks and compliance requirements. This knowledge allows organizations to harness the potential of no-code solutions without exposing themselves to unnecessary risks.

Data privacy regulations, such as the General Data Protection Regulation (GDPR) and the California Consumer Privacy Act (CCPA), should be a primary consideration. No-code platforms must incorporate features that enable users to manage and protect sensitive information effectively. When using platforms like Airtable or Bubble, it's crucial to examine how they handle data storage, access controls, and user consent mechanisms. Organizations need to ensure that these platforms provide robust compliance support; otherwise, they risk incurring hefty fines and damaging their reputations.

Take Bubble, for example. While this platform allows users to control privacy settings for their applications, developers must actively implement best practices. It's vital to configure data permissions carefully within Bubble's database and workflows, restricting access based on user roles. A common oversight is failing to set these permissions correctly, which could lead to the exposure of sensitive user data.

Next, consider how Zapier manages security within its automation environment. While Zapier connects various apps through workflows, organizations must remain vigilant about the data being transferred between these services. When using Zapier with applications that handle sensitive information, it's essential to understand each service's data protection policies and whether they comply with relevant regulations. Opting for integrations where both the sending and receiving applications have strong security measures in place can significantly reduce the risk of data breaches during automated transfers.

The mobile app development space also introduces additional security considerations, particularly with platforms like Adalo. Although Adalo simplifies mobile application creation, developers need to manually integrate authentication features to protect user accounts from unauthorized access. Implementing measures such as two-factor authentication or single sign-on capabilities is crucial for enhancing security while still taking advantage of Adalo's no-code features.

For chatbots created using Chatbot.com, ensuring secure

interactions is vital, especially since these bots often handle personal customer information. Developers must evaluate how the platform encrypts conversations and stores user data. Compliance with applicable privacy laws is essential when managing user queries and retaining conversation histories.

Similarly, while Airtable provides versatile database management, careful thought around data protection strategies is necessary. Users should employ encryption for sensitive fields and regularly audit sharing permissions across their bases. The simplicity of Airtable can create a false sense of security; therefore, maintaining vigilance about who has access to what information is crucial.

Fostering a culture of security awareness within your organization can significantly enhance compliance efforts. Employees should receive training focused on recognizing potential vulnerabilities associated with no-code tools—such as social engineering attacks targeting application users—and understand how their actions impact overall security posture.

Incorporating third-party audits and assessments can further strengthen compliance measures within your chosen no-code platform. Platforms that voluntarily undergo rigorous testing demonstrate a commitment to security that aligns with industry standards; this commitment should be a key factor in your decision-making process when selecting a platform for your projects.

And, monitoring tools play an integral role in maintaining ongoing compliance after deployment. Implementing analytics dashboards that track user activity can help identify unusual patterns indicative of a breach or misuse of sensitive information—addressing such issues swiftly is essential for upholding trust with users while safeguarding organizational integrity.

prioritizing security and compliance as you navigate the landscape of no-code AI solutions will lay a strong foundation for your projects' success. By understanding how different platforms approach these challenges, you can mitigate risks and unlock greater value from your investments, fostering trust among users who engage with your AI-driven systems.

Testing and Evaluation Methods

Testing and evaluation methods are essential for ensuring that no-code AI agents operate as intended. While these platforms simplify the development of intelligent systems, they do not eliminate the need for thorough testing. The effectiveness of AI agents depends on a clear understanding of their capabilities, the identification of potential issues, and the validation of their performance against defined requirements.

Begin by establishing clear objectives for your AI agent. What specific tasks should it perform? Take this example, if you're creating a customer service chatbot using a platform like Chatbot.com, specify the expected interactions, such as responding to frequently asked questions or addressing complaints. By defining these benchmarks early on, you can guide your testing process and accurately measure success.

With your objectives in place, develop a detailed test plan that outlines various testing phases: unit testing, integration testing, and user acceptance testing (UAT). Unit testing focuses on individual components of your AI agent—such as response accuracy or data retrieval methods—ensuring that each part functions correctly before they are integrated into the larger system. For example, if your agent is designed to fetch order statuses from a database, verify its ability to retrieve this information accurately under various conditions.

Next comes integration testing, which assesses how well the individual components work together. Suppose you've created a multi-step workflow in Zapier that involves pulling data from an online form and sending automated email responses. Testing this entire flow is crucial to confirm that data transfers seamlessly between services and triggers the intended actions.

Any failure points identified during this phase should be addressed immediately to ensure smooth operation.

User acceptance testing plays a critical role in validating that the final product meets user needs. Gather a group of target users to interact with your AI agent in real-world scenarios and collect feedback on usability and performance. This step provides valuable insights into any necessary modifications before full deployment. Engaging users early not only refines the system but also fosters a sense of ownership among potential end-users.

In addition to user feedback, incorporate performance metrics into your evaluation process. Tools like Google Analytics can track user interactions with your AI agent, providing valuable data on engagement levels and identifying areas for improvement. For example, if users consistently drop off during a specific interaction flow within your chatbot, analyze the reasons—perhaps the responses are unclear or the conversation takes unexpected turns.

A/B testing can further enhance your understanding of user preferences. By creating variations of responses or workflows within your no-code solution—such as different greeting messages or follow-up questions—you can determine which options yield better engagement rates. This method enables data-driven decisions rather than relying on assumptions about what users might prefer.

It's also important to monitor long-term performance after launch. Establish key performance indicators (KPIs) relevant to your objectives—like response time or accuracy rate—and set up alerts to notify you of any significant deviations from expected behavior as users begin interacting with your AI agent at scale.

Documentation is equally vital throughout this process. Keep thorough records of test results, feedback from UAT, and any adjustments made based on evaluations. This documentation serves multiple purposes: it provides transparency for stakeholders and creates a reference point for future iterations of your AI project.

As you navigate through testing and evaluation, adopt an iterative mindset. The first version of your no-code AI agent may not be perfect; using feedback constructively fosters continuous improvement. Iteration isn't just about fixing bugs; it's also about enhancing functionality based on real-world usage patterns—this is where true innovation happens.

By incorporating these testing and evaluation methods into your development process, you can ensure that your no-code AI agents deliver effective value while meeting user expectations and operational standards. rigorous testing lays the foundation for successful implementation and builds confidence in deploying intelligent systems across various applications.

CHAPTER 4: SETTING UP YOUR NO-CODE ENVIRONMENT

Initial Configuration and Settings

S etting the stage for your no-code AI project begins with the critical initial configuration and settings of your chosen platform. This foundational step can significantly influence the smooth progression of your entire project. Start by exploring the platform's dashboard, where you'll encounter various settings that require your careful attention. Rather than viewing this as a mere checklist, approach it as an opportunity to customize your environment to align with your project's specific needs.

Begin by defining user roles and permissions. Every no-code platform offers options for determining who has access to which features. Take this example, if you're using a tool like Airtable, it's essential to clearly delineate roles—designers may need different access levels compared to developers or stakeholders. By addressing these settings early on, you can ensure sensitive data is protected while enabling effective collaboration among team members without unnecessary barriers.

Once user roles are established, turn your attention to configuring your data sources. If your AI agent relies on external databases or APIs, establishing these connections at the outset is crucial. For example, if you're integrating Google Sheets as a data source for an AI-driven analytics dashboard, navigate to the integrations section of your platform and follow the prompts to securely link your Google account. It's wise to test this connection immediately; a well-configured setup allows for seamless real-time data retrieval.

With user roles and data sources in place, shift your focus to customizing the interface of your no-code tool. An intuitive interface significantly enhances usability. Whether you're designing a customer-facing chatbot or an internal process automation tool, consider how users will interact with it. In platforms like Webflow, drag-and-drop features enable you to create a visually appealing layout without any coding knowledge. Experiment with various elements until the design feels just right—this is where form meets function.

After addressing aesthetics, delve into workflow automation settings. Most no-code platforms feature visual flow editors that allow you to map out processes graphically. Take this example, when building an order processing system with Bubble.io, visually lay out each step—from receiving an order to sending confirmation emails—within the workflow editor. Ensure that each node clearly reflects an action or decision point based on the logic you've established.

Next, consider notification settings. Keeping users informed is paramount, especially if your AI agent serves customers. Configure alerts so users are notified when their queries have been addressed or when new features become available. Integrating platforms like Slack can facilitate real-time notifications, ensuring communication remains fluid across all touchpoints.

As you progress through these configurations, remember that testing should be an ongoing process rather than a one-time task. After establishing connections with external databases or configuring workflows, conduct preliminary tests to verify functionality. This might involve checking whether inputs correctly trigger responses in a chatbot setup or validating data integrity in automated report generation.

Don't overlook privacy and compliance settings during this initial configuration phase—especially if you're handling personal data under regulations like GDPR. Familiarize yourself with the privacy features offered by your chosen platform; many provide templates for consent forms or automated solutions designed specifically for compliance.

Documentation also plays a vital role at this stage. As configurations evolve through iterations of testing and feedback, maintain detailed records of changes made and the rationale behind those decisions. This transparency not only streamlines future adjustments but also serves as valuable training material for new team members who may join later in the project.

Throughout this initial configuration phase, embrace flexibility and adaptability in your approach. The digital landscape evolves rapidly; being open to making necessary adjustments based on user feedback or emerging best practices is essential for long-term success.

By thoughtfully executing these foundational steps in configuration and settings adjustments, you set yourself up for smoother development ahead—allowing creativity and innovation to flourish within your no-code AI environment while ensuring alignment with user needs and business objectives.

Customizing User Interface

Customizing the user interface of your no-code AI agent is

where your vision truly begins to take shape. This process goes beyond aesthetics; it's about creating an experience that resonates with users, allowing them to engage with your system intuitively and effectively. As you embark on this journey, remember that every design element serves a purpose —contributing to overall functionality and user satisfaction.

Start by assessing your target audience. Understanding who will interact with your AI agent is crucial, as it informs your design choices. For example, if your agent is aimed at tech-savvy users, a sleek, minimalistic interface may be sufficient. In contrast, if your audience includes less experienced users, incorporating guided tutorials or tooltips can significantly enhance usability. This user-centric approach ensures that your interface not only looks appealing but also effectively meets the needs of its users.

Next, consider the layout design. Employing grid systems can create a structured environment that enhances visual harmony and directs user attention to key functionalities. Tools like Figma or Adobe XD allow you to prototype layouts before implementation. Take this example, when designing a dashboard for data insights, prioritize placing critical metrics front and center while ensuring that supporting features remain accessible yet unobtrusive.

The choice of colors and fonts also plays a vital role in user experience. A coherent color palette fosters familiarity and trust, creating a sense of belonging within the platform you've built. Tools like Coolors can help generate aesthetically pleasing color schemes that align with your brand identity. Meanwhile, selecting legible fonts enhances readability and accessibility; consider using sans-serif fonts for body text paired with distinct typefaces for headings.

Interactive elements like buttons and forms require careful consideration as well. Clarity is essential when designing buttons; labels should convey actions without ambiguity—

think "Submit," "Cancel," or "Learn More." For example, if you're creating a feedback form within your AI agent's interface, ensure that the submit button stands out visually while maintaining consistency with the overall design.

Incorporating user feedback mechanisms is crucial for continuous improvement. Simple pop-up surveys or embedded feedback forms can provide valuable insights into what works and what doesn't from the user's perspective. This real-time input helps refine your design based on actual usage rather than assumptions.

Responsive design principles are equally important, especially given the variety of devices users may employ to interact with your AI agent. A responsive layout adjusts seamlessly across screens—from desktops to smartphones—ensuring a consistent experience regardless of access method. Platforms like Bubble.io offer templates optimized for responsiveness, saving time while ensuring high-quality user experiences.

Strategically integrating multimedia elements such as images or videos can significantly enrich user engagement. Thoughtfully placed tutorial videos can demonstrate complex functionalities, alleviating confusion for new users while encouraging exploration of advanced features.

Finally, throughout this customization process, prioritize thorough testing across various devices and diverse user groups before launch. Conducting usability tests will reveal unforeseen challenges or areas for enhancement—perhaps certain buttons are difficult to find on mobile devices or text appears crowded in specific layouts. Gathering this feedback early enables you to make necessary adjustments before unveiling the final product.

In summary, customizing the user interface involves much more than aesthetics; it's about creating an engaging environment that enhances interaction and supports the functionality of your no-code AI agent. By carefully considering user needs, organizing layouts effectively, ensuring interactivity and responsiveness, and incorporating personalization features—all informed by ongoing testing—you'll create an experience that stands out as both effective and enjoyable for its users.

User Roles and Permissions

Creating a robust framework for user roles and permissions in your no-code AI agent is crucial for both security and a seamless user experience. As you embark on this task, you will be establishing an architecture that specifies who can access various functionalities and data, fostering a structured environment that enhances trust and efficiency within your system.

Start by clearly defining the different user roles essential to your application. This begins with understanding the unique needs of each user group. Take this example, administrators typically require comprehensive access to all features for management purposes, while end-users should have limited access focused on their specific tasks. By mapping out these roles early in the development process, you can prevent conflicts that may arise when users attempt actions outside their permissions.

Once you've established the user roles, the next step is to define the permissions associated with each role. A permission matrix—a table detailing what actions each role can perform—can help clarify this structure. For example, an administrator might have the authority to create or delete AI agents, whereas a content creator may only edit existing ones. Many no-code platforms offer built-in tools for managing these permissions visually, making it easy to set up configurations without writing code. Tools like Airtable or AppSheet facilitate this process and enhance user intuitiveness.

In addition, consider implementing conditional access controls. That means certain features or data may only be visible to users based on their role or status. Take this example, support staff could be restricted to viewing user queries relevant to their department while sensitive information remains concealed. These controls not only safeguard sensitive data but also simplify the user interface by reducing unnecessary clutter for different roles.

Next, develop an efficient onboarding process that includes training about users' roles and permissions. It's vital for users to comprehend their capabilities and limitations within the platform. You might create a straightforward onboarding checklist or tutorial within your AI agent that guides users through the functionalities pertinent to their specific roles. This strategy ensures users feel empowered rather than confused about what they can achieve.

Integrating feedback loops into your system is also essential for managing roles and permissions effectively. Encourage users to share insights about their experiences—what aspects they find intuitive and which areas may need clarification. Utilizing tools like Typeform or Google Forms can simplify gathering feedback related to usability issues tied to permissions or access rights. This input will inform refinements and necessary adjustments.

Monitoring user activity is another vital element in maintaining security and optimizing performance within your no-code AI environment. Most platforms provide built-in analytics tools that track user interactions based on their roles, helping identify unusual behaviors that could signal security risks or inefficiencies. For example, if a standard user repeatedly attempts actions typically reserved for administrators, it may indicate a need for improved training or adjustments in permission settings.

And, consider empowering users with self-service capabilities where appropriate. Allowing users to request changes in their permissions through an automated workflow not only gives them more control but also streamlines administrative tasks. No-code tools like Zapier can automate notifications for admin approval, ensuring any adjustments are efficiently logged and managed.

Finally, don't underestimate the importance of regular audits of user roles and permissions as part of your overall maintenance strategy. Over time, team structures may shift or project requirements may evolve, necessitating updates in how roles are defined or what access they require. Scheduling routine reviews every few months ensures that your system remains secure and aligned with current operational needs.

In summary, developing user roles and permissions involves striking a balance between functionality and security within your no-code AI agent. By clearly defining roles, creating detailed permission matrices, implementing conditional access controls, facilitating comprehensive onboarding processes, encouraging feedback loops, monitoring activity patterns, enabling self-service capabilities, and conducting regular audits—you lay a solid foundation for an effective framework that enhances user experience while protecting critical information within your system.

API Integrations

API integrations act as the essential link between your no-code AI agents and external systems, significantly enhancing functionality and broadening the capabilities of your applications. As you enter this crucial phase, think about how these integrations will enable your AI agent to interact with various platforms, retrieving data or delivering results as needed. This integration process is vital; it can greatly elevate the effectiveness of your no-code solutions.

Start by identifying the external systems that can provide valuable data or functionality for your AI agent. Common options include customer relationship management (CRM) platforms, social media networks, e-commerce solutions, and data analytics services. Take this example, if you're developing a customer support AI agent, integrating it with a CRM like Salesforce can allow direct access to customer information, facilitating personalized interactions. This not only enhances the user experience but also streamlines workflows.

Next, familiarize yourself with the APIs of these systems. An API, or Application Programming Interface, consists of a set of rules and protocols for building and interacting with software applications. Most platforms offer comprehensive documentation that explains how to authenticate requests, format data, and handle errors. Gaining a solid understanding of these specifications will empower you to connect your no-code AI agent with external services effectively, minimizing potential roadblocks.

Once you grasp the APIs involved, turn to no-code tools that simplify the integration process. Platforms like Zapier and Integromat are designed to seamlessly connect various applications without requiring any coding skills. For example, with Zapier, you could create a workflow that automatically generates a corresponding entry in your no-code AI database every time a new lead is added to your CRM. This automatic synchronization ensures that your AI agent always operates with the most up-to-date information.

As you integrate APIs, it's crucial to be mindful of data handling practices. Compliance with data privacy regulations such as GDPR is essential when transmitting sensitive user information between systems. Implement secure authentication methods like OAuth 2.0 to safeguard data exchanges and prevent unauthorized access. Clearly communicating how user data will be used is also vital for maintaining trust.

Additionally, consider establishing fallback mechanisms to address potential integration failures. External services may experience downtime or changes in their API endpoints that could disrupt your application's functionality. Designing your no-code AI agent to handle such scenarios gracefully ensures a smooth experience for users. For example, if an API call fails, having predefined responses or alternative actions can help maintain user satisfaction.

Testing is another critical aspect of ensuring successful API integrations. After setting up an integration, rigorously test each connection to confirm that data flows as expected and that any triggers or actions execute correctly. Create test cases that simulate real-world scenarios to identify potential issues early on. This proactive approach allows you to refine integrations before they go live, reducing the likelihood of complications once users begin interacting with the system.

Documentation is also vital for managing API integrations within your no-code environment. Keep clear records detailing how each integration works, including parameters used, error handling procedures, and specific configurations. This not only aids in troubleshooting but also assists team members who may need to modify or expand upon these integrations in the future.

Finally, leverage monitoring tools to track API performance and usage metrics after deployment. Many no-code platforms include built-in analytics features that provide insights into how often integrations are utilized and whether they encounter any errors during operation. Monitoring these metrics enables timely adjustments based on actual usage patterns and can highlight areas where additional training may be needed for users.

Crafting effective API integrations requires attention to detail and foresight but offers immense rewards in terms of functionality and enhanced user experience for your no-code AI agents. By identifying essential external systems, utilizing user-friendly integration platforms, prioritizing data privacy and security protocols, implementing fallback strategies for failures, thoroughly testing connections, maintaining robust documentation, and monitoring performance over time, you create a powerful framework that maximizes the potential of your AI solutions while simplifying interactions across diverse ecosystems.

Incorporating these strategic elements will empower you not only to build intelligent systems but also to ensure their seamless operation within broader digital landscapes—an essential aspect of modern technology applications today.

Managing Data Sources

Data management is the backbone of your no-code AI agent, ensuring it operates efficiently and delivers accurate results. Properly managing data sources not only enhances your AI's functionality but also bolsters its reliability and responsiveness. Consider data sources as the fuel that powers your agent's decision-making capabilities, enabling it to provide insightful interactions.

Start by evaluating the types of data your AI agent will require. This can include structured datasets, such as those in spreadsheets or databases, as well as unstructured data from social media or customer feedback. Take this example, if you're developing a marketing AI agent, gathering historical campaign performance data is vital. This information allows the agent to analyze trends and recommend optimizations based on past successes or failures. Clearly defining your data needs will streamline the setup process and ensure that you collect relevant information.

Once you've pinpointed your data requirements, think about where this information will be stored. Many no-code platforms offer built-in databases or allow connections to external ones like Google Sheets, Airtable, or SQL databases. For example, if you choose Airtable, you'll benefit from its user-friendly interface for managing data through easily created tables. Integrating Airtable with your AI agent enables you to update records effortlessly, track customer interactions, and trigger responses based on specific inputs.

Next, focus on keeping this data fresh and relevant. Establishing a regular update schedule is essential for maintaining accuracy over time. If you're relying on dynamic market research data for an analytics agent, set up automated updates to refresh this information weekly or monthly. Tools like Zapier can facilitate these updates by syncing new entries across platforms without requiring manual intervention.

Another critical aspect is ensuring data quality. Inconsistent or erroneous data can lead to misguided insights and poor decision-making by your AI agent. Implement validation checks at the point of entry to ensure that only accurate information is captured. For example, when users submit feedback through a form linked to your AI agent, use dropdown menus for categories instead of free text fields whenever possible—this minimizes variations in how information is recorded.

With quality assurance in place, consider how you will manage large volumes of incoming data. If you're integrating with a system that generates significant amounts of information—like social media feeds—ensure that your architecture can handle this influx without degrading performance. Cloud storage solutions like AWS S3 can provide scalable options for storing large datasets while maintaining quick and efficient retrieval times.

Data privacy is paramount throughout this process. As you gather sensitive user information—from personal identifiers to payment details—ensure compliance with regulations such as GDPR or CCPA. This involves securing consent for data collection and implementing strong encryption methods during both transmission and storage.

After establishing how you'll collect and manage data, it's crucial to create pathways for utilizing this information within your AI agent's functionality. Design workflows where specific triggers lead to defined actions based on incoming data patterns. For example, if sales figures exceed a predetermined threshold in your database, program the AI to generate alerts for team members or automatically suggest follow-up actions.

Once everything is set up and running smoothly, monitoring and evaluation become essential. Continuously analyze the effectiveness of your data management strategies by reviewing performance metrics regularly. Look at processing error rates or response times from the AI—these insights help identify areas for improvement that can significantly enhance user experience.

Finally, fostering a culture of ongoing learning within your organization can refine how you manage data over time. Encourage team members to share observations about current strategies' effectiveness and brainstorm innovative ways to leverage new datasets as they emerge.

Effectively managing data sources requires diligence but opens doors to enhanced functionality within your no-code AI agents—laying the groundwork for robust interactions that meet user needs while respecting their privacy concerns. By thoughtfully selecting sources, implementing rigorous quality controls, adhering to legal standards, seamlessly integrating workflows, continuously monitoring performance, and collaborating on improvements; you establish an intelligent framework ready to adapt alongside evolving demands in today's fast-paced digital landscape.

Deployment Options

Deploying your no-code AI agent is a critical step that significantly impacts its overall effectiveness and performance. This process involves careful consideration of various deployment options, each designed to address specific operational needs and user expectations. Rather than simply launching a product, think of deployment as orchestrating an experience that integrates smoothly into the environments where users will interact with your agent.

Start by assessing the environment in which your AI agent will operate. Consider whether it will be embedded in a web application, accessible via mobile devices, or integrated into existing software systems. Take this example, if you're developing an AI-driven customer support agent, you might choose to deploy it on your company's website using a chat interface. Tools like Landbot can facilitate straightforward integration of such chatbots without requiring extensive technical expertise.

Next, evaluate the advantages of cloud-based versus on-premises deployment models. Cloud solutions offer flexibility and scalability, typically allowing for easier updates and maintenance while ensuring high availability. If you decide on cloud deployment, services like AWS Lambda or Google Cloud Functions can support a serverless architecture, meaning you won't have to manage any servers yourself. For example, deploying your agent on AWS enables it to automatically scale according to user demand, ensuring optimal performance during peak times.

On the other hand, an on-premises setup may be more suitable for organizations with strict data privacy requirements or compliance regulations. If your AI agent will handle sensitive information—such as financial records or health data—keeping everything on-site can provide additional security assurances. However, this approach often requires more resources for maintenance and may limit scalability compared to cloud solutions.

Another vital aspect of deployment is integrating APIs. APIs allow your AI agent to communicate effectively with other applications and services. If your AI processes customer inquiries from email and social media platforms, ensure it can seamlessly pull data from those sources through well-defined API connections. Platforms like Zapier can help bridge gaps between various services without the need for coding skills, empowering you to create robust workflows that respond dynamically to user interactions.

Once you've established the basic architecture and integration points, prioritize user accessibility. A user-friendly interface is essential; if users find the deployment cumbersome or unintuitive, they may disengage quickly. No-code platforms like Bubble or Wix offer intuitive design capabilities that enable you to create interfaces where users can easily interact with your AI agent.

After deploying your AI agent, monitoring its performance is crucial for ensuring its long-term effectiveness. Set up analytics tools to track user interactions—what questions are frequently asked? Where do users tend to drop off? Tools like Google Analytics or Hotjar can provide valuable insights into user behavior, revealing interaction patterns that inform necessary adjustments or enhancements.

Incorporating continuous improvement into your deployment strategy is also important. Actively seek feedback from users about their experiences with the AI agent and use this information to refine functionalities. Creating mechanisms for easy feedback collection directly within the application ensures you stay aligned with user needs while fostering engagement.

Finally, plan for regular updates post-deployment to keep your AI agent relevant and functional as technology evolves and user expectations change. Schedule periodic reviews of both system performance and content accuracy to maintain high-quality interactions over time.

In summary, deploying a no-code AI agent involves strategic planning across multiple dimensions—from selecting the right environment to ensuring seamless integrations and ongoing enhancements based on user feedback. Each decision not only influences the initial launch but also determines how well the agent adapts in a rapidly changing digital landscape, laying a strong foundation for future success in delivering value through intelligent automation.

Maintenance and Troubleshooting

Maintaining your no-code AI agent is an ongoing commitment that ensures its continued effectiveness and adaptability in today's fast-paced digital landscape. Once deployed, the journey evolves into a cycle of monitoring, troubleshooting, and enhancing. This dynamic process not only helps sustain optimal performance but also aligns your AI agent with changing user needs and technological advancements.

To start, establish a robust monitoring system. This entails selecting the right tools to effectively track performance metrics. Platforms like Datadog or New Relic can provide real-time insights into system performance. These tools alert you to anomalies—such as increased response times or unexpected errors—allowing you to respond promptly and minimize disruptions for users. Regularly reviewing these analytics will uncover patterns, such as peak usage times or frequently asked questions, enabling you to make proactive adjustments.

Post-deployment, integration failures can be a common challenge. When your AI agent interacts with multiple APIs or data sources, changes in these external systems can lead to disruptions. Take this example, if an API that provides customer data experiences downtime, your AI may deliver incomplete or outdated information. To mitigate these risks, establish a process for regularly testing integrations. Create a checklist to periodically verify that all connections function correctly, ensuring seamless communication between your AI agent and other services.

Troubleshooting is particularly crucial when users report issues. Equip your team with a clear protocol for addressing common problems to streamline this process. Document frequently encountered issues along with their solutions in a shared knowledge base. For example, if users struggle to log in to access the AI interface, providing a straightforward guide or video walkthrough can quickly resolve frustrations and enhance user satisfaction.

User feedback is another invaluable resource for maintenance and improvement. Actively seek insights from users about their experiences by incorporating features like pop-up surveys or feedback forms directly within the application interface. By asking targeted questions—such as "What features do you find most useful?" or "What could be improved?"—you gain actionable data that guides your next steps. Engaging users this way fosters a sense of ownership and investment in the evolution of the AI agent.

In addition to gathering user feedback, conducting routine audits of your AI agent's performance and functionality is essential. Schedule regular reviews to assess both user interactions and the underlying algorithms driving your AI's responses. This practice helps identify areas needing retraining or updates based on shifts in user behavior or preferences. If certain queries yield unsatisfactory answers, it may be time to refine your training datasets or adjust the logic behind specific functionalities.

Another critical aspect of maintenance involves ensuring compliance with relevant regulations and standards, especially when handling sensitive data. Regularly review your AI's data practices against applicable laws such as GDPR or HIPAA to avoid potential legal pitfalls. Staying informed about these regulations is crucial not just for compliance but also for building trust with your users.

As technology advances, so should your AI agent's capabilities. Keep abreast of new tools and features offered by no-code platforms that could enhance your existing systems.

Whether incorporating advanced machine learning models or leveraging new integration options, exploring these innovations can keep your AI agent competitive and relevant.

Finally, consider fostering a culture of ongoing learning within your team regarding best practices for managing and improving AI solutions. Encourage members to participate in forums, attend workshops, or engage with communities focused on no-code development and AI technologies. This shared knowledge base empowers individual growth while strengthening your collective capacity to maintain and innovate around your AI systems.

To wrap things up, effective maintenance of a no-code AI agent requires vigilance across multiple fronts—from monitoring performance metrics and troubleshooting issues to actively engaging users for feedback and ensuring compliance with regulatory standards. Each layer of this process builds upon the previous ones, creating a resilient framework that preserves functionality while enhancing user satisfaction and paving the way for continuous improvement in an ever-evolving technological landscape.

Enhancing Performance

Optimizing the performance of your AI agent goes beyond simply increasing its speed; it's about improving its overall efficiency, accuracy, and user experience. Think of this optimization process as tuning a musical instrument—each adjustment contributes to a more harmonious outcome. The effectiveness of your AI agent relies on several factors, including the quality of data, the efficiency of algorithms, and the capabilities of your infrastructure.

A critical starting point is the data that feeds into your AI agent. High-quality, well-structured data significantly enhances the agent's ability to perform its tasks. For example, if you're developing a chatbot to manage customer inquiries, equipping it with a comprehensive dataset containing diverse conversation examples will enable it to grasp nuances and respond appropriately. Regularly revisiting and updating this dataset ensures that the chatbot remains relevant and responsive to emerging queries or trends in customer behavior.

Next, focus on algorithm optimization. Many no-code platforms allow you to adjust algorithms without delving into complex coding. If you're using platforms like Bubble or Airtable that integrate machine learning capabilities, you can modify parameters related to prediction models or even switch between different algorithms based on performance metrics from prior iterations. Take this example, you might transition from a basic regression model to a more advanced neural network when working with complex datasets that require deeper insights.

Infrastructure also plays a vital role in enhancing performance. Assess whether your current setup can accommodate increased demands from your AI agent. Utilizing cloud services such as AWS or Google Cloud can provide scalable solutions that adapt dynamically to your needs. This flexibility means that during peak periods—such as a product launch—the AI agent can access additional resources for processing without compromising speed or response quality.

Monitoring tools are essential for tracking performance metrics over time. Setting up dashboards in platforms like Microsoft Power BI or Google Data Studio allows you to visualize key indicators such as response times and user satisfaction ratings at a glance. By regularly analyzing these metrics, you can identify bottlenecks or underperforming areas in real-time, enabling proactive adjustments rather than reactive fixes after issues arise.

Incorporating feedback loops directly into your AI systems further enhances their ability to learn from interactions continuously. For example, after each customer interaction with your AI-powered support system, collecting feedback through quick surveys allows users to rate their experiences. This information can then be integrated back into the system's training process, refining responses based on what users found helpful or unhelpful.

Additionally, employing A/B testing methodologies within your setup can provide valuable insights. If you're uncertain about which version of an interaction—such as two different greetings for customers—works better, running A/B tests allows you to compare their effectiveness directly with real users. This empirical approach fosters continuous improvement based on actual user interactions rather than theoretical predictions.

Lastly, consider how collaboration across teams can enhance performance outcomes even further. Engaging developers and data scientists alongside marketing teams creates a holistic approach that balances technical efficiencies with user expectations. Workshops where these groups collaborate on refining use cases foster an environment ripe for innovation while ensuring that all perspectives are considered in decision-making processes.

each enhancement decision should align with clear objectives rooted in user needs and business goals. Whether you're optimizing data quality or upgrading infrastructure capabilities, maintaining strategic foresight is crucial—balancing immediate improvements with long-term growth aspirations is essential for sustained success in the rapidly evolving landscape of no-code AI agents.

CHAPTER 5:
BUILDING YOUR
FIRST AI AGENT

Identifying Your Use Case

I dentifying the right use case for your AI agent is a crucial step that lays the foundation for success. The clarity of your purpose directly influences how effectively you can utilize no-code tools to create a system that truly meets specific needs. This journey begins with a deep understanding of the problems you aim to solve or the efficiencies you wish to achieve.

Start by exploring existing pain points within your organization or personal workflow. For example, if a small business is struggling with slow customer service response times, an AI agent designed to manage initial inquiries can significantly lighten the workload while preserving service quality. Conducting surveys or interviews with team members can help identify common challenges and priorities, providing firsthand insights into where automation could have the most substantial impact.

After identifying potential use cases, it's essential to

assess their feasibility. Not every challenge requires an AI solution; some issues may be better addressed through simpler automation or manual processes. Evaluate whether the expected benefits justify the time and resources needed for development. Take this example, when considering automating inventory management, analyze current practices to see if they are complex enough to warrant AI intervention. If the processes are relatively straightforward, a basic inventory software may suffice.

Understanding your target audience's needs and expectations is equally important. If you're developing an AI agent for end-users, their preferences will significantly shape your design decisions. Engaging directly with users during this phase can provide valuable insights about their experiences and desires. Take this example, if customers express frustration with long wait times for support tickets, designing an AI agent that prioritizes speed in responses could prove invaluable.

Once you have narrowed down potential use cases, prioritize them based on their impact and feasibility. A simple matrix can help visualize this: one axis represents potential impact (from high to low), while the other reflects feasibility (from easy to hard). This visual aid allows you to concentrate on projects that promise significant returns without excessive complexity or investment.

Consider leveraging existing frameworks or case studies during this evaluation stage. Many organizations have successfully implemented no-code AI agents across various sectors—ranging from chatbots in retail that offer personalized shopping experiences to automated systems in healthcare that streamline patient scheduling. Learning from these examples can provide essential guidance on effective strategies and potential pitfalls.

Collaboration is vital in this process; involving stakeholders from different departments early on enriches your understanding of diverse perspectives and aligns objectives across teams. Take this example, discussing potential use cases with both marketing and technical teams could uncover new engagement opportunities that might not have been initially considered.

With a clear primary use case established, it becomes essential to articulate specific goals associated with it. Defining measurable outcomes not only guides development but also sets benchmarks for success once the AI agent is deployed. If your goal is to enhance customer engagement through a chatbot, establishing metrics such as response accuracy rates and user satisfaction scores should be prioritized at this stage.

Documenting these elements ensures that everyone involved shares a unified vision moving forward—a critical aspect when transitioning ideas into actionable strategies using no-code platforms later in the process.

identifying your use case is about aligning technology with real-world challenges—discovering intersections where innovation meets necessity leads not only to improved efficiency but also fosters a culture of creativity within teams eager to embrace change. Each decision made here builds upon insights gained through analysis and collaboration, weaving together a coherent narrative that drives toward impactful solutions tailored for today's dynamic environments.

Designing the Workflow

Designing the workflow for your AI agent is where your vision begins to take shape. After identifying a relevant use case, the next step is to map out how your AI agent will operate within that context. This process clarifies not only the functionality of your agent but also paves the way for seamless integration with existing systems and processes.

Start by outlining the specific tasks your AI agent will perform. For example, if your use case involves automating customer inquiries, detail each step of the interaction—from receiving an inquiry to providing a response. Flowcharts can be particularly useful at this stage, as they visually represent the sequence of actions and decision points in the process. A simple flowchart might illustrate how an AI chatbot identifies user intent, retrieves information from a knowledge base, and delivers personalized responses.

Next, think about user interactions and touchpoints within this workflow. An effective AI agent should not only complete tasks but also engage users in a manner that feels intuitive and satisfying. Consider how users initiate interactions: Is it through a website chat interface, email, or mobile app? Understanding these preferences helps shape the agent's design to fit seamlessly into user behaviors. Take this example, if users are accustomed to texting for support, creating a conversational interface that mimics natural dialogue can significantly enhance their experience.

As you design these workflows, pay close attention to potential bottlenecks or pain points that may arise during interactions. For example, if your chatbot is programmed to escalate complex queries to human representatives after two unsuccessful attempts at resolution, ensure that this handoff process is clear and efficient. Users should feel confident that they won't be left hanging—clarity in communication is essential.

Incorporating feedback mechanisms into your workflow design is another critical aspect. Providing users with options to rate their experiences or report issues fosters a loop for continuous improvement. Imagine implementing a feature where users can quickly indicate whether their questions were answered satisfactorily after interacting with your AI agent. This real-time feedback can inform ongoing adjustments and enhancements to both the AI's capabilities and its overall performance.

Once you have drafted the initial workflow design, testing

it in smaller segments before full deployment is essential. Prototyping tools enable you to create interactive models of your AI agent's workflows without requiring extensive coding knowledge. Platforms like Bubble or Airtable allow you to visually simulate conversations or workflows, providing insights into user navigation and decision-making patterns.

User testing plays a pivotal role during this phase. Invite actual users to interact with your prototype while observing their behaviors and collecting feedback on their experiences. This approach not only helps identify unforeseen challenges within the workflow but also fosters user buy-in by making them feel included in the development process.

Additionally, consider scalability while designing workflows. As businesses grow and evolve, so too do their needs; ensuring that your AI agent's workflows can adapt accordingly will help you avoid future headaches. Design with modularity in mind: breaking tasks into smaller components allows for easier updates or adjustments as requirements change over time.

Documentation remains crucial throughout this design phase as well. Keep records of every iteration and decision made regarding workflows—this not only aids team communication but also provides valuable insights for revisiting designs later on. Establishing clear guidelines for development will facilitate consistency as you expand functionalities or onboard new team members.

As you finalize the workflow design for your AI agent, focus on aligning technical aspects with user experience principles. The goal is not just functionality but creating an engaging interaction model that resonates with users while effectively fulfilling operational objectives.

With a well-defined workflow in place, you're not just preparing for deployment but also embarking on an iterative journey ahead—where each interaction with your AI agent yields insights that lead to further refinements and efficiencies. This foundation will empower you to build intelligent systems that not only meet immediate needs but also adapt seamlessly as those needs evolve over time.

Selecting the Right Tools

Choosing the right tools for your no-code AI agent is a crucial step that significantly impacts both its effectiveness and usability. With so many options available, it can be overwhelming; however, prioritizing your specific needs will guide you in making informed decisions.

Start by assessing the core functionalities you require from your AI agent. Are you aiming for natural language processing, data analytics, or the automation of repetitive tasks? Each tool has its unique strengths, so clearly defining your objectives will simplify the selection process. For example, if conversational capabilities are essential, you might consider platforms like Dialogflow or Microsoft Bot Framework, which excel in natural language processing.

Next, think about integration capabilities. The tools you select should seamlessly connect with your existing systems and data sources. Opting for tools that offer API access or pre-built integrations can save you significant time and effort during deployment. If you're working within a specific ecosystem, such as Salesforce for customer relationship management, choosing tools that integrate well with that environment will reduce friction and enhance overall functionality.

Ease of use is another important consideration. While no-code platforms are designed to make technology accessible to non-technical users, the intuitiveness of different interfaces can vary. Take the time to read user reviews and, if possible, conduct hands-on tests. This firsthand experience will help you understand how easy it is to create workflows and customize functionalities.

Cost is a critical factor that shouldn't be overlooked. Different platforms have varying pricing structures based on features, usage limits, or subscription models. Conducting a cost-benefit analysis can help you identify which tools fit your budget while meeting essential needs. Some platforms even offer free tiers that allow for experimentation before making a significant financial commitment.

Community support and resources are invaluable when exploring new technologies. Engaging with active user communities can offer insights into best practices and potential pitfalls. Platforms like Bubble or Zapier have large user bases where individuals share experiences, templates, and solutions to common problems. This network can be particularly beneficial during initial setup and ongoing development.

As you evaluate specific platforms, create a comparison matrix focusing on how they align with your identified needs. List key attributes such as automation capabilities, customization options, scalability features, and customer support availability for each tool you're considering. This visual representation will help you easily weigh the pros and cons at a glance.

As you narrow down your options, take advantage of demos or trial versions of your chosen platforms. Practical exposure allows you to assess usability and determine whether the tools fit seamlessly into your intended workflows. Take this example, if you're exploring an AI-powered chatbot platform, testing its conversational abilities in real time can provide valuable insights into its effectiveness in addressing user inquiries.

Don't forget to consider long-term scalability as well. The ideal tool should not only meet your current demands but also accommodate future growth or changes in strategy without necessitating a complete system overhaul. Look for platforms that are known for their flexibility—those that enable easy modifications or additions as your needs evolve will save you considerable resources down the line.

Finally, ensure that comprehensive documentation is a part of your tool selection process. The accessibility of tutorials, guides, and customer service channels can greatly influence how quickly you can get up to speed and troubleshoot issues as they arise. Tools that prioritize thorough documentation empower you to resolve challenges independently.

In summary, selecting the right no-code tools requires balancing immediate requirements with a vision for future growth and adaptability. By taking a thoughtful approach grounded in practical considerations—such as functionality, integration potential, usability, and cost-effectiveness—you'll be well-positioned to build an AI agent that not only meets today's needs but is also equipped for tomorrow's challenges. Remember: each decision builds upon the last, shaping the foundation for what's possible ahead as you embark on this journey of developing intelligent systems without traditional coding barriers.

Drag-and-Drop Elements

The appeal of no-code platforms lies in their user-friendly interfaces, which empower individuals without programming experience to create sophisticated applications. A standout feature that enhances this accessibility is the drag-and-drop functionality. This tool allows users to visually construct their AI agents by simply repositioning elements within a workspace, thus eliminating the complexities of coding syntax and lowering the barriers to entry.

Consider the process of building an AI-driven customer service chatbot. Rather than writing countless lines of code to define its behavior, you can effortlessly drag and drop components such as text input fields, response buttons, and conversation flow connectors into your project area. This visual approach not only speeds up development but also encourages creativity. Users can experiment with different configurations in real time, seeing how their changes affect the overall flow without being bogged down by technical intricacies.

When you first engage with a no-code platform equipped with drag-and-drop elements, you'll encounter a palette or sidebar filled with options. Each option represents a component—like triggers, actions, or conditions—that can be seamlessly integrated into your workflow. For example, if you're using a platform like Integromat (now known as Make), you might find modules designed for connecting various apps and services. The process is straightforward: click on a module and drag it into your workspace to establish a connection between two applications.

To illustrate this further, let's build a simple task automation agent using Zapier. You begin by selecting a trigger event from one app—let's say receiving an email in Gmail—and then drag that trigger onto your workspace. Next, you introduce an action from another app, like creating a task in Trello whenever that email arrives. The intuitive layout enables you to visualize the entire workflow at once, making it easier to grasp how data flows from one element to another.

While drag-and-drop interfaces are designed for simplicity, understanding certain nuances can significantly enhance your experience. Take this example, recognizing the hierarchy of actions is crucial; some components may rely on others to function correctly. When constructing workflows that involve conditional logic—such as sending notifications only if specific criteria are met—acknowledging these dependencies will save you time and frustration later on.

Another advantage of this approach is the immediate feedback it provides during development. As you build out your agent's capabilities by connecting components and adjusting settings through user-friendly menus, you'll often see live previews or instant simulations of what users might experience. This feature is invaluable because it helps you identify potential issues before deployment; catching errors early ensures smoother operation once your AI agent goes live.

Customization is yet another area where drag-and-drop functionality excels. Many platforms allow users to modify properties directly within the interface; for example, you can effortlessly change colors, fonts, or add custom branding elements with just a few clicks instead of delving into code adjustments. This capability ensures that you not only create functional solutions tailored to specific tasks but also design polished outputs that reflect your brand's identity.

Don't overlook the value of community resources when navigating these tools. Most no-code platforms have vibrant user communities that share templates and workflows created with drag-and-drop features. By exploring these shared resources—such as pre-configured chatbot flows—you can gain insights into best practices while accelerating your learning curve.

Additionally, consider documenting your workflow as you develop it through drag-and-drop interactions. Having a visual representation of how components connect can assist in future modifications or troubleshooting efforts. Screenshots or flowcharts illustrating your design choices will serve as helpful references for others who may engage with or expand upon your work later.

In summary, drag-and-drop functionality transforms how we interact with technology by making complex processes accessible and engaging for everyone—from novices crafting their first AI solutions to experienced professionals refining advanced systems. It simplifies creation while fostering experimentation and innovation.

As you embrace this methodology within no-code environments, remember that each interaction shapes not only immediate functionality but also informs broader strategies for developing intelligent systems tailored specifically to your objectives and vision for success.

Setting Agent Behaviors and Triggers

Defining the behaviors and triggers of your AI agent is a crucial step in transforming a static system into one that intelligently responds to user inputs and environmental changes. This process shapes how your agent behaves, interacts, and evolves in response to specific conditions. Rather than hardcoding every response or action, no-code platforms offer intuitive interfaces that let you establish these functionalities effortlessly, without needing to write a single line of code.

To get started, pinpoint the core actions your AI agent should perform. For example, if you're creating a virtual assistant for scheduling appointments, think about the prompts that will trigger its responses. Is it as simple as asking for an appointment time, or does the assistant need to analyze existing calendar events to suggest optimal times? Mapping these interactions clarifies the necessary triggers for your workflow.

In most no-code platforms, triggers serve as the initial catalysts for any action your AI agent will take. These can be event-based, such as receiving a message or entering data into a form. Imagine building an AI agent using a platform like Bubble or Adalo; here, you could set up a trigger based on user input—like clicking a button to schedule an appointment. The platform's visual interface allows you to easily drag this trigger into place and configure its parameters without delving into complex coding languages.

Once you've established your triggers, the next step is to define the corresponding behaviors. These behaviors dictate how your agent responds when activated by the triggers. Using our scheduling assistant example again, once the trigger (the button click) occurs, you can configure multiple behaviors: sending confirmation messages via email, updating a shared calendar, and notifying team members through messaging apps like Slack. Each behavior can be easily set up using simple dropdown menus or sliders in the platform's interface.

To further enhance your AI agent's intelligence, consider incorporating conditional logic. With conditional statements —often framed as "if-then" scenarios—you can create dynamic responses based on various inputs. Take this example, if a user specifies they want to meet only during certain hours (like 9 AM to 5 PM), you could program your assistant to check available slots during those times before confirming an appointment. This approach adds depth to your AI's functionality while keeping its foundational structure straightforward.

Another key element in setting up behaviors and triggers effectively is integrating actions with feedback mechanisms. For example, after successfully scheduling an appointment based on user input and available slots, your assistant could immediately send a confirmation message while offering options for rescheduling or canceling directly within that communication channel. This continuous interaction loop not only makes users feel valued but also streamlines their experience.

Testing these interactions in real-time is essential to ensure they function as intended before going live. Most no-code platforms provide simulation tools that allow you to observe how triggers activate behaviors under various conditions without needing actual users to interact with the system at first. Take this example, platforms like Zapier or Make (formerly Integromat) enable you to run test scenarios where specific inputs simulate user actions to verify that all components work together seamlessly.

Documentation is also vital throughout this process. As you visually define behaviors and configure triggers within the platform, take notes on key decisions and logic flows you've implemented; this record will prove invaluable if you need to revisit or expand functionalities later.

One of the significant advantages of setting up these systems without code is their adaptability over time. Your AI agent isn't limited by fixed capabilities; instead, it can evolve based on feedback and changing needs by simply adjusting existing behaviors or adding new triggers directly through the interface.

At its core, establishing agent behaviors and triggers creates a responsive ecosystem where artificial intelligence can interact meaningfully with users while remaining flexible enough to adapt over time—all without requiring extensive programming knowledge. By embracing this approach, you position yourself not just for effective deployment but also for ongoing enhancement as needs shift and technologies advance around you.

Testing and Iterating

After establishing the foundational behaviors and triggers for your AI agent, it's time to focus on testing and iteration. This phase is crucial as it transforms your conceptual framework into a functional reality, allowing you to refine your AI agent's capabilities through real user interactions and feedback. Engaging in this iterative process ensures that your agent not only operates as intended but also adapts to the evolving needs of its users.

Begin by conducting thorough tests of each behavior linked to the triggers you've set up. For example, if your scheduling assistant is designed to confirm appointments via email, simulate user actions to test that specific functionality. Input various appointment times and observe how the agent responds. Does it send an email confirmation? Are all details accurate? By carefully scrutinizing these elements, you can identify potential issues early, preventing complications once the system is live.

Take advantage of the built-in testing tools offered by your no-code platform. Many platforms provide options to create test environments where you can safely evaluate your AI agent's performance under various scenarios. If you're using a platform like Bubble, look for a "preview" mode that allows you to interact with your agent in a controlled setting. Engage with the interface as if you were an actual user: click buttons, input data, and navigate different pathways. This hands-on approach helps you understand how users will experience your AI agent in practice.

Gathering feedback from real users is another essential component of this process. Once you've thoroughly tested in a controlled environment, consider launching a beta version of your AI agent to a small group of users who can provide insights into its functionality and user experience. Collect qualitative feedback through surveys or direct conversations and analyze their interactions with the agent. Are they finding it intuitive? Are there features they wish it included? Their insights will be invaluable in shaping future iterations.

View iteration as a cyclical process rather than a linear one. Based on user feedback and test results, adjust both behaviors and triggers as needed. Take this example, if users struggle to find available appointment slots due to overly complex filtering options, consider simplifying those conditions or providing clearer guidance within the interface. Thoughtfully incorporate their suggestions; even minor tweaks can significantly enhance user satisfaction and engagement.

Establish metrics to continuously assess performance. Metrics such as response time, accuracy of scheduled appointments, and user satisfaction ratings can highlight areas for improvement. Regularly review these metrics after each iteration cycle. If certain behaviors are underperforming— such as an email confirmation not being sent reliably—take immediate action to troubleshoot that issue. Adopting an agile mindset—where rapid testing and adjustments are pivotal— can be highly beneficial.

Additionally, don't underestimate the importance of documentation during this iterative process. Keep detailed records of changes made after each round of testing. Documenting decisions related to behaviors, triggers, and user feedback will streamline future revisions or expansions of your AI agent's capabilities.

As new technologies emerge and user expectations evolve, regularly revisit your AI agent's functionalities to ensure it remains relevant. Continuous learning is integral to the lifecycle of your AI project; incorporate new features based on market trends or technological advancements without needing drastic overhauls. This flexibility is one of the core strengths of no-code platforms—your AI solutions can remain dynamic without being constrained by extensive coding requirements.

To wrap things up, testing and iterating are key to transforming your initial vision into an effective tool that adeptly responds to real-world use cases. By maintaining rigorous testing methods alongside ongoing user feedback loops, you pave the way for enhancements that keep pace with evolving needs and expectations—ensuring that your no-code AI agent not only meets but exceeds user demands over time. Embracing this iterative mindset empowers you to build robust systems capable of thriving in dynamic environments while remaining accessible without code.

Launching Your AI Agent

After meticulously testing and refining your AI agent, you're ready to take the pivotal step of launching it into the world. This phase is more than simply making your AI agent available; it's a strategic endeavor that requires careful planning and execution. The way you launch sets the tone for user engagement and significantly influences the overall success of your system.

Before you hit that launch button, ensure that every aspect

of your AI agent is polished and ready for user interaction. Review the user interface to confirm that it is intuitive and adheres to best practices in user experience design. A clean, user-friendly interface minimizes confusion and enhances adoption rates. Take this example, if your AI agent includes a chatbot feature, conduct extensive tests on the conversation flow. Users should receive clear responses to simple queries without feeling lost or overwhelmed.

Timing is another critical factor in your launch strategy. Choose a period when your target audience is most likely to engage with your new system. Take this example, if you're developing an agent for business applications, steer clear of launching during busy seasons or holidays when potential users may be preoccupied. Instead, aim for quieter times when users can fully explore and interact with your AI solution.

Once you've determined the right timing, create a comprehensive launch plan that includes marketing strategies designed to generate excitement and awareness around your AI agent. Utilize social media platforms to build buzz by posting engaging content that highlights its features and benefits. Consider producing video demos that showcase how the agent operates in real-world scenarios, helping potential users visualize its practical applications. Additionally, hosting a webinar can formally introduce the tool while providing live demonstrations and opportunities for Q&A sessions.

As you approach launch day, gather resources like tutorials or FAQs to support users as they begin interacting with your AI agent. New technology can often feel intimidating; providing robust support materials helps ease this transition and empowers users to maximize their experience from day one.

Post-launch activities are equally vital as they present an opportunity to collect initial feedback from early adopters. Encourage users to share their experiences through surveys or direct communication channels such as chat or email. This feedback can be invaluable, revealing any pain points or unexpected behaviors that may not have surfaced during testing.

Monitoring performance metrics from the moment of launch is crucial for ensuring ongoing success. Utilize analytics tools within your no-code platform to track user engagement with different functionalities of your AI agent. Metrics such as active user counts, session durations, and interaction frequencies provide valuable insights into user behavior. If certain features are well-received while others fade into obscurity, these findings can guide future development priorities.

Be prepared for potential issues post-launch; having a dedicated support team available to address questions or troubleshoot problems can significantly enhance user satisfaction and build trust in your AI solution. Quick resolutions contribute to the credibility of your product and help maintain momentum generated during the launch phase.

As time goes on after the launch, remember that this is not just a finish line but rather the beginning of an ongoing journey with your AI agent. Engage with users regularly by sharing updates about new features or improvements based on their feedback—this ongoing dialogue fosters a sense of community around your project.

The insights gained from real-world interactions will allow you to continuously refine functionalities and introduce enhancements that align with evolving user needs. In doing so, you transform what began as an initial idea into a robust tool capable of adapting alongside its user base—a testament to the power of no-code development approaches.

Launching an AI agent marks both an exciting milestone and a critical moment for growth and adaptation throughout its lifecycle. By strategically planning this process, maintaining open lines of communication post-launch, and committing to ongoing improvement based on feedback, you lay the foundation for long-term success in the dynamic landscape of no-code solutions. With each interaction and iteration, you deepen sophistication—empowering you to create systems that evolve alongside their users while fulfilling their intended purpose more effectively than ever before.

Collecting Feedback and Monitoring

Once your AI agent is live and engaging with users, the next critical step is to implement a robust system for collecting feedback and monitoring performance. This process is not just a routine task; it plays a pivotal role in shaping the evolution of your AI solution. By actively engaging with users, you can refine their experience and enhance the overall effectiveness of the agent.

To facilitate this, it's essential to create multiple channels for user feedback. Start by integrating brief surveys directly within the user interface, allowing users to share their experiences or feature requests as they interact with the AI. Additionally, set up a dedicated feedback channel—like a chat function or an email link—where users can communicate their thoughts in real time. This two-way communication not only provides valuable insights but also fosters greater user engagement and loyalty.

Monitoring performance metrics should accompany your feedback collection efforts. Utilize analytics tools available in your no-code platform to track user interactions with your agent. Metrics such as user retention rates can reveal how many users return after their initial interaction; a high retention rate suggests that users find value in your agent, while a low rate may indicate confusion or dissatisfaction. Also consider session durations, as longer interactions typically reflect deeper engagement.

Another key metric to examine is the frequency of interactions with specific features. If analytics show that certain functions are being used significantly more than others, it may highlight what users value most about your agent. Conversely, if some features remain unused, this could signal a need for improvement or clearer communication regarding their purpose.

Real-time performance monitoring is crucial for swiftly identifying and addressing potential issues. Set up alerts for unusual activity or spikes in user complaints so you can respond proactively rather than reactively. Take this example, an uptick in negative feedback about response times warrants an investigation into backend processes to ensure they meet user expectations.

Engagement doesn't end at launch; it's an ongoing conversation. Establish a routine for regularly reviewing collected data and user feedback—consider weekly or bi-weekly assessments to keep abreast of trends and make timely adjustments. These reviews can uncover patterns that inform future updates or feature enhancements.

User feedback should be seamlessly integrated into your development cycle. If users consistently request specific functionalities or report difficulties with existing features, prioritize these insights in your roadmap for iterative improvements. Real-world usage often reveals context that testing alone may overlook; it is through these lived experiences that your AI agent can evolve into a tool that truly meets its audience's needs.

Consider implementing a public-facing changelog where users can see updates and enhancements made based on their feedback. This transparency not only demonstrates that their voices matter but also builds trust in your commitment to continuous improvement.

Building an engaged community around your AI agent can further amplify opportunities for feedback. Create forums or social media groups where users can share experiences, ask questions, and collaboratively offer suggestions. Such environments foster a sense of ownership among users and encourage them to actively contribute to the product's evolution.

collecting feedback and monitoring performance transforms your initial release into a living project—one that grows and adapts over time based on genuine user interactions and preferences. By establishing clear channels for communication and closely analyzing engagement metrics, you lay the foundation for creating an agile AI solution capable of thriving in ever-changing environments.

In this way, gathering feedback is not merely an operational step; it becomes an integral part of crafting a responsive system that resonates deeply with its audience—ensuring lasting relevance and utility in a landscape that demands innovation and adaptability at every turn. Embrace this ongoing dialogue as both an opportunity and responsibility; through attentive listening and proactive adjustments, your no-code AI agent will evolve from functional to exceptional in fulfilling its purpose.

CHAPTER 6:
ADVANCED AI
AGENT FEATURES

Automated Decision-Making

Automated decision-making is at the forefront of modern AI applications, revolutionizing how businesses and individuals tackle challenges. By emulating human cognitive processes, AI agents can swiftly analyze vast datasets, identify patterns, and make informed decisions. In an environment where speed and accuracy are critical, this capability becomes essential for success.

Consider an AI agent implemented by a retail company to predict stock requirements based on seasonal trends and real-time sales data. By synthesizing historical data with current market conditions, the agent can autonomously reorder items before they run out, ensuring that shelves remain stocked without human intervention. This level of automation not only streamlines operations but also enhances inventory management, effectively minimizing costs associated with both overstocking and stockouts.

To successfully implement automated decision-making, a

structured approach is necessary. Begin by setting clear objectives for your AI agent: What specific decisions do you want it to make? Establish metrics for success—whether the aim is to increase sales, boost customer satisfaction, or enhance operational efficiency. Take this example, if your goal is to drive sales through targeted promotions, your AI agent should analyze customer purchasing behaviors to create personalized offers that resonate with individual shoppers.

Next, gather the relevant data that will fuel your decision-making model. The quality of this data is paramount; remember that poor data leads to poor outcomes. In our retail example, this could include historical sales figures, customer demographics, and even external influences like economic trends. Tools such as Google Analytics or CRM software can provide valuable insights into consumer behavior and preferences.

With your data in place, the next step is selecting appropriate algorithms. Decision trees, neural networks, and reinforcement learning models are popular options for facilitating automated decision-making. Take this example, if you choose a decision tree model, it organizes your dataset into branches based on feature values until it arrives at outcomes that guide decisions—such as determining which product to recommend to specific customer segments. No-code platforms often allow you to configure these algorithms without requiring programming skills.

Once you've established your setup, testing and validation are crucial. You must assess how well your AI agent performs its tasks across various scenarios using historical datasets or simulated environments. This evaluation ensures that the decision-making process aligns with expected outcomes before launching live. Running simulations can help determine whether promotions generated by the AI effectively drive increased purchases or fail to engage customers.

Once operational, continuous monitoring becomes vital for maintaining your AI agent's effectiveness. Automated decision-making is not a one-time effort; it must adapt alongside evolving trends and consumer behaviors. Create dashboards that provide real-time analytics on how the AI's decisions impact your business objectives. Are customers responding positively to targeted promotions? Are certain products frequently overlooked? These insights will guide necessary adjustments for maintaining the model's relevance.

Additionally, incorporating mechanisms for learning from new data enhances decision-making accuracy over time. This could involve simple feedback loops where user interactions inform future recommendations or more complex adaptive algorithms that autonomously evolve based on emerging patterns in user behavior.

A prime example is Amazon's recommendation system, which continually refines its suggestions based on users' browsing and purchasing habits. The underlying algorithms adapt by analyzing millions of transactions daily—an approach that not only personalizes user experiences but also significantly boosts sales through intelligent cross-selling techniques.

A key element of successful automated decision-making lies in transparency and user trust. It's essential for users to understand how decisions are made—especially when those choices can significantly impact their experiences or transactions. Clear communication about the AI's processes fosters confidence in its capabilities; consider sharing insights into how recommendations are formulated or what data informs specific decisions.

In summary, automated decision-making empowers businesses to operate more efficiently while enhancing user experiences through personalization and rapid responses to market dynamics. Embrace this technology as a powerful ally that simplifies complex processes and provides insights driving informed strategic choices. With careful planning, effective data management, and ongoing evaluation, your AI agent will become an invaluable asset in navigating today's fast-paced landscape—turning challenges into opportunities with ease.

Natural Language Processing

Natural Language Processing (NLP) stands out as one of the most transformative capabilities in artificial intelligence. This technology allows machines to comprehend, interpret, and generate human language in ways that are both meaningful and contextually relevant. As companies work to enhance customer interactions and streamline operations, the implementation of NLP is proving invaluable across a variety of sectors.

Consider a customer service scenario in which an AI agent can handle inquiries from thousands of customers simultaneously. By leveraging NLP, this agent can process incoming messages, discern user intent, and provide accurate responses without requiring human intervention. Such automation not only boosts efficiency but also significantly enhances the customer experience by minimizing wait times. Take this example, a banking institution might implement an NLP-driven chatbot to answer common questions about account balances or transaction histories, freeing up human agents to address more complex customer needs.

To effectively harness the power of NLP, start by identifying the specific challenges you want your AI agent to tackle. Are you aiming to automate customer support, analyze sentiment in social media posts, or generate marketing content? Each application has distinct requirements and nuances that will shape your approach. For example, a sentiment analysis tool focused on social media would need to accurately identify emotional tones—like joy or frustration—through subtle linguistic cues.

Once you've defined your use case, gather the necessary data. This could include transcripts from past customer interactions, public comments on social media, or product reviews. High-quality data is essential; it serves as the foundation for your NLP model. Open-source datasets available on platforms like Kaggle can be excellent resources for training your AI model without requiring extensive proprietary data.

Next, consider which NLP techniques align best with your objectives. Foundational methods such as tokenization, named entity recognition (NER), and part-of-speech tagging can be effectively combined to enhance understanding. Tokenization breaks text into smaller units—such as words or phrases—while NER identifies specific entities like dates or names within that text. For example, when analyzing product reviews, NER can highlight key aspects such as product features or consumer sentiments related to those features.

If you choose a no-code platform for building your NLP applications, you'll find many user-friendly interfaces that allow you to implement these techniques without needing programming skills. Tools like Bubble or Airtable enable users to create workflows that seamlessly integrate these functionalities. With drag-and-drop features, users can easily set up processes for automating text classification or sentiment analysis with minimal effort.

Testing your NLP model is crucial to ensure it operates as expected. Run the AI through sample inputs that mirror real-world scenarios to observe how it interprets language nuances. Take this example, if you're developing a chatbot for travel bookings, simulate various user inquiries—from simple questions like "What are my options?" to more complex ones such as "Can you help me find a flight that leaves after 5 PM?" Evaluating its performance across these diverse inputs will help ensure it understands context and provides appropriate responses.

Continuous improvement is vital for NLP applications. As language evolves and new slang or expressions emerge, your AI must adapt accordingly. Incorporating feedback mechanisms where users can rate responses enhances performance over time. If your chatbot frequently misunderstands requests related to "last minute bookings," for example, adjusting its training with additional data reflecting those scenarios can yield significant improvements.

Transparency also plays a crucial role in building trust with users who interact with NLP-driven solutions. When customers understand how their queries are processed and what data informs responses, they are more likely to engage confidently. Providing insights into how certain responses are generated—such as indicating which keywords triggered specific answers—can help demystify the technology.

Take Google Assistant as an example; it continuously learns from user interactions and refines its conversational abilities based on recognized patterns over time. By leveraging vast amounts of user data while respecting privacy standards, Google has developed an assistant that feels increasingly intuitive.

Natural Language Processing empowers organizations not only by automating tasks but also by unlocking deeper insights into customer sentiment and behavior. By comprehending language at scale, businesses can tailor their services in ways previously unimaginable. Embrace this technology as a fundamental component of your AI strategy; with thoughtful implementation and ongoing refinement, you can transform language barriers into bridges that foster meaningful connections with your audience.

Image Recognition Capabilities

Image recognition technology stands at the forefront of artificial intelligence, unlocking a myriad of innovative applications across diverse industries. This capability enables machines to interpret and understand visual information, allowing them to recognize objects, faces, and even actions within images or video streams. The implications are profound, ranging from enhanced security systems to personalized shopping experiences.

In the retail sector, for example, image recognition has the potential to transform customer interactions with products. Imagine walking into a store and simply pointing your smartphone at an item; the app could instantly recognize the product, display its details, and present related promotions— all without any manual searching. This seamless experience not only boosts user engagement but can also drive sales through targeted recommendations based on visual cues.

To embark on your journey in building image recognition applications using no-code tools, start by identifying your specific use case. Are you aiming to develop a security system that monitors public areas? Or perhaps you're interested in creating an application for a health clinic that identifies skin conditions from photographs? Each scenario presents unique challenges and requires tailored approaches.

Once you've pinpointed your use case, gather a robust dataset relevant to your project. High-quality images that reflect the diversity of scenarios your application will encounter are crucial for effective training. Consider utilizing publicly available datasets like ImageNet or COCO, which provide annotated images across various categories. If your application is niche-specific—such as identifying types of plants—you may need to compile your own dataset by collecting images under controlled conditions to ensure accuracy.

With your dataset in place, choose a no-code platform that offers image recognition capabilities. Tools like Microsoft PowerApps or Google AutoML provide user-friendly interfaces where you can upload images and define parameters without writing any code. These platforms often include pre-built models that can be fine-tuned for specific tasks, making it easier for those without technical backgrounds to get started.

The next step involves configuring image recognition by training the model with your dataset. During this phase, you'll input labeled images so the system can learn to distinguish different classes of items—such as recognizing whether an image contains a cat or a dog based on their unique characteristics. Take this example, in a medical diagnosis app focused on dermatology, you would train the model with images labeled according to specific conditions like eczema or melanoma.

Testing is a critical part of the development process. Run diverse sets of images through your trained model to evaluate its accuracy and performance. For example, if you're developing a security system, simulate real-world scenarios by testing with various lighting conditions or angles—does it accurately identify faces in low light? Assessing these variables helps refine the model's efficacy and ensures it performs well under varying conditions.

Continuous refinement is equally important; as new data becomes available or trends change (for instance, evolving fashion styles), updating your model helps maintain its relevance. Implement feedback mechanisms that allow users to report inaccuracies or provide insights on misidentified objects. This ongoing interaction not only enhances the model's accuracy but also builds trust among users who depend on its functionality.

Consider how leading companies effectively leverage image recognition technology. For example, Amazon Go stores utilize this technology extensively; cameras throughout the store track what items customers pick up and automatically charge them upon exit—eliminating friction from the shopping experience while gathering invaluable data on consumer behavior.

And, transparency regarding how image recognition models operate is vital for user trust. Providing insights about data usage and processing—for instance, reassuring users that their images aren't stored long-term unless necessary—can alleviate privacy concerns. Clear communication around these aspects fosters confidence in using AI-driven solutions.

In summary, embracing image recognition capabilities empowers businesses to innovate rapidly while dramatically enhancing user experience. Whether improving efficiency in security applications or personalizing retail interactions, these technologies can transform our visual engagement with the world around us. By understanding both the technical aspects involved and user-centric strategies for deployment, you position yourself at the forefront of this powerful domain within artificial intelligence.

Predictive Analytics

Predictive analytics leverages historical data and statistical algorithms to forecast future outcomes, providing businesses with a powerful tool for informed decision-making. In today's information-driven world, the ability to predict trends, behaviors, and preferences can transform operations across various sectors, including finance, healthcare, and marketing.

To grasp the essentials of predictive analytics, we can break it down into three core components: data collection, analysis, and interpretation. Data is the foundation of predictive models; thus, identifying relevant datasets is vital. For example, a retail company might analyze past sales figures, customer demographics, and purchasing patterns to anticipate future buying behavior. This insight enables them to tailor their inventory and marketing strategies effectively.

Once the data is collected, the next step is to choose a no-code platform that specializes in predictive analytics. Tools such as Google Cloud AutoML and Microsoft Power BI offer user-friendly interfaces that allow users to upload datasets without needing extensive coding skills. These platforms come equipped with built-in algorithms for regression analysis or classification tasks, making it easier for non-technical users to create robust predictive models.

After selecting a platform, you'll need to prepare your data for analysis. Data cleaning is a crucial phase where you remove inconsistencies and irrelevant information that could distort results. Take this example, if you're analyzing customer transaction records, ensuring all entries are uniformly formatted (such as dates) will enhance your model's accuracy.

The next phase is modeling, where you define your variables and select the appropriate algorithm for your prediction task. A common starting point is linear regression for predicting continuous values like sales figures. Alternatively, logistic regression may be used for binary outcomes, such as whether a customer will make a purchase. Many no-code platforms simplify this process by allowing users to drag-and-drop selected features into predefined model structures.

Once your model is established with historical data inputs, it's time to train it. Training involves feeding your model data so it can learn the relationships between input variables and target outcomes. For example, when predicting customer churn in a subscription service based on usage metrics and demographic factors, training helps the model identify patterns that lead to cancellations.

Following training is the validation phase, which assesses how well your model performs using unseen datasets known as test sets. By conducting these tests, you can evaluate metrics like accuracy and precision to see how closely your predictions align with actual outcomes. This iterative process often uncovers opportunities for improvement; perhaps incorporating additional features could enhance performance or adjusting parameters might yield better results.

Post-launch monitoring is essential since external factors can shift consumer behavior or market conditions over time. For example, seasonality significantly impacts sales predictions; therefore, regularly updating models with fresh data ensures their continued relevance. Implementing feedback mechanisms allows users to flag inaccurate predictions, thereby informing future iterations of your model while fostering user trust.

Consider an illustrative case: Netflix employs predictive analytics extensively to personalize viewing recommendations based on user behavior patterns such as viewing history and ratings given by similar users. This strategic use of predictive modeling not only enhances user engagement but also influences content acquisition decisions —if predictions indicate strong interest in certain genres or themes, Netflix may choose to invest more heavily in those areas.

In another instance, healthcare providers utilize predictive analytics for forecasting patient readmissions. By analyzing past admissions alongside social determinants of health (such as socioeconomic status), they can identify high-risk patients who may require additional support after discharge— ultimately improving patient outcomes while reducing costs.

As organizations increasingly adopt AI-driven predictive analytics tools that require little to no coding expertise, they gain agility in their decision-making processes—an essential advantage in today's fast-paced environment. By effectively leveraging these insights within their operations or client services—whether through targeted marketing campaigns or optimized resource allocation—businesses position themselves not just as reactive entities but as proactive leaders ready to tackle future challenges. Embracing this technology shifts the paradigm from mere response mechanisms to intelligent forecasting strategies that thrive in an unpredictable landscape where foresight becomes invaluable.

Chatbot Integration

Integrating chatbots into your no-code AI systems can transform how you engage with users, streamline processes, and elevate customer service experiences. These intelligent agents are capable of handling a wide range of tasks, from addressing frequently asked questions to processing transactions, all while delivering personalized interactions. The key to success lies in effectively leveraging existing no-code platforms to create and deploy chatbot solutions tailored to your unique needs.

To start, it's important to clarify the primary objective of your chatbot. Are you looking to enhance customer support, offer product recommendations, or gather feedback? Each goal will influence the design and functionality of your bot. For example, a customer support chatbot should feature a comprehensive FAQ database and quick response capabilities to efficiently address common inquiries. Conversely, a recommendation bot may require integration with an inventory system to suggest products that align with user preferences.

Once you've identified the main purpose of your chatbot, choosing the right no-code platform becomes essential. Tools like Chatfuel, ManyChat, and Landbot enable you to design and deploy chatbots effortlessly, even without coding experience. Take this example, Chatfuel allows you to create a Facebook Messenger bot by simply dragging and dropping elements on a visual canvas, making it easy to set up conversation flows intuitively. If you're interested in linking various applications without writing code, platforms such as Zapier can seamlessly connect your chatbot to email services or CRM systems.

After selecting your platform, designing conversation flows is a key next step. This process involves mapping out potential dialogues between users and the bot. Utilizing flowcharts or conversational maps can help you visualize interactions effectively. Start by scripting common user questions and defining appropriate responses. A rule-based approach can be useful initially; for example, if a user inquires about store hours, a straightforward response could be: "Our store is open from 9 AM to 9 PM.

Incorporating natural language processing (NLP) further enhances user interactions. Many no-code platforms come with built-in NLP capabilities that facilitate understanding user intents—recognizing phrases like "What are your business hours?" and "When do you close?" as equivalent inquiries. For more advanced functionalities, consider integrating services like Dialogflow or Wit.ai through APIs, which can enable your chatbot to engage in more natural conversations rather than adhering strictly to predefined paths.

Thorough testing of your chatbot before launch is crucial. Engaging real users in beta testing can help identify areas where the bot may struggle or where conversations could derail. Using their feedback to iterate on dialogue flows will improve both user satisfaction and functionality. Additionally, A/B testing different responses can provide insights into which approaches resonate best with users.

Once deployed, monitoring interactions will yield valuable insights into performance metrics such as engagement rates and resolution times. Most no-code platforms offer analytics tools that track these metrics directly within their dashboards. Regularly reviewing this data allows for ongoing refinement of responses and optimization of user experiences based on actual usage patterns.

And, integrating chatbots into broader digital ecosystems significantly enhances their effectiveness. By connecting them with other applications through APIs or workflows established on platforms like Integromat or Zapier, you empower your chatbot not only to respond but also to perform actions—such as sending confirmation emails after bookings or updating databases when collecting customer information.

The final aspect of successful chatbot integration is the ongoing evolution of its capabilities based on user interactions and established feedback loops. As users engage with your bot over time, their behaviors will inform necessary adjustments in conversation design or feature enhancements—ensuring it remains relevant and useful.

Chatbot integration represents a dynamic opportunity within no-code AI environments. It focuses on creating engaging experiences that foster relationships while maintaining efficiency. By thoughtfully designing chatbots that meet specific needs and continuously refining them using analytics-driven insights, businesses can develop a powerful tool that boosts both customer satisfaction and operational performance without requiring extensive coding knowledge.

Sentiment Analysis

Sentiment analysis acts as a vital link between human emotions and machine understanding, enabling AI to interpret the feelings expressed in textual data. As businesses increasingly turn to digital communication, grasping sentiment becomes a significant competitive advantage. This capability transcends basic data processing; it explores customer emotions, perceptions, and even brand loyalty. By integrating sentiment analysis into your no-code AI strategies, you can uncover valuable insights that inform decision-making and enhance user experiences.

To embark on sentiment analysis, defining your objectives is crucial. Are you looking to monitor brand perception on social media, assess customer satisfaction through feedback surveys, or analyze product reviews? Your specific goals will guide the type of data you collect and the methods of analysis you choose. Take this example, if your aim is to gauge customer sentiment about a new product launch, gathering social media mentions and review comments will be essential.

Once your objectives are clear, the next step is selecting a no-code platform that offers sentiment analysis capabilities. Tools like MonkeyLearn or Google Cloud Natural Language provide intuitive interfaces for text analysis without requiring programming skills. With MonkeyLearn, for example, you can upload your text data or seamlessly integrate with platforms like Zapier to automatically pull in data from various sources. The platform uses pre-built models to classify text as positive, negative, or neutral—enabling swift insights into public sentiment.

After choosing a platform, you'll need to prepare your data for analysis. This step often involves cleaning the raw text by removing irrelevant information such as URLs or special characters that could distort results. For example, when analyzing tweets about your brand, focusing solely on original tweet content—while excluding retweets or unrelated replies—ensures that your analysis accurately reflects genuine sentiments.

With clean data in hand, it's time to configure the sentiment analysis model within your chosen platform. Many no-code tools allow you to train custom models tailored to specific vocabularies or industry jargon relevant to your field. Take this example, in the tech industry, terms like "bug" might indicate negative sentiment while "update" could convey positivity. Customizing your model to recognize these nuances leads to more accurate insights.

Once configured, running the sentiment analysis on your dataset will yield results that provide a clearer understanding of public sentiment regarding your subject matter. The outputs typically include percentages indicating how much content was categorized as positive, negative, or neutral, along with examples of specific comments driving those conclusions. This actionable data empowers businesses to adapt strategies accordingly—whether it's amplifying positive sentiments through targeted marketing campaigns or addressing concerns highlighted by negative feedback.

Following the initial analysis, visualizing the findings is essential for comprehension and presentation. Most no-code platforms feature built-in visualization tools that enable you to create graphs and charts illustrating sentiment trends over time. Take this example, a line graph displaying monthly sentiment shifts can effectively demonstrate how a recent marketing campaign impacted public perception. Presenting this data visually helps stakeholders quickly grasp complex insights.

The next critical step is integrating these insights into broader business strategies. If customer feedback consistently points out dissatisfaction with a particular product feature, this insight can prompt immediate action from product development teams to implement necessary changes. Conversely, if certain aspects generate excitement and praise among users, those strengths can be leveraged in future marketing efforts.

Ongoing sentiment monitoring is equally important. Establishing a continuous feedback loop ensures that you remain attuned to shifts in public perception and can respond swiftly to emerging trends or issues before they escalate. Setting up alerts within your no-code platform can notify you of sudden changes in sentiment—whether it's an increase in negative comments following a product issue or a surge in positive feedback after a successful campaign.

sentiment analysis is not just about understanding emotions; it's about translating them into strategic actions that enhance user engagement and drive growth. By seamlessly incorporating this capability into no-code AI environments, organizations position themselves not only to respond proactively but also to cultivate deeper relationships with their audiences.

In today's digital communication landscape—where every comment carries potential significance—leveraging sentiment analysis enables informed decision-making and fosters stronger connections between brands and customers. Embracing these insights allows businesses to respond intelligently rather than reactively—shaping narratives based on what truly matters: human emotion and experience.

Personalization and Recommendations

Personalization has become an essential component of the digital landscape, transforming how businesses connect with their audiences. By customizing experiences to align with individual preferences and behaviors, organizations can significantly boost customer satisfaction and loyalty. This process not only captures users' attention but also nurtures deeper connections, ultimately driving increased engagement and conversions. A key element in leveraging the power of personalization is the implementation of recommendation systems.

Recommendation systems analyze user data to suggest products or content that resonate with individuals based on their past interactions. Consider platforms like Netflix and Amazon; they rely on sophisticated algorithms that assess viewing habits or purchase history to provide relevant suggestions. This personalized approach fosters a sense of understanding and appreciation among users, making them feel valued.

To embark on building a recommendation system using no-code tools, start by defining your goals. Are you aiming to recommend products based on browsing behavior or suggest articles that align with user interests? Clarifying your

NO-CODE AI AGENTS: BUILD SMART SYSTEMS WITHOUT WRITING A LIN...

objectives will shape your data collection methods and the framework of your recommendation engine.

Once your goals are established, select a no-code platform that facilitates the development of recommendation systems. Options like Airtable, Zapier, or specialized platforms such as Bubble offer features for integrating recommendation capabilities without requiring coding expertise. Take this example, Airtable can help manage user profiles and interactions, while Zapier can connect various apps to gather the necessary data.

Data preparation is a critical step in this journey. Begin by collecting relevant information from diverse sources—this could include user activity logs, purchase histories, or explicit preferences obtained through surveys. Ensure you clean this data by removing duplicates and irrelevant entries; for example, when tracking user purchases for recommendations, focus solely on completed transactions rather than abandoned carts.

With clean data ready for analysis, proceed to create your recommendation model within the chosen no-code platform. Many of these solutions offer templates or pre-built models that can be customized to meet your specific needs. A common approach is collaborative filtering, which identifies similarities among users or items to make recommendations. Take this example, if User A and User B exhibit similar purchasing habits, User A may be encouraged to explore items purchased by User B.

After configuring your model, it's important to test its effectiveness before a wider rollout. Simulate scenarios using historical data to evaluate how well the recommendations align with actual user preferences. You might find that certain products are suggested more frequently than intended; refining these parameters can enhance the accuracy of outputs.

Once validated, you can deploy the recommendation engine into your existing platform so users can begin receiving personalized suggestions. Ensure that these recommendations integrate seamlessly into their browsing experience—whether as product suggestions at checkout or tailored content feeds within an app.

Ongoing performance monitoring is crucial for long-term success after deployment. Analyzing user interactions with recommendations helps identify trends and refine strategies accordingly. For example, if certain recommendations lead to higher conversion rates while others underperform, you can adjust those less effective aspects based on feedback collected.

Establishing user feedback loops is vital as well; actively solicit input regarding the relevance of the recommendations provided. Tools like surveys or feedback forms can help gauge whether users find value in suggested items—this insight is invaluable for continuous improvement of your system.

In addition to basic recommendations based on past behavior, consider employing dynamic personalization techniques that adapt in real-time as new data becomes available. By utilizing machine learning algorithms offered by some no-code platforms, you can continually enhance the system's ability to deliver relevant suggestions tailored precisely for each unique user.

The journey doesn't stop here; exploring advanced features such as contextual recommendations—where suggestions shift based on current trends or events—can significantly enrich the user experience. This level of personalization positions businesses not just as service providers but as insightful partners who anticipate customer needs.

embedding personalization through effective recommendation systems empowers organizations to cultivate lasting relationships with customers while driving growth through meaningful engagement. By adopting these strategies within no-code frameworks, businesses can unlock potential previously thought reserved for tech-savvy developers alone—ushering in an era where every interaction feels tailored and intentional.

Workflow Automation

Automation of workflows has become essential for enhancing efficiency in both business and personal settings. By streamlining repetitive tasks, automation not only saves time but also minimizes the risk of human error, allowing individuals and organizations to concentrate on higher-value activities. In this landscape, no-code platforms have emerged as powerful tools that democratize access to technology once reserved for coding experts, making workflow automation accessible to everyone.

To embark on your journey into workflow automation with no-code tools, begin by mapping out the processes you wish to automate. Identify tasks that are repetitive or tedious—these are ideal candidates for automation. Consider scenarios such as onboarding new clients, processing invoices, or sending follow-up emails after meetings. By pinpointing these workflows, you establish a solid foundation for an efficient system that can free up valuable resources.

After identifying your processes, the next step is to choose a suitable no-code platform that meets your needs. Tools like Zapier or Integromat (now Make) offer user-friendly interfaces and integrate seamlessly with a variety of applications. Take this example, you can set up Zapier to automatically create a Trello card whenever a new lead fills out a form on your website—all without writing a single line of code.

Once you've selected your platform, it's time to design your workflow. The drag-and-drop functionalities typical of no-code platforms make this phase intuitive and straightforward. You might start by creating triggers—specific events that initiate actions within your workflow. For example, a new form submission in Google Forms could trigger an email notification via Gmail. This orchestration can be further refined by adding filters, ensuring that only relevant submissions prompt specific actions.

Before launching your automated workflows, thorough testing is crucial. No-code tools allow you to run tests using sample data to confirm that everything functions as intended. This process is similar to debugging in traditional coding but much simpler; if something doesn't work correctly, you can easily revisit your setup and make necessary adjustments.

After testing, deploy your automated workflows into live environments. As users begin interacting with these systems, actively monitor their performance. Analyze key metrics such as completion times and error rates associated with automated tasks; this data provides valuable insights into how effectively the automation fulfills its purpose.

Incorporating feedback mechanisms into your automated workflows is also important. Take this example, if you're automating client onboarding processes, consider including touchpoints where users can share their experiences with the system. This feedback is invaluable for continuous improvement and ensures that the automation not only meets expectations but exceeds them.

Also, keep scalability in mind from the outset. As businesses grow or personal needs evolve, workflows may need adjustments or enhancements over time. No-code platforms typically allow for easy modifications, so be ready to iterate on your designs based on changing demands or user feedback.

As you explore workflow automation techniques further, consider advanced capabilities such as conditional logic— allowing workflows to adapt based on specific criteria. For example, you might want different email sequences triggered depending on whether a lead originated from an online ad or organic search traffic. This level of customization fosters targeted communications and enhances user engagement.

Don't overlook the potential of integrating AI elements into your automated workflows; many no-code platforms now support AI-driven features that improve task execution. Imagine utilizing machine learning algorithms to analyze past interactions and suggest optimizations for future outreach strategies—adding significant value without requiring extensive technical knowledge.

Embracing workflow automation through no-code solutions signifies not just an operational shift but a cultural transformation as well—encouraging innovation and efficiency at all levels of an organization or individual endeavor. By demystifying complex processes and empowering everyone with user-friendly tools, organizations can cultivate an environment where creativity flourishes alongside productivity.

Nowadays, automation has become synonymous with progress. Adopting these strategies enables individuals and teams not just to keep pace but to thrive amidst evolving challenges and opportunities. Through careful planning and effective use of no-code capabilities, anyone can revolutionize their approach to work—shifting the focus from manual tasks to innovative possibilities waiting just around the corner.

Cross-Platform Compatibility

The ability to develop applications across various platforms without requiring advanced coding skills is a game-changer. Cross-platform compatibility has become essential for ensuring that no-code solutions function smoothly, regardless of the environment in which they are used. This shift liberates users from being tied to a single operating system or device, allowing them to create applications that deliver a consistent experience across desktops, tablets, and mobile devices.

To effectively leverage cross-platform compatibility, it's crucial to choose no-code tools specifically designed for this purpose.

Many contemporary platforms come equipped with features that enable users—whether seasoned developers or novices —to create responsive designs with ease. For example, tools like Bubble and Adalo allow users to build applications that automatically adapt their layouts based on the screen size of the device in use. So, whether someone accesses your application on a smartphone or a laptop, they enjoy a fluid and intuitive experience.

Start by exploring the unique functionalities offered by these platforms. Familiarize yourself with features like drag-and-drop interfaces that simplify layout adjustments for different screen types. While building your application, remember to test it on multiple devices and operating systems. This practice helps identify layout discrepancies and ensures that functionality remains consistent across various environments.

Consider a practical scenario: imagine creating an event registration application with a no-code platform. By utilizing built-in templates optimized for different devices, you can design forms that look great on both mobile and desktop views. You might initially create your layout on your computer but then test it on your phone to ensure buttons are easy to tap and forms are user-friendly. Making adjustments is quick and straightforward, eliminating the need for complex coding.

Integrating third-party APIs significantly enhances cross-platform compatibility as well. Many no-code platforms offer simple ways to incorporate external services such as payment gateways or email marketing tools, each with its own specific requirements. Using platforms like Zapier or Integromat can facilitate seamless data transfer between your app and other systems, ensuring all components work harmoniously regardless of their source.

As you build cross-platform applications, prioritize user experience at every stage. Today's users expect instant access and smooth functionality, no matter how they engage with technology. This expectation highlights the importance of performance optimization; slow-loading applications or inconsistent behaviors can lead to frustration and disengagement. Conducting thorough performance tests across devices helps pinpoint bottlenecks so you can implement solutions before launch.

Accessibility features should also be integral to your design process. Adapting applications for users with disabilities not only enhances inclusivity but also broadens your audience base. No-code platforms often provide tools that help implement accessibility best practices—such as adjustable text sizes or alternative text for images—making it easier for everyone to engage with your content.

Keeping your software up-to-date is another key aspect of this process. Many no-code solutions continuously improve their features and compatibility; staying informed about updates allows you to leverage the latest advancements without extensive technical adjustments. Regularly reviewing release notes from your chosen platform ensures you can take advantage of new functionalities that enhance cross-platform capabilities.

As you immerse yourself in creating cross-platform applications using no-code tools, remember that adaptability is vital in today's rapidly changing technological landscape. Embrace shifts in user preferences and emerging technologies; this flexibility will empower you to refine your approach and introduce enhancements based on real-world feedback.

In summary, cross-platform compatibility is not just a technical necessity but also a strategic advantage when developing user-centric applications. By embracing this capability within no-code environments, you unlock opportunities for innovation while fostering an inclusive approach to technology. As industries evolve towards greater digital integration, leveraging these principles empowers creators from all backgrounds to effortlessly bring their visions to life across diverse platforms and devices.

CHAPTER 7: DATA PREPARATION AND MANAGEMENT

Cleaning and Preprocessing Data

C leaning and preprocessing data is a crucial step that establishes the foundation for any successful AI project. During this phase, raw information is transformed into a structured format suitable for analysis or modeling. Without proper cleaning, even the most advanced algorithms can produce misleading results, undermining the entire effort.

To begin, identify the sources of your data. Whether it originates from forms, spreadsheets, or APIs, understanding its source is vital for assessing its quality and relevance. For example, if you're aggregating user feedback from a web application, you may encounter data entry errors such as typos or inconsistent formatting. Before proceeding with analysis, it's important to review these entries; this initial inspection helps gauge the extent of cleaning required.

One common challenge in data preprocessing is addressing missing values. Gaps in your dataset can skew analyses and lead to inaccurate conclusions. There are various strategies for handling missing data, including imputation, deletion, and interpolation. If you opt for imputation, replacing missing values with the mean or median of the dataset can be effective. Using Python's Pandas library simplifies this process:

```python
import pandas as pd
```

\#\# Load your data

```python
data = pd.read_csv('user_feedback.csv')
```

\#\# Fill missing values with the mean of their respective columns

```python
data.fillna(data.mean(), inplace=True)
```

Next, focus on ensuring consistent formatting throughout your dataset. Inconsistencies—such as varying date formats or text casing—can create confusion during analysis. Take this example, if some entries are formatted as 'MM/DD/YYYY' while others use 'DD/MM/YYYY,' this inconsistency could lead to incorrect date interpretations. Standardizing these formats early on will save time and prevent errors down the line.

Once you've completed basic cleaning, it's time to explore outliers—values that significantly deviate from the rest of the dataset. These anomalies can distort statistical analyses and predictions if not addressed. Visualizations like box plots or scatter plots are effective tools for detecting outliers:

```python
import matplotlib.pyplot as plt
```

\#\# Create a box plot to visualize outliers

```python
plt.boxplot(data['column_of_interest'])

plt.title('Box Plot of Column of Interest')

plt.show()
```

If you find that an outlier represents a valid observation —such as a high sales figure resulting from a successful marketing campaign—consider how it fits within your analysis framework before deciding whether to remove it.

At this stage, data normalization and scaling are also essential. Different variables may operate on varying scales; some might range from 0 to 1 while others could span hundreds or thousands. Applying techniques like Min-Max scaling or Z-score normalization can align these variables, allowing algorithms to perform more effectively.

Here's an example of how to normalize a dataset using Scikit-learn in Python:

```python
from sklearn.preprocessing import MinMaxScaler


scaler = MinMaxScaler()

normalized_data    =    scaler.fit_transform(data[['column1', 'column2']])
```

Additionally, consider encoding categorical variables if they play a role in your AI models. Since many algorithms require numerical input, converting categories into dummy variables can facilitate processing. This task can also be easily accomplished with Pandas:

```python
```

\#\# Convert categorical variable into dummy/indicator variables

```
data = pd.get_dummies(data, columns=['category_column'])
` ` `
```

Throughout this process, maintain rigorous documentation of your steps and decisions made during cleaning and preprocessing. Not only does this support reproducibility, but it also aids future collaborators who may work with your dataset.

As you conclude the cleaning phase, ensure you have a robust validation strategy in place. This involves checking whether your preprocessing has genuinely enhanced data quality —using statistical summaries and visualizations to verify expectations against outcomes.

In summary, effective data cleaning and preprocessing demand diligence and strategic decision-making at every step. By establishing clear procedures for handling missing values, standardizing formats, detecting outliers, normalizing data ranges, and encoding categorical variables—all while meticulously documenting changes—you create a solid foundation for subsequent analysis or modeling tasks within AI projects. Remember that the quality of your input directly influences the output; prioritize this stage to enhance overall project success and reliability.

Handling Large Datasets

Handling large datasets comes with distinct challenges that necessitate tailored strategies to keep the data both manageable and useful. As organizations increasingly depend on data to inform decision-making, efficiently processing and analyzing extensive datasets becomes essential. This complexity is often heightened by the diverse sources and formats of data encountered in real-world applications.

The first step in managing large volumes of data is to evaluate your infrastructure capabilities. Cloud services like AWS, Google Cloud, and Azure provide robust solutions for storing and processing these datasets. By leveraging cloud storage, organizations can achieve scalability while ensuring efficient access and computation. Take this example, combining Amazon S3 for storage with AWS Lambda functions allows for the automation of processing tasks without overwhelming local systems.

It's also important to consider the architecture of your data handling processes. Implementing a distributed computing framework, such as Apache Spark, enables you to process big data across multiple nodes, significantly accelerating analysis. Spark's capacity for in-memory data processing makes it a preferred option for operations that require rapid computation.

Now, let's explore some practical techniques for effectively managing large datasets:

1. Chunking: Instead of loading an entire dataset into memory at once, break it into smaller chunks. This method reduces memory overload and allows for more manageable processing times. For example, when dealing with a massive CSV file in Python, you can use the Pandas read_csv method with the chunksize parameter:

```python
import pandas as pd


\#\# Process a large CSV file in chunks

for chunk in pd.read_csv('large_data.csv', chunksize=10000):

\#\# Perform operations on each chunk

process(chunk)
```

` ` `

1. Data Sampling: When analyzing an entire dataset is impractical, consider using a representative sample. Techniques like stratified sampling can help ensure that key characteristics of the overall dataset are maintained while working with a more manageable subset.

2. Efficient Data Formats: The format in which data is stored can significantly impact performance during loading and processing. Formats like Parquet or Avro are optimized for performance; they compress data effectively and allow for faster reads compared to traditional formats such as CSV or JSON.

3. Indexing: For databases containing vast amounts of information, implementing indexing strategies can greatly enhance query response times. Proper indexing enables quick retrieval of specific records without scanning the entire dataset.

4. Batch Processing: Similar to chunking but focused on aggregating records for efficiency, batch processing reduces overhead by allowing multiple transactions or updates to be handled simultaneously rather than individually.

5. Data Pipeline Automation: Utilize tools like Apache NiFi or Airflow to automate workflows for continuously collecting and processing data streams. Automating these pipelines ensures timely updates without manual intervention while maintaining consistent quality control measures.

6. Monitoring Resource Usage: Tracking resource consumption—such as CPU usage, memory allocation, and I/O throughput—is crucial when managing large datasets. Tools like Grafana can

visualize these metrics in real-time, allowing for dynamic adjustments based on system performance.

As you refine your approach to handling large datasets, consider fostering collaborative practices as well. Engaging team members in discussions about best practices not only promotes knowledge sharing but also encourages diverse perspectives in problem-solving.

The importance of well-managed datasets cannot be overstated; they form the backbone of effective AI models and analyses within modern businesses. By strategically managing these datasets from inception through analysis, you enhance your ability to extract actionable insights that drive value across various applications—from predictive analytics to real-time decision-making support systems.

transitioning from raw information management to actionable insights hinges on these foundational steps. By embracing techniques designed for large-scale operations, you can fully harness the potential of your data landscape while remaining adaptable to evolving technological demands.

Data Annotation Techniques

Building upon the foundational understanding of large datasets, data annotation emerges as a crucial process that enables AI models to learn accurately and effectively. By transforming raw data into structured information, data annotation ensures that machine learning algorithms can interpret and utilize the data meaningfully. The quality and clarity of these annotations play a direct role in shaping the performance of your models.

The first step in data annotation is to identify the type of data you are working with—whether it be images, text, audio, or video. Each category presents its own unique challenges and requires specific annotation techniques. For example, annotating image datasets may involve using bounding boxes to pinpoint objects within photos, whereas text datasets often necessitate labeled categories to convey sentiments or topics. This specificity is vital for enhancing the relevance and accuracy of your machine learning outputs.

Different methods are employed for annotating various types of data:

1. Image Annotation: In computer vision tasks, image annotation is typically achieved through techniques like bounding box annotations or polygonal segmentation. Tools such as LabelImg allow users to draw bounding boxes around objects in images and export results in formats like YOLO or Pascal VOC. Take this example, when using LabelImg, one might annotate an image containing cars and pedestrians by enclosing each object in a bounding box and labeling it according to its category.

2. Text Annotation: For text classification tasks, either manual or semi-automated techniques can be utilized to label sections of text for applications such as sentiment analysis or named entity recognition (NER). Platforms like Prodigy simplify this process by providing user-friendly interfaces for creating training datasets. An example would be annotating customer feedback sentences as positive, negative, or neutral using Prodigy's tagging feature, which helps establish clear labels for training your sentiment analysis model.

3. Audio Annotation: Audio data often necessitates transcription for speech recognition tasks or labeling for sound classification. Tools like Audacity can be used to segment audio clips and apply relevant labels. For example, you might annotate different segments of an audio file where various speakers are talking or specific sounds occur (like laughter or applause),

marking each segment with appropriate tags.

4. Video Annotation: Video data adds an extra layer of complexity due to its combination of visual and audio elements. Annotating videos may involve frame-by-frame analysis or action recognition tasks. Software like CVAT can help automate some of these processes. Take this example, you might annotate a video sequence depicting a soccer match by tracking player movements and actions (such as passing or shooting) across multiple frames.

Establishing clear annotation guidelines is essential for maintaining consistency throughout your dataset. When multiple annotators are involved, varying interpretations of guidelines can lead to discrepancies. A well-defined set of rules outlining how each type of data should be annotated minimizes variability and enhances quality control.

To further streamline the annotation process, consider integrating automation tools that leverage machine learning models trained on smaller sets of annotated data to predict labels for unannotated examples. This approach can significantly accelerate the workflow, particularly when managing large datasets.

Once your dataset has been annotated, validation becomes imperative. Randomly sampling annotated entries helps ensure that labels are accurate and adhere to established guidelines. Take this example, having a peer review a subset of annotations can uncover inconsistencies that need to be addressed before incorporating your dataset into training workflows.

dedicating time to proper data annotation equips your AI agents with the clarity they need for effective learning. As you refine your approach to this vital step, remember that high-quality annotations go beyond mere labeling; they lay a strong foundation for machine learning models that can adapt and excel in real-world applications. By carefully considering techniques tailored to your specific dataset types, you will not only enhance the learning capabilities of your AI systems but also increase their practical utility across diverse domains.

Data Privacy and Security Considerations

Data privacy and security have become crucial considerations in the age of AI, especially as organizations increasingly depend on large volumes of sensitive data to power their intelligent systems. With every dataset comes the responsibility to protect personal information and comply with regulations governing data use. Neglecting these responsibilities can lead to serious consequences, including legal repercussions and a loss of trust among users.

To grasp the importance of data privacy, it's essential to understand the types of data being collected. Personally identifiable information (PII)—which includes names, addresses, social security numbers, and even biometric data— must be handled with the utmost care. Organizations should prioritize minimizing data collection, gathering only what is necessary for specific purposes. This approach not only reduces risks but also aligns with various data protection regulations, such as the General Data Protection Regulation (GDPR) in Europe.

Closely linked to privacy is data security; protecting sensitive information from unauthorized access is critical. Implementing strong security measures, such as encryption, serves as a vital first line of defense. For example, encrypting sensitive customer data ensures that even if unauthorized individuals gain access, the information remains unreadable without decryption keys. Widely used solutions like AES (Advanced Encryption Standard) offer robust encryption capabilities for this purpose.

Establishing clear access controls within your organization is equally important. Identifying who can view or manipulate different types of data is essential for preventing breaches and ensuring accountability. Role-based access control (RBAC) allows organizations to assign permissions based on users' roles, minimizing unnecessary exposure to sensitive information. Take this example, marketing teams may require access to anonymized user behavior data for analysis but should not have access to raw PII.

Regular audits of data handling practices and security protocols can help identify vulnerabilities before they escalate into serious issues. These audits might involve reviewing access logs for unusual activity or verifying that encryption standards are consistently applied across all stored datasets. Tools like Splunk can assist in monitoring efforts by providing real-time insights into user activity and potential threats.

Beyond technical measures, cultivating a culture of security awareness among employees is vital. Training sessions that cover best practices for handling sensitive information empower team members to recognize potential risks, such as phishing attacks or improper data sharing. For example, periodic workshops can teach employees how to identify suspicious emails and understand the implications of sharing unencrypted files over unsecured networks.

Regulatory compliance adds another layer of complexity to managing data privacy and security. Staying informed about evolving laws and standards related to data protection is essential for any organization operating across multiple jurisdictions. GDPR, for instance, imposes strict guidelines concerning user consent and rights regarding personal data; failure to comply can result in significant fines that impact your organization's bottom line.

To build user confidence in your AI solutions, transparency about your data handling practices is crucial. This could involve publishing clear privacy policies that outline how users' data will be used, shared, and protected. Providing mechanisms for users to opt-out or control their data enhances trust and demonstrates a commitment to ethical practices.

As you develop AI agents that utilize diverse datasets, embedding strong privacy and security frameworks from the outset will yield long-term benefits. These principles not only protect individuals but also uphold your organization's integrity in an increasingly scrutinized digital landscape. By incorporating stringent measures around both privacy and security into every phase—from development through deployment—you create an environment where innovation flourishes alongside ethical responsibility.

In a rapidly evolving technological landscape, maintaining robust privacy and security protocols serves as a foundation for building trust with users while exploring the limitless possibilities AI offers in transforming industries and enhancing lives.

Implementing Data Pipelines

Implementing data pipelines is essential for effectively managing and leveraging the vast amounts of data that AI agents require. As organizations increasingly depend on these agents to drive decision-making and automation, establishing a seamless flow of data—from collection to processing and storage—becomes crucial. A well-designed data pipeline ensures that the right information reaches the appropriate systems at the right time, thereby facilitating intelligent insights and actions.

The first step in this process is identifying your specific data sources. These can include internal databases, APIs, third-party services, user-generated content, and IoT devices. Understanding where your data originates allows you to map its journey through the pipeline. For example, if your AI agent needs customer feedback from social media platforms, it is essential to set up an automated mechanism for pulling that data. Tools like Apache Kafka or Apache NiFi can help streamline this process, enabling real-time ingestion from multiple channels.

Once you've identified your data sources, the next step is transforming raw data into a format suitable for analysis or processing. Data often comes in various forms—structured, semi-structured, or unstructured—and may require cleaning or preprocessing before it can be utilized effectively. Take this example, when aggregating user behavior logs from different websites, it's vital to standardize timestamps and eliminate duplicates to maintain consistency across datasets.

To facilitate this transformation stage, consider leveraging ETL (Extract, Transform, Load) tools such as Talend or Informatica. These platforms simplify complex transformations with user-friendly interfaces that allow you to create workflows with minimal coding effort. With Talend, you can set up a job that extracts relevant fields from incoming JSON files and loads them into a structured database like PostgreSQL without requiring extensive programming knowledge.

After transformation is complete, loading the processed data into a centralized storage solution simplifies access for analysis and reporting. Cloud-based options like AWS S3 or Google Cloud Storage provide scalable solutions for storing both structured and unstructured data. By utilizing these services, organizations can manage storage costs effectively while ensuring high availability of their datasets.

Monitoring and maintaining data pipelines are also crucial for their long-term functionality. Implementing automated checks helps identify bottlenecks or failures before they affect downstream processes. Tools like Apache Airflow make it easy to schedule tasks and define dependencies between them; you can set alerts based on performance metrics so that if a task fails—such as failing to pull new sales records—you receive immediate notifications.

Additionally, version control plays a key role in managing changes to both your data schema and the underlying code of your pipeline. Incorporating software development practices into your data management approach enhances collaboration among team members working on different aspects of the pipeline. Solutions like Git enable effective tracking of changes over time while allowing multiple contributors to collaborate without conflicts.

Security should be integral to every aspect of your pipeline design. Implementing data encryption during transit and at rest ensures that sensitive information remains protected against unauthorized access. Using methods such as TLS (Transport Layer Security) when transmitting data across networks minimizes vulnerabilities associated with exposure during transfers.

Testing is another critical component of effective data pipeline implementation; thorough testing helps catch anomalies early in development rather than after deployment when they could disrupt operations or lead to erroneous conclusions drawn from faulty datasets. Create test scenarios that mimic real-world conditions using sample datasets representative of actual usage patterns.

With an established workflow in place, automation becomes achievable—significantly reducing manual effort while increasing efficiency across all stages of the pipeline's operation. Automating repetitive tasks not only frees up resources but also minimizes human error associated with manual handling.

Finally, incorporating feedback loops where insights gained from analytics inform improvements in subsequent iterations fosters continuous optimization of both the pipeline itself and its outputs. This dynamic approach enables organizations to adapt quickly as their needs evolve alongside advancements in technology and shifts in market demands.

By meticulously implementing robust data pipelines tailored specifically for AI agent operations, organizations empower themselves to harness real-time insights—ultimately enhancing decision-making capabilities while paving the way for innovative applications driven by intelligent automation.

Tools for Data Management

Data management is a fundamental element in the realm of no-code AI, transforming raw information into actionable insights that drive intelligent systems. To effectively leverage the capabilities of AI agents, it's crucial to understand and utilize the right tools for managing data. These tools simplify processes, enhance accuracy, and increase speed, ultimately laying the groundwork for robust decision-making.

The first step in this journey is to assess the nature of your data. Whether it consists of structured data from databases, unstructured data from social media platforms, or semi-structured formats like JSON files, understanding these characteristics will inform your choice of management tools. Take this example, if you're handling large datasets that require frequent updates, platforms such as Google BigQuery or Amazon Redshift can be invaluable. They enable efficient querying and management of vast amounts of structured data, all without needing complex SQL knowledge.

After identifying your data types, the next step is to integrate them seamlessly using appropriate tools. Solutions like Zapier and Integromat offer user-friendly interfaces that connect various applications and services effortlessly. For example, you can create a Zap to automatically transfer lead information from a web form into your CRM system—no coding needed. This automation not only saves time but also minimizes the risk of manual errors that could compromise data integrity.

Alongside integration tools, having reliable options for

data cleaning and preprocessing is essential. Raw data often requires careful curation before analysis. Tools like OpenRefine simplify this task by helping users explore and clean datasets, identifying inconsistencies and allowing for bulk edits with ease. Imagine having customer feedback collected from multiple platforms with varied formatting; OpenRefine can help standardize this information quickly and efficiently.

Once your datasets are clean and consistent, consider how they will be stored and accessed. Cloud storage solutions like Microsoft Azure Blob Storage provide scalable options suited to diverse needs, whether managing small text files or large video uploads. Their built-in security features protect sensitive information while ensuring easy access across teams.

To maintain effective oversight of your data management processes, implement monitoring solutions such as DataDog or Grafana. These platforms track performance metrics in real-time, alerting you to potential issues before they escalate. Take this example, if a dataset begins encountering upload errors, early alerts can prompt immediate investigation and resolution.

Regular updates are crucial for keeping your tools current and aligned with evolving organizational requirements. Integrating DevOps practices within your data management strategy—using version control systems like Git—enables efficient change management while fostering collaboration among team members working on different project components.

Security should always be a priority in your tool selection and implementation process. Beyond employing encryption protocols like TLS during transmission, consider exploring Identity Access Management (IAM) solutions available through cloud providers to restrict access based on user roles effectively. This guarantees that only authorized personnel can modify sensitive datasets.

Testing remains an indispensable part of this cycle; establishing comprehensive test environments allows you to simulate real-world scenarios using representative sample datasets. This approach not only identifies bugs early but also ensures that workflows perform as expected under various conditions.

Automation serves as a powerful ally in streamlining operations across all stages of your data management strategy. For example, utilizing Apache NiFi allows users to automate complex workflows involving multiple sources while minimizing human intervention—a crucial factor for enhancing efficiency.

Finally, establishing feedback loops is essential for refining both processes and outputs over time. Analyzing insights gained from user interactions with AI agents can inform adjustments in how your data is managed or presented. This iterative approach fosters a culture of continuous improvement where innovation can thrive.

By strategically deploying these tools tailored for managing data within no-code AI frameworks, organizations can unlock deeper insights efficiently—transforming mundane tasks into streamlined operations while empowering their teams with reliable information needed for smart decision-making on demand. Effective data management not only enhances operational efficiency but also elevates the overall intelligence of AI agents deployed across diverse applications.

Ensuring Data Quality

Data quality serves as the backbone of any successful no-code AI initiative. When data lacks quality, the insights generated by AI agents can become misleading or even harmful. To ensure high data quality, several dimensions must be considered: accuracy, consistency, completeness, and relevance. Each of these aspects is critical in shaping the effectiveness of your AI systems.

Starting with accuracy, it's vital to implement mechanisms that verify the correctness of your data. For example, when collecting customer information through website forms, validation checks can help ensure entries are accurate. Tools like Google Forms allow you to set rules that automatically reject invalid inputs—such as email addresses missing an "@" sign or phone numbers with incorrect lengths—right at the point of entry.

Equally important is consistency across datasets. Disparate data sources often lead to variations in formats and terminology. Take this example, one department may refer to a product as "Widget A," while another might call it "A Widget." Standardization tools like Data Ladder can help harmonize naming conventions across databases. When all teams use the same terminology and format, collaboration improves and confusion decreases.

Next, completeness pertains to having all necessary data points available for analysis. Missing information can result in skewed results or limit the potential of your AI applications. Tools such as Talend can identify gaps within datasets and fill them using predefined rules or machine learning predictions based on existing data patterns. By employing these strategies, you ensure that your datasets are not only complete but also rich enough to provide valuable insights.

Relevance focuses on filtering out noise from your datasets—excluding data points that do not meaningfully contribute to your AI project objectives. This often requires periodic reviews of your data sources and their contributions. Automating checks using platforms like Segment can streamline this process by collecting only relevant user interaction metrics that feed directly into your decision-making frameworks.

Once you establish high standards for quality across these dimensions, continuous monitoring becomes crucial.

Automated monitoring systems can help catch deviations early on. Take this example, if a sudden spike in missing values occurs after an update in how data is collected from users, a tool like Apache Airflow can alert you immediately so you can implement corrective measures swiftly.

Training your team on best practices in data management further enhances quality assurance efforts. Encouraging the use of collaborative platforms like Notion or Confluence for documenting processes related to data entry and management fosters accountability and raises awareness about maintaining high standards within teams responsible for managing datasets.

Regular audits of both datasets and processes are another pivotal step in ensuring ongoing data quality. Establishing a quarterly audit schedule allows you to review how well your strategies are working and make necessary adjustments based on evaluation findings. These audits should assess not only the datasets themselves but also how effectively they are being utilized within AI systems.

Additionally, creating feedback loops with users interacting with AI agents helps identify pain points related to data usage in real-time scenarios. Systematically collecting feedback— using tools like SurveyMonkey—can provide insights into how accurately the AI meets user expectations and where gaps may exist regarding input or output quality.

Finally, integrating machine learning techniques can enhance quality control by enabling predictive analytics on incoming data streams. For example, if historical patterns indicate that certain fields are often left blank during specific periods (like holiday seasons), machine learning models trained on past behavior can suggest likely values based on similar contexts.

By focusing relentlessly on these facets of data quality— from accuracy through relevance—you empower your no-code AI initiatives with robust foundations capable of yielding significant insights and driving intelligent actions across various applications. This commitment not only elevates operational efficiency but also strategically positions organizations for sustainable growth in an increasingly competitive landscape where intelligent decision-making is paramount.

Real-Time Data Processing

The demand for real-time data processing has never been greater. In today's fast-paced business environment, organizations need immediate insights to make informed decisions. This need has led to the development of sophisticated systems designed to handle data as it flows in. Real-time data processing empowers organizations to respond dynamically to changes, optimize operations, and enhance customer experiences. However, achieving effective real-time processing requires a nuanced understanding of the entire data lifecycle, from ingestion to analysis and action.

Essentially of real-time data processing lies the concept of continuous data streams. Unlike traditional batch processing, which collects and processes data at fixed intervals, real-time systems work with data as it arrives. For example, an e-commerce platform monitoring transactions can analyze every purchase in real time, extracting valuable information such as transaction amounts, customer IDs, and timestamps. By employing tools like Apache Kafka or Amazon Kinesis, businesses can efficiently ingest and process these data streams.

To fully harness the advantages of real-time processing, it is essential to establish a robust architecture. A common strategy involves leveraging a combination of event-driven architecture (EDA) and microservices. In an EDA setup, events trigger actions throughout the system. Take this example, when a customer places an order, this event can initiate multiple actions simultaneously: updating inventory levels, sending confirmation emails, and logging analytics data—all executed seamlessly in real time.

Despite its benefits, managing large volumes of streaming data presents challenges. One significant concern is latency—the delay in processing data—which can greatly affect decision-making. To address this issue, organizations need low-latency systems in place. Techniques like edge computing can help by bringing computation closer to the data source, thereby reducing the distance that information must travel before being processed and accelerating response times.

Once data is ingested in real time, it is crucial to use analytics engines capable of delivering insights quickly. Stream processing frameworks such as Apache Flink or Apache Storm excel in this area by enabling complex event processing (CEP). This allows businesses to identify patterns as they emerge. For example, financial institutions employ CEP to monitor transactions for potential fraud by establishing rules that flag unusual activity—such as multiple high-value transactions from different locations within a short timeframe.

Integrating machine learning further enhances real-time systems. Predictive models can be deployed directly within streaming pipelines using frameworks like TensorFlow Extended (TFX). Take this example, a retail company could utilize machine learning models trained on historical purchasing behavior to forecast which products are likely to sell well during an upcoming holiday season based on current sales trends observed in their streaming data.

Data visualization is also vital for interpreting real-time analytics effectively. Dashboards created with tools like Tableau or Power BI offer dynamic views of key performance indicators (KPIs), enabling teams to monitor metrics live as they evolve. This capability not only supports quick decision-making but also helps stakeholders visualize trends over time, fostering proactive rather than reactive strategies.

Equally important is ensuring that your system is resilient against failures. Real-time processing must incorporate redundancy and failover mechanisms to prevent severe disruptions during outages. Techniques such as distributed consensus algorithms (e.g., Paxos or Raft) help maintain consistency across distributed components in the face of failures.

Monitoring is crucial throughout this process; maintaining system performance requires vigilance over metrics like throughput and error rates. Integrating tools such as Prometheus or Grafana into your architecture provides comprehensive monitoring solutions that alert teams when performance dips below acceptable thresholds.

Real-time processing goes beyond technology; it also necessitates a cultural shift within organizations towards agility and rapid iteration. By building cross-functional teams capable of swiftly pivoting based on live insights, organizations create an environment where innovation can thrive.

In summary, mastering real-time data processing involves a delicate balance of technological infrastructure, analytical capabilities, and a readiness for cultural change. The ability to process and act on data as it arrives opens up countless opportunities for businesses willing to innovate and adapt quickly in today's competitive landscape, where every second counts in seizing opportunities and addressing challenges effectively.

CHAPTER 8:
CUSTOMIZING AI
AGENT BEHAVIOR

Understanding Behavior Rules

Behavior rules form the foundation of AI agents, enabling them to perform tasks while aligning with user expectations and operational goals. These rules dictate how an agent reacts to stimuli, interacts with users, and adapts to changing environmental conditions. Understanding behavior rules can be compared to teaching a child how to respond appropriately in various situations —a blend of guidance, learned experiences, and adjustments based on feedback.

At the heart of any effective AI agent lies the clear definition of behaviors. Take, for instance, a chatbot designed for customer service. Its behavior rules might include responding politely to inquiries, escalating unresolved issues after three attempts, or providing alternative resources when the answer is unknown. Each response can be customized according to context, such as the urgency of a query or the sentiment expressed in user messages.

An essential element of defining these behavior rules is identifying triggers that prompt specific actions. A trigger could be a keyword like "urgent" or a user action, such as clicking a button. In our chatbot scenario, if a customer types "I need help now," it could trigger an immediate escalation to a human representative. This approach not only boosts user satisfaction but also ensures that the agent operates dynamically rather than statically.

And, behavior rules must allow for flexibility and adaptability. An AI agent should not just react but also anticipate user needs based on historical interactions or predictive analytics. Take this example, if an e-commerce AI recognizes that a user regularly buys athletic wear every six months during seasonal sales, it could proactively send reminders about upcoming discounts or suggest new products tailored to that user's preferences.

To implement these behavior rules effectively, using decision trees or state machines within your no-code platform is crucial. Decision trees provide a clear mapping of various pathways based on different conditions and outcomes. Let's illustrate this with a simple decision tree for our customer service chatbot:

1. User Inquiry: The chat opens with "How can I assist you today?

2. If the user says "I have an urgent issue," escalate the conversation.

3. If the user asks "I have a question about my order," request the order number.

4. Order Inquiry:

5. If the order number is provided, check its status.

6. If the order number is not provided, ask for it and offer assistance in locating it.

7. Resolution Outcome:

8. If the issue is resolved, inquire if there's anything else.

9. If unresolved after three attempts, escalate automatically.

This structured approach ensures clarity in interactions while allowing personalization based on individual user behaviors.

Incorporating feedback loops into your behavior design is also vital. Feedback loops enable your AI agent to continuously learn from interactions, offering opportunities for improvement without extensive reprogramming. For example, if users frequently express frustration over certain automated responses—perhaps indicated by keywords like "not helpful"—this data can inform adjustments to behavior rules.

A practical example of this concept can be seen in digital assistants like Siri or Alexa, which continually learn from user interactions and adapt their responses based on preferred communication styles or common requests over time.

In summary, behavior rules provide both structure and guidance for AI agents, defining their capabilities while allowing them to evolve in response to user needs and preferences. By grounding your design decisions in solid behavioral principles and adaptive learning strategies, you enhance functionality and foster genuinely valuable interactions between technology and its users.

Designing Custom Algorithms

Designing custom algorithms for AI agents is essential for creating intelligent systems that effectively meet user needs and adapt to their environments. These algorithms act as the brain behind the behaviors we define, translating abstract rules into actionable processes that guide an agent's decisions and interactions. The journey begins with a clear understanding of the specific objectives your AI agent aims to achieve, laying a solid foundation for algorithmic design.

Establishing clarity around your agent's purpose is crucial. For example, if you're developing a health-monitoring AI for personal wellness, the algorithm should include features like data collection from wearables, analysis of user habits, and generation of personalized feedback. Each of these components requires distinct algorithmic pathways that dictate how data flows through the system and shapes user interactions.

During the design phase, consider utilizing flowcharts or pseudocode as foundational tools. Flowcharts can help visualize decision-making processes, allowing you to outline potential scenarios your agent might encounter. Pseudocode, on the other hand, presents algorithm logic in a human-readable format without getting bogged down in programming syntax. In our health-monitoring scenario, a simple pseudocode snippet could look like this:

```
` ` `

IF heart_rate > threshold THEN

send_alert("High heart rate detected")

ELSE IF activity_level < recommended THEN

suggest_activity("How about a walk?")

END IF

` ` `
```

This approach allows you to concentrate on what the AI should accomplish before delving into coding specifics.

Once you establish your basic structure, it's important to consider integrating machine learning components where appropriate. Machine learning can enhance an AI agent's performance by enabling it to learn from past interactions rather than relying solely on predefined rules. Take this example, in our health-monitoring example, this might involve analyzing trends over time to recognize patterns in when users typically experience elevated heart rates and adapting responses accordingly.

To make these learning capabilities more accessible without requiring extensive coding knowledge, many no-code platforms now offer built-in machine learning functionalities. These platforms often feature drag-and-drop interfaces that allow you to input training data sets and specify outcomes easily. Tools like Google AutoML or Microsoft Azure ML can facilitate the upload of datasets related to user health metrics while helping you define desired outcomes for predictions or recommendations.

As you develop your algorithms, it's vital to remain mindful of ethical considerations and potential biases that may arise during both design and implementation phases. Every choice made while crafting algorithms can significantly impact user experience and trust in your AI system. For example, an algorithm designed for loan approvals that inadvertently favors certain demographics due to biased training data could lead to serious ethical concerns.

Testing is another critical step in designing algorithms for AI agents. Conducting rigorous tests against real-world scenarios ensures that your algorithms perform as expected under various conditions. Create environments that simulate user interactions—through simulated users or A/B testing methodologies—to assess how well your algorithms respond before full deployment.

And, it's essential to iterate based on user feedback after launching your AI agents into production. Monitoring performance metrics will highlight areas needing adjustments —whether in response speed or recommendation accuracy —and enable continuous refinement of the underlying algorithms.

In summary, designing custom algorithms transcends mere rule creation; it involves crafting experiences that resonate with users while remaining adaptable to their evolving needs. By prioritizing clarity of purpose, leveraging accessible design tools, incorporating machine learning where suitable, upholding ethical standards, and committing to ongoing testing and refinement, you set your AI agents up for success in an increasingly complex digital landscape. With these guiding principles, you're not just building technology; you're fostering meaningful relationships between users and intelligent systems that evolve alongside them.

Adding Personality to Chatbots

Creating a chatbot with personality is an exciting endeavor that enriches user interactions. Unlike standard bots that respond mechanically, a personality-infused chatbot engages users in a more relatable manner, making conversations feel more human-like. This journey begins with defining the traits you want your chatbot to embody—whether friendly, formal, humorous, or empathetic. These attributes will guide the design of responses and behaviors throughout its lifecycle.

Take, for instance, a customer service chatbot for an e-commerce platform. If the desired personality is friendly and supportive, its responses should reflect warmth and approachability. Rather than simply stating product information, the bot might say, "I'd love to help you find that perfect pair of shoes! Do you have any styles in mind?" This subtle shift creates a conversational tone that enhances the user experience and fosters trust.

Once you've outlined the core personality traits, the next step is to develop a consistent voice across all interactions. Consistency is key; users should feel as if they are speaking with the same entity every time they interact with your bot. Creating a style guide that includes specific phrases, emojis, and punctuation styles can help ensure uniformity.

For example, if the bot frequently uses exclamation marks to convey enthusiasm—like "Awesome! Let's get started!"—this tone should be maintained throughout all replies.

Adapting language to fit different contexts while retaining defined character traits is another critical aspect of personality development. A humorous chatbot might use light-hearted jokes or playful puns in casual conversations but should adopt a more serious tone when addressing pressing issues. For example, when responding to inquiries about order delays, it could say, "I'm really sorry for the wait! Let me check on that for you right away." Here, humor takes a backseat to understanding and reassurance.

Building scenarios is vital for shaping how your chatbot responds under various circumstances. By anticipating user inquiries and crafting tailored responses, you create a rich conversational flow. Utilizing decision trees or dialogue maps can help visualize potential conversation paths. Imagine a customer asking about product returns; your bot could follow this pathway:

1. **User asks about returns.

2. Bot replies: "Returns are easy! I can guide you through the process."

3. If the user responds positively: "Great! Can I have your order number?"

4. If the user seems frustrated: "I understand returns can be tricky sometimes. Let's make this as smooth as possible!"

This flexibility allows your chatbot to effectively handle diverse emotional tones from users.

Integrating user feedback mechanisms is another powerful way to refine your chatbot's personality over time. Encourage users to rate their interactions or provide comments after chats. This feedback not only identifies areas needing improvement but also reveals how well the bot's personality resonates with users. Take this example, if users consistently enjoy the chat's humor but express frustration during complex inquiries, adjustments can be made accordingly.

And, leveraging machine learning tools on no-code platforms can facilitate ongoing enhancements without requiring deep programming skills. Many platforms allow chatbots to learn from previous interactions, helping them understand which responses work best in specific contexts or user moods.

For example, if data shows that customers often ask about shipping times right after placing an order, adding proactive responses about shipping updates could enhance overall satisfaction. You might configure your bot to automatically inform users: "Hey there! Just wanted to let you know that your order is on its way and should arrive by Tuesday!"

Finally, ethical considerations are paramount when designing personalized chatbots. Ensure that personality traits do not lead to misunderstandings or reinforce biases—especially when humor or cultural references are involved. Testing with diverse user groups can help validate whether your bot's personality resonates positively across various demographics.

In summary, adding personality to chatbots involves thoughtful design focused on creating relatable interactions that reflect clearly defined traits while adapting language and tone according to context. By utilizing structured scenarios for conversation flow and harnessing user feedback for continuous improvement, you can create engaging experiences that elevate user satisfaction and loyalty towards your brand or service. Embrace this opportunity not just to build technology but also to foster meaningful connections between users and intelligent systems crafted for human-like interaction.

Managing User Interactions

Creating a seamless interaction experience for users is crucial in the development of AI agents. The way users engage with these systems profoundly influences their overall satisfaction and trust. By understanding user behavior, preferences, and emotional states, we can tailor AI responses to enhance the user experience. This approach involves multiple layers, including the development of user personas and the implementation of adaptive responses based on real-time data.

The foundation of effective user interactions begins with a clear recognition of who the users are and what they need. Developing detailed user personas is essential; these personas encapsulate demographics, goals, challenges, and preferred communication styles. Take this example, a customer support agent might interact differently with a tech-savvy millennial compared to a less tech-oriented senior citizen. Understanding your audience allows you to customize interactions, making them more relevant and effective.

Once user personas are established, mapping out the typical user journey can reveal key interaction points where your AI agent can have the most significant impact. This journey encompasses everything from initial contact—such as asking a question or seeking assistance—to the resolution or completion of a task. By identifying these touchpoints, you can design responses that guide users smoothly through their experiences.

For example, consider a user who needs help with account recovery. A well-structured flow might unfold as follows:

1. User initiates: "I forgot my password."

2. AI Agent responds: "No problem! I can help you reset it. Can you please provide your email address?"

3. If the email is valid: "Great! A reset link has been sent to your inbox."

4. If the email is not found: "I'm sorry, but I couldn't find that email in our system. Would you like to try another one?"

Each response is designed to keep the conversation moving forward while effectively addressing potential roadblocks.

Real-time analytics play an essential role in managing user interactions by providing insights into how users engage with your AI agent. Implementing tracking tools to monitor engagement metrics—such as response times, drop-off rates, and common queries—can highlight areas for improvement. Take this example, if analytics show that users frequently abandon conversations after inquiries about returns or refunds, it may indicate that those responses require refinement for clarity and reassurance.

Incorporating sentiment analysis tools can further enhance responsiveness by gauging the emotional tone of user inputs in real time. If sentiment analysis detects frustration during an interaction about billing issues, your AI agent could adjust its approach: "I understand billing can be confusing; let's work together to resolve this." This sensitivity not only improves engagement but also builds trust between users and the AI system.

User feedback loops are another invaluable resource for optimizing interaction management. Prompting users for feedback at various stages of their journey fosters continuous improvement. You might use simple rating systems post-interaction or follow up with emails asking how well their issues were resolved and how they felt about their experience.

Take this example:

- After resolving an issue, ask: "Was this helpful? Rate us from 1 to 5!"

- If feedback indicates dissatisfaction: "I'm sorry we didn't meet your expectations! Can you tell us what went wrong?"

Such proactive measures not only facilitate adjustments but also demonstrate that you value user opinions.

Another important layer involves integrating contextual understanding into interactions—a feature increasingly enabled by no-code platforms today. Contextual understanding allows your AI agent to recognize prior interactions or pull relevant information into current conversations seamlessly. If a returning customer had previously asked about product specifications last week, instead of starting from scratch during their next inquiry about similar products, the bot could say: "Welcome back! Last time you were interested in our wireless headphones; do you have any specific features in mind this time?" This level of personalization adds depth to interactions that standard bots lack.

Ethical considerations are also paramount; ensuring inclusivity across diverse demographics is essential to prevent alienation of any user group while promoting positive engagement strategies is critical for maintaining integrity in design choices.

effective management of user interactions through thoughtful design leads not only to improved functionality but also to a significant enhancement in overall satisfaction with AI agents. By recognizing diverse needs through persona development and carefully mapping experiences while dynamically adapting using real-time analytics and feedback mechanisms—all these elements contribute to building strong connections between users and technology-based solutions tailored specifically for them.

To wrap things up, prioritizing user interaction management transforms mere functionality into engaging experiences that resonate on personal levels—essentially crafting intelligent systems that feel more human than mechanical at every touchpoint.

Setting Up Feedback Loops

Establishing effective feedback loops is essential for enhancing AI agents. Feedback not only sheds light on user experiences but also steers your iterations, ensuring the AI evolves in harmony with user expectations and needs. To achieve this, proactive feedback collection should be woven into every interaction, rather than treated as an afterthought.

Begin by integrating subtle prompts throughout the user journey. Take this example, after an interaction, consider asking users for their thoughts: "Did I help you find what you were looking for?" This question can be posed immediately after providing a solution or included in a follow-up message. Such inquiries seamlessly fit into the conversation, demonstrating to users that their opinions matter and fostering rapport and trust.

Once feedback is gathered, categorize it to extract actionable insights. Different types of responses can highlight various areas for improvement. User ratings provide quantitative data, while open-ended comments can offer deeper insights into emotional responses or points of confusion. For example, if multiple users express frustration with the navigation of an agent's responses, it indicates that reorganizing the conversation flow could be beneficial.

A practical approach might involve implementing a simple rating system paired with follow-up questions. After interacting with your AI agent, prompt users to rate their experience on a scale from 1 to 5 and ask them to elaborate on what influenced their rating: "Please share any suggestions for improving our service." This not only helps gauge satisfaction levels but also yields concrete suggestions for refinement.

Continuous monitoring is crucial in establishing these feedback loops. Utilize analytics tools to track user interactions in real-time, focusing on metrics like engagement duration, common queries leading to drop-offs, and recurring themes in feedback. Such data enables you to identify trends; if numerous users inquire about similar topics or seem confused at specific points in their interactions, it serves as a signal for further investigation.

Consider employing A/B testing for different versions of your feedback queries or interaction flows. By systematically altering one variable—such as the phrasing of a response— you can assess which version elicits higher satisfaction ratings or more detailed feedback submissions. For example, if asking "Was this helpful?" generates fewer responses than "How would you rate my assistance today?" it suggests that users respond better to more engaging prompts.

It's equally important to ensure that feedback loops are closed; inform users how their input has influenced changes within the system. If users report confusion over certain responses that lead to improvements in the bot's conversational flow, communicate these changes through an engaging message during their next interaction: "Thanks for helping us improve! We've made some changes based on your valuable input." This transparency builds trust and encourages ongoing participation in your feedback processes.

Incorporating machine learning algorithms can further enhance feedback loops. With sufficient historical data from user interactions and inputs, your AI agent can begin to learn preferences over time—adapting its responses without the need for manual reprogramming whenever shifts occur in user behavior or preferences. Take this example, if data reveals that users often ask about delivery times shortly after making purchases, your AI could proactively include that information in relevant conversations.

Finally, don't underestimate the importance of emotional intelligence within AI conversations shaped by feedback loops. Utilize sentiment analysis tools to gauge how users feel during their interactions. If frustration levels rise during exchanges related to technical issues or product inquiries, consider adjusting response strategies—perhaps by incorporating more empathetic language or offering additional reassurances regarding resolution timelines.

Feedback loops act as both a mirror reflecting current performance and a compass guiding future improvements. By embedding these mechanisms deeply into your AI systems —from proactive querying and responsive adaptations to leveraging analytics for strategic enhancements—you create an intelligent ecosystem that continuously learns and evolves alongside its users.

effective feedback loops transform passive observations into dynamic dialogues between technology and humanity— ensuring that each interaction remains meaningful while paving the way for continuous improvement through direct engagement with user needs and experiences.

Adapting to Changing Environments

Adapting your AI agent to changing environments is not just a technical necessity; it's essential for its ongoing success and relevance. In a world that is constantly evolving—where user preferences shift, market dynamics change, and new technologies emerge—your AI systems must remain agile and responsive. While a static agent may have been effective at launch, it risks becoming obsolete without continual adaptability.

One effective strategy for fostering this adaptability is through real-time data analysis. By continuously monitoring user interactions, feedback, and emerging trends, you provide your AI with the insights necessary to pivot when needed. Take this example, if analytics reveal an increasing user interest in sustainability, you can adjust the AI's responses or resources to align with this trend. This might involve creating tailored content that addresses eco-friendly practices or integrating features that highlight sustainable options available to users.

Consider an e-commerce AI agent initially designed to assist with order tracking. If data analytics indicate that users are increasingly inquiring about return policies after making purchases, recognizing this shift allows you to enhance the agent's capabilities. By adding functionality that informs users about return options immediately after they complete an order, you not only improve the customer experience but also reduce confusion—reinforcing trust in your brand.

Flexibility in design is another key element of adaptability. By building your AI agent with a modular architecture, you facilitate easy updates or feature additions without needing a complete system overhaul. Leveraging microservices or APIs allows for the independent introduction of new functionalities. For example, if you want to integrate live chat support, a modular setup enables this enhancement without disrupting existing services.

Machine learning algorithms further empower your AI agent by enabling it to learn from historical interactions and adapt its responses based on user behavior patterns. If data shows that certain phrases lead to better engagement, your AI can gradually adjust its conversational style toward those successful approaches without requiring manual intervention at every step.

Regular performance reviews also play a vital role in adaptation. Establish routines to assess how well your AI meets current user expectations compared to actual performance. This process involves analyzing both qualitative feedback from users and quantitative metrics such as interaction completion rates and satisfaction scores. If you find that users disengage during specific tasks—like product searches—it signals that adjustments are necessary, whether through refining search algorithms or improving the user interface's intuitiveness.

Creating an environment where users feel empowered to share insights about their experiences is equally important. By cultivating a community around your AI, you not only foster loyalty but also generate valuable qualitative data for adaptation efforts. Running surveys focused on user satisfaction after interactions can yield direct suggestions for improvement while simultaneously making users feel valued and heard.

It's also crucial to incorporate seasonal or contextual changes into your AI's functionality to maintain relevance. An adaptive AI should reflect current events or trends pertinent to its domain. Take this example, a travel booking assistant can significantly benefit from adjusting its offerings based on holidays or local events occurring in popular destinations throughout the year.

Lastly, implementing continuous testing as part of your adaptive strategy is essential—what works today may not work tomorrow. Utilizing A/B testing across different components of the user experience allows you to gather data on which variations yield better results in terms of engagement and satisfaction. This iterative approach enables organic refinement of features while remaining sensitive to evolving user needs.

Effective adaptation isn't just about reacting to change; it's about anticipating shifts before they occur and embedding flexibility into your design philosophy from the outset. Every enhancement should stem from a deep understanding of both current conditions and projected shifts in user behaviors or market trends.

By fostering an agile mindset within your development practices—and grounding decisions in robust data—you create an intelligent feedback system capable of thriving amid constant change. Adaptability thus transforms from a daunting challenge into a strategic advantage, keeping your AI agent at the forefront of innovation and responsiveness while ensuring long-term success and satisfaction for its users.

Using AI for Dynamic Decision Making

Leveraging AI for dynamic decision-making is revolutionizing how organizations operate in today's fast-paced environment. As both businesses and individuals face an ever-growing volume of data, AI's ability to process information swiftly and efficiently has become essential. Unlike traditional methods that rely on static rules or predetermined paths, dynamic decision-making allows systems to adjust in real-time, responding to user interactions and changing external conditions.

Central to this approach is AI's capability to analyze vast datasets at remarkable speeds. For example, consider a customer service AI that engages with users across multiple channels. By analyzing historical chat logs, purchase behaviors, and customer feedback in real-time, it can swiftly identify emerging trends or potential issues. If a sudden influx of inquiries about product availability arises from a marketing campaign, the AI can prioritize those questions and provide timely updates on stock levels or alternatives. This not only expedites responses but also enhances user satisfaction by addressing their immediate needs effectively.

In addition, integrating predictive analytics into your AI framework significantly amplifies its effectiveness. Utilizing machine learning algorithms to assess past behaviors enables systems to forecast future actions. Take this example, in the finance sector, a banking AI could examine transaction histories to predict when a customer might require assistance or express interest in new financial products. If data suggests that customers who exceed certain spending thresholds are likely to inquire about investment opportunities, targeted outreach can be initiated proactively. This approach fosters stronger relationships and increases conversion rates.

Context-aware computing further enhances AI's decision-making capabilities by allowing it to operate based on situational awareness. Picture an urban transport app that tailors its recommendations according to real-time traffic data, weather conditions, and local events. If heavy rain is forecasted alongside a nearby sports event, the app can suggest alternative routes or transportation modes to help users avoid delays. Such contextual adaptability not only enriches the user experience but also establishes your service as vital during critical times.

Collaboration across various organizational functions is also essential for effective decision-making. An AI designed for sales teams can integrate insights from marketing initiatives while accessing inventory management systems. By consolidating these perspectives, it can deliver tailored recommendations regarding promotional strategies or upselling opportunities based on current stock levels and customer preferences—optimizing performance across the organization instead of in isolated silos.

Real-time feedback loops are crucial for refining decision-making processes as well. When users interact with your system—whether through inquiries or ratings—this data should be continuously captured and analyzed. Take this example, if customer ratings decline after launching a new feature, immediate investigations can determine whether adjustments are necessary or if additional training for the AI is needed to meet user expectations effectively.

Incorporating user-generated insights into your dynamic decision-making toolkit is equally important. Collecting qualitative feedback through user surveys after interactions provides direct input on what resonates with users and what leaves them wanting more. This feedback can inform iterative improvements rather than relying solely on assumptions about user preferences.

As you implement these strategies, it's essential to recognize how automated decision frameworks enhance speed without compromising quality. Automated rule sets informed by machine learning models facilitate rapid responses while ensuring alignment with overarching business objectives—striking a balance between efficiency and thoughtful analysis.

And, ethical considerations must underlie every decision made by your AI system. As these systems grow increasingly autonomous—particularly in sensitive areas like healthcare or finance—transparency and accountability throughout the decision-making process become crucial. Establishing clear guidelines for how decisions are made fosters trust among users and mitigates risks associated with unintended consequences.

utilizing AI for dynamic decision-making shifts organizations from reactive processes to proactive strategies that anticipate user needs before they arise. This transformation creates competitive advantages across industries while enhancing overall service quality. Embracing this evolution not only positions organizations favorably within their markets but also nurtures deeper connections between technology and its daily users—a potent combination for success in today's digital landscape.

Continuous Learning and Improvement

The journey of continuous learning and improvement is essential for anyone aiming to harness the full potential of AI agents. In an era where technology evolves at a rapid pace, the ability to adapt and grow is imperative. Continuous learning isn't merely an optional endeavor; it is a fundamental principle that ensures your AI systems remain relevant, efficient, and capable of meeting user expectations.

To begin, foster a culture that embraces experimentation. Encouraging team members to explore new features, tools, or approaches can yield unexpected insights. For example, a marketing team might test various messaging strategies in their AI-driven campaigns. By analyzing performance data—such as click-through rates and conversion metrics—they can identify what resonates with their audience. This iterative process cultivates an environment where learning from both successes and failures is valued, ultimately enhancing AI capabilities.

Engaging with the broader AI community also provides invaluable learning opportunities. Participate in forums, attend webinars, and follow industry leaders on platforms like LinkedIn or Twitter. Staying connected with others in the field allows you to gain insights into emerging trends, best practices, and potential pitfalls. Many organizations share case studies detailing their successful AI implementations; learning from these real-world experiences helps you avoid common mistakes while adopting proven strategies.

Training your AI systems should be an ongoing commitment. Regularly updating models with new data ensures they adapt to shifting patterns in user behavior and market conditions. Take this example, consider a retail AI agent that predicts customer preferences based on past purchases. As shopping habits evolve—perhaps influenced by seasonal trends or economic changes—feeding updated sales data into the model maintains its accuracy. This proactive approach prevents stagnation and enhances the system's responsiveness.

Implementing feedback mechanisms is another crucial aspect of continuous improvement. Actively seek input from users interacting with your AI systems; their perspectives are valuable insights that can guide enhancements. If users frequently express confusion about a specific feature in your chatbot interface, understanding this pain point enables targeted adjustments that improve usability and satisfaction.

Incorporating metrics into your improvement strategy is vital for effectively gauging progress. Define key performance indicators (KPIs) relevant to your AI initiatives—such as response time, accuracy rates, or user satisfaction scores—and track these over time. This quantitative approach not only identifies areas needing attention but also celebrates achievements as improvements are realized.

Training sessions focused on the latest advancements in AI can further bolster team expertise. Whether it's understanding new machine learning algorithms or exploring advanced data processing techniques, ongoing education empowers your team to leverage cutting-edge tools effectively. Consider partnering with educational institutions for workshops or online courses tailored specifically for no-code platforms and AI technologies.

The continuous integration of user feedback into development cycles strengthens your approach even more. Implementing agile methodologies allows teams to iterate quickly based on real-time user insights while staying aligned with business objectives. Agile practices promote flexibility; adjusting priorities based on immediate feedback ensures projects meet actual user needs rather than rigidly adhering to predefined plans.

Lastly, remain mindful of ethical implications as you innovate continuously. Establishing ethical guidelines should be integral to your improvement framework—ensuring every iteration respects user privacy and promotes fairness in decision-making processes builds trust over time.

As you embark on this journey toward continuous learning and improvement, remember to keep sight of the bigger picture: each small enhancement contributes to creating a more intelligent system capable of delivering exceptional experiences tailored to users' needs. Your commitment to refining processes not only benefits technology but also enhances relationships with users who interact with it daily—an essential ingredient for sustained success in today's rapidly evolving landscape.

Case Studies of Custom AI Behavior

Customizing AI behavior empowers organizations to align their agents with specific user needs and business objectives. This process goes beyond mere technical adjustments; it involves harmonizing technology with the values and preferences of end users. Every decision made in shaping an AI agent's responses can profoundly impact user experience and satisfaction.

Consider a customer service AI implemented by a major retail company. Initially, the chatbot offered generic responses based on frequently asked questions. However, user feedback indicated that customers felt disconnected from this impersonal approach. To foster engagement, the company decided to infuse personality into the chatbot. By programming it with a friendly tone and playful language, they transformed a basic tool into a virtual assistant that felt more relatable. This shift not only enhanced customer interactions but also boosted resolution rates for initial inquiries.

Creating personalized experiences through AI necessitates a thoughtful analysis of user data and preferences. Take this example, an online learning platform could leverage user data to tailor course recommendations based on previous enrollments or expressed interests. When users receive suggestions that resonate with their unique learning journeys, engagement flourishes. This approach transcends simply pushing content; it's about understanding each learner's context and crafting pathways that feel intuitive and relevant.

Effective management of user interactions is another crucial aspect, especially in chatbots or voice assistants. The way these systems interpret and respond to human input directly affects their success. Implementing natural language processing (NLP) can significantly enhance comprehension by enabling AI agents to grasp nuances like sarcasm or emotional tone. For example, a health-focused app might use this capability to offer empathetic responses when users express frustration about managing chronic pain, illustrating how technology can connect on a human level.

Feedback loops play a vital role in continuously refining AI behavior. Imagine conducting A/B tests with different versions of a chatbot's conversation flow. One version may prioritize efficiency—leading users to answers as quickly as possible—while another focuses on rapport-building through casual conversation starters. By analyzing which version yields higher satisfaction ratings or conversion rates for specific queries, you can adjust your AI's behavior accordingly. Such experimentation not only fine-tunes performance but also fosters an iterative culture where every interaction becomes an opportunity for growth.

When adapting AI behavior, it's essential to consider how external factors can necessitate changes over time. During the pandemic, for instance, many businesses had to pivot rapidly to address new customer concerns regarding safety protocols or delivery options. An e-commerce platform that updated its chatbot to provide real-time information on shipping delays due to logistics disruptions found that proactive communication significantly improved customer trust and loyalty.

Incorporating algorithms designed for dynamic decision-making enables AI agents to adapt their responses based on real-time data analysis rather than adhering strictly to pre-set rules. An intelligent financial advisory bot, for example, could adjust its recommendations in response to market fluctuations, ensuring clients receive timely advice tailored to their current situations.

As customization efforts evolve, maintaining a commitment to continuous learning is crucial for ensuring that

AI agents keep pace with changing expectations and technologies. Regularly revisiting training data, exploring new methodologies for behavior adjustment, and encouraging team brainstorming sessions around potential enhancements create an environment where innovation thrives.

building a successful customized AI agent involves more than just coding responses; it's about forging meaningful connections with users through thoughtful design and responsive adaptations. As organizations embrace this holistic approach, they discover that well-crafted AI behaviors fulfill functional roles while also resonating emotionally with users —a dual advantage in today's competitive landscape where personalization drives loyalty and satisfaction.

To wrap things up, the journey of customizing AI behavior is an ongoing process rooted in understanding human needs while creatively leveraging technological capabilities. Through active engagement with user feedback, experimentation with interaction styles, and awareness of external influences, companies can shape AI agents that not only serve but also inspire confidence among those they aim to assist—an essential ingredient for long-term success in the digital age.

CHAPTER 9:
INTEGRATION WITH
EXISTING SYSTEMS

Identifying Integration
Opportunities

I dentifying integration opportunities is essential for effectively leveraging AI agents within an organization. This process begins with a comprehensive understanding of existing systems and workflows. Rather than simply adding new tools, the focus should be on fostering synergistic relationships that enhance overall functionality. Successful integrations can revolutionize team operations, boosting productivity and simplifying complex tasks.

To pinpoint potential integration points, start by mapping current processes. For example, consider a retail business that utilizes various software solutions for inventory management, customer relationship management (CRM), and sales analytics. Each system contains valuable data that, when integrated with an AI agent, can create a unified interface. This allows employees to access real-time insights without switching between platforms, enabling customer service representatives to quickly check inventory levels while addressing customer inquiries. The result is reduced wait times and improved service quality.

Next, evaluate which workflows experience the most friction. If teams are spending excessive time manually transferring data between systems, this presents a prime opportunity for automation. Take this example, if an HR department faces challenges in onboarding new hires due to repetitive administrative tasks spread across various applications, implementing an AI agent that centralizes information can streamline the process. Such an agent could automatically send welcome emails, schedule training sessions, and facilitate paperwork completion.

Gathering direct feedback from users is also crucial for identifying integration opportunities. Engaging stakeholders from different departments can provide valuable insights into their daily challenges and desired tools. For example, marketing teams may find it frustrating to analyze customer data scattered across platforms without easy access to analytical reports. By integrating these disparate data sources into a cohesive AI-driven dashboard tailored to their needs, marketing professionals can gain actionable insights in real time, leading to more informed decision-making.

Application Programming Interfaces (APIs) are vital in enabling these integrations by allowing different software applications to communicate seamlessly. Consider an e-commerce business that integrates its payment processing systems with inventory management software using APIs. This guarantees real-time updates on stock availability whenever a purchase occurs, preventing overselling and enhancing customer satisfaction.

Additionally, leveraging cloud services can expand integration capabilities. Cloud-based platforms often provide pre-built connectors or integrations that save time and reduce development efforts compared to custom solutions. If your organization uses platforms like Salesforce or Shopify, explore their ecosystems for available integrations with AI tools that facilitate functions such as predictive sales forecasting or personalized customer outreach based on behavior analysis.

However, it's essential to evaluate the technical readiness of your existing infrastructure when identifying integration opportunities. Assess whether your current systems can handle the added complexity introduced by AI agents. If they cannot accommodate new functionalities without significant modifications or hardware investments, it may be wise to reconsider your approach before proceeding.

Security considerations are equally important during the planning phase of any integration project. A well-integrated system must ensure that sensitive data remains protected throughout its lifecycle; thus investing in security protocols like encryption is critical.

User experience also plays a vital role in successful integrations; seamless interfaces can significantly boost engagement. An intuitive design helps users feel empowered by enhanced capabilities rather than overwhelmed by technological changes.

recognizing integration opportunities requires both analytical thinking and creative problem-solving—combining technical feasibility with an understanding of user needs creates environments where AI agents can thrive. The outcome is not only improved operational efficiency but also enriched experiences for users interacting with these systems— fostering buy-in across teams as they witness tangible benefits in their daily work lives.

Identifying these integration possibilities is a crucial step toward maximizing the impact of no-code AI agents within any organization; it lays the foundation for transformative change across all operational facets while elevating strategic goals through thoughtful execution. Embracing this perspective will lead organizations toward more intelligent processes that evolve in response to changing needs and market dynamics over time.

API and Webhooks

Integrating AI agents into your existing workflows relies heavily on understanding how APIs and webhooks connect disparate systems. APIs, or Application Programming Interfaces, are sets of rules and protocols that facilitate communication between different software applications, allowing for seamless data sharing and functionality across platforms. On the other hand, webhooks provide a way for real-time updates, enabling one application to automatically notify another when specific events occur. Together, these tools create a powerful framework for integration that can significantly boost operational efficiency.

Imagine a company that uses an email marketing tool alongside a customer relationship management (CRM) system. By leveraging APIs, the marketing platform can directly access customer data from the CRM, ensuring that campaigns are informed by the most current information available. For example, when a customer makes a purchase, their data can be automatically updated in the CRM without any manual input. This allows sales teams to maintain up-to-date insights into customer behavior.

To implement this integration effectively, start by identifying the specific API endpoints within each system you want to connect. An endpoint in an API represents a particular function or data point accessible through the API. In the case of our email marketing example, you might utilize endpoints that retrieve customer lists or update user preferences. Defining these details is crucial as it establishes how information will flow between your systems.

Following this identification phase is configuration, which

often requires writing scripts to call these API endpoints when triggered by specific events. Take this example, using JavaScript or Python, you might create a function that activates whenever a new customer signs up through your website. Here's a simple Python example:

```python
import requests

def add_new_customer(customer_data):
api_url = 'https://api.your-crm.com/customers'
response = requests.post(api_url, json=customer_data)

if response.status_code == 201:
print("Customer added successfully!")
else:
print("Error adding customer:", response.content)
```

In this example, the add_new_customer function sends new customer data to your CRM's API endpoint. Using RESTful APIs like this allows for seamless integration without requiring extensive backend development.

Webhooks can enhance this integration by facilitating real-time communication between systems. Take this example, if your e-commerce platform needs to inform your inventory management system each time an order is placed, you would set up a webhook on your e-commerce platform to send an HTTP POST request with order details whenever an order occurs. The inventory management system would then listen for these requests and update stock levels accordingly.

Configuring a webhook typically involves adjusting settings on the sending application (your e-commerce platform) to direct notifications to an endpoint on the receiving application (your inventory management system). For example:

```json
```

url": "https://api.your-inventory.com/update-stock",

event": "order_placed

```
```

This JSON structure indicates where to send updates whenever an order is placed.

As organizations increasingly adopt cloud-based tools, understanding how APIs and webhooks facilitate integration becomes essential. Many popular platforms offer comprehensive documentation and community support for their APIs, which can significantly speed up development efforts. For example, platforms like Zapier enable users to connect applications without coding through pre-built integrations that leverage APIs behind the scenes.

While integrating these technologies offers substantial benefits—such as improved data accuracy and operational efficiency—it's important to consider potential pitfalls as well. Security is paramount; improperly exposing APIs or misconfiguring webhooks could lead to unauthorized access or data breaches. Therefore, implementing security measures like OAuth for API authentication and validating incoming webhook requests is critical for protecting sensitive information.

Monitoring becomes vital once integrations are set up. Tracking API calls and webhook events helps ensure everything runs smoothly. Tools like Postman can assist with testing API requests, while logging libraries in various programming languages help monitor success and error rates in real time.

The synergy created through effective use of APIs and webhooks not only streamlines operations but also equips teams with actionable insights derived from interconnected systems. By enabling diverse tools to work together harmoniously, organizations position themselves to respond more effectively to market demands and customer needs.

In summary, leveraging APIs and webhooks transforms isolated systems into cohesive units that drive productivity and enhance user experience. While the integration process requires careful planning and execution, it ultimately establishes a foundation for innovative solutions powered by no-code AI agents—allowing businesses to adapt quickly while maximizing their existing technological investments.

Synchronization with Databases

To fully harness the potential of AI agents within your organization, database synchronization is essential. This process enables your intelligent systems to access, store, and manipulate data effectively, resulting in a seamless experience for both users and systems. Think of your database as the backbone of your AI agent's functionality, housing critical information from which actionable insights can emerge.

When embarking on database synchronization, the first step is to identify the types of databases you'll be working with. Whether you choose a SQL-based system like MySQL or PostgreSQL or a NoSQL solution such as MongoDB, understanding the unique architectures of these databases will guide you in creating efficient workflows. Each type has its strengths: SQL databases excel in managing structured data and complex queries, while NoSQL systems offer flexibility and scalability for handling unstructured data. Recognizing these distinctions will shape your approach to synchronization and data retrieval.

Consider the example of a retail business that operates an online store alongside a customer database. Whenever a customer places an order, this event triggers updates in both the inventory database and the customer relationship management (CRM) system. To achieve this synchronization, you can establish a structured workflow using webhooks and database triggers.

Take this example, if you're using PostgreSQL, you could create a trigger that activates whenever a new order is inserted into your orders table. The following SQL command illustrates how to set up such a trigger:

```sql
CREATE OR REPLACE FUNCTION notify_order_placed()

RETURNS TRIGGER AS ()

BEGIN

PERFORM pg_notify('order_placed', row_to_json(NEW)::text);

RETURN NEW;

END;

() LANGUAGE plpgsql;

CREATE TRIGGER order_placed_trigger

AFTER INSERT ON orders

FOR EACH ROW EXECUTE PROCEDURE notify_order_placed();
```

In this scenario, when a new order is placed, the trigger invokes a function that sends a notification through PostgreSQL's pg_notify mechanism. Your application can capture this notification and use it to update inventory levels and relevant customer records accordingly.

The next step involves integrating these updates into your AI agent's workflows. Depending on the no-code platform you're using, establishing these connections may be as simple as utilizing visual tools to define actions that occur when an event takes place—such as placing an order. Many platforms offer intuitive drag-and-drop interfaces that connect database actions directly with AI functionalities.

For example, if you're using Airtable as your database, you could automate updates where new entries in the "Orders" table automatically trigger modifications in another table called "Inventory." An automation workflow might look like this:

1. Trigger: When a new record is created in the Orders table.

2. Action: Update Inventory table records based on product IDs listed in the Order record.

Such setups significantly reduce manual data entry errors and ensure that your inventory reflects real-time sales without requiring extensive coding efforts.

Data integrity is also crucial during synchronization processes. Implementing constraints within your databases helps maintain consistency. Take this example, foreign key constraints in relational databases ensure that only valid product IDs can be referenced in order records, while unique indexes prevent duplicate entries from compromising data accuracy.

As you refine these synchronization processes, monitoring becomes vital for maintaining optimal performance. Tools like Grafana or Tableau can visualize database activity, allowing you to identify bottlenecks or issues early on. Regularly analyzing these insights enables teams to make informed decisions regarding potential upgrades or adjustments needed to improve efficiency.

Additionally, keeping track of synchronization logs

is invaluable for troubleshooting discrepancies between systems. If an inventory update fails or there are delays in reflecting changes across platforms, these logs provide crucial context for diagnosing issues swiftly.

By employing effective synchronization techniques between databases and AI agents, organizations not only enhance operational efficiencies but also enrich their capacity to deliver timely and relevant user experiences. As data flows seamlessly across systems, businesses become more agile and better equipped to respond to evolving market demands.

This interconnectedness empowers organizations to leverage AI capabilities fully while ensuring their foundational data structures robustly support these innovations—transforming data into actionable intelligence without sacrificing accuracy or user experience.

Cross-Platform Data Sharing

Cross-platform data sharing is essential for organizations aiming to harness the full potential of AI agents. By ensuring that information flows seamlessly and accurately across various systems, organizations can enable their AI applications to access real-time data from multiple sources, avoiding the bottlenecks that often arise in siloed environments. This interconnectedness significantly enhances both operational efficiency and user experience.

Imagine a marketing department leveraging an AI agent to analyze customer engagement across different platforms— such as social media, email, and the company website. If data from these channels is stored in separate systems without a streamlined sharing process, the AI agent may miss valuable insights. For example, if your email marketing tool records open rates but doesn't share that information with your CRM or analytics platform, you lose the ability to understand how email interactions impact website traffic and sales conversions.

To establish effective cross-platform data sharing, begin by clearly identifying which systems need to communicate. This may include databases, cloud storage services, and external APIs. After pinpointing these systems, consider implementing integration solutions like Zapier or Integromat (now known as Make) that enable you to connect disparate tools without the need for complex coding.

Take this example, suppose your organization tracks sales leads in Google Sheets while using Slack for internal communications. You could automate a process with Zapier so that any new row added in Google Sheets triggers a message in a specific Slack channel:

1. Trigger: New row added in Google Sheets.

2. Action: Send a message to the "Sales Updates" Slack channel detailing the new lead's information.

This automation keeps your team informed in real time and reduces the risk of manual errors by eliminating the need for updates.

Integrating APIs can further enhance cross-platform capabilities. For example, when utilizing RESTful APIs, it's important to ensure seamless request handling between platforms. Consider an AI-powered chatbot on your e-commerce site that needs access to customer purchase history stored in another application; it should be able to call that API directly as needed.

Here's a simplified example of how you might structure such an API request in JavaScript using the Fetch API:

```javascript
fetch('https://api.example.com/customer/purchase-history?customerId=12345')

.then(response => response.json())

.then(data =>
```

```
console.log('Purchase History:', data);
)
.catch(error =>
console.error('Error fetching purchase history:', error);
);
` ` `
```

This method allows your chatbot to retrieve necessary data on-the-fly, providing customers with personalized assistance based on their past interactions without delay.

While prioritizing integration, it's crucial to consider data security and privacy. Adhere strictly to compliance requirements such as GDPR or CCPA when handling personal data. This may involve implementing encryption during data transmission and ensuring that only authorized users can access sensitive information across platforms.

Regular audits of shared data pathways are also essential for identifying potential vulnerabilities. Tools like Postman can be valuable for testing API endpoints for security and functionality before they go live.

By focusing on effective cross-platform data sharing strategies, organizations can significantly improve the performance and reliability of their AI agents. This approach not only dismantles silos between departments and tools but also fosters a comprehensive view of business operations —allowing insights to be harnessed quickly and efficiently across various functions.

To wrap things up, as we navigate this increasingly interconnected digital landscape, investing thoughtfully in cross-platform solutions will empower businesses to leverage their data more effectively than ever before—ultimately driving innovation through collaboration and shared intelligence.

Overcoming Integration Challenges

Overcoming integration challenges is essential for unlocking the full potential of no-code AI agents. While these platforms simplify development, the task of integrating them with existing systems can often feel overwhelming. The diverse landscape of technology today—spanning legacy software to modern cloud applications—introduces complexities that require thoughtful navigation.

To begin with, it's important to clearly identify integration points. Assess your current technology stack and determine where your new AI agent will fit in. For example, if you're deploying a chatbot to enhance customer service, examine your existing customer relationship management (CRM) system. Understanding the data flow between systems will enable you to create seamless interactions. Utilizing APIs (Application Programming Interfaces) can facilitate communication between your AI agent and existing software, allowing real-time data sharing without the need for manual intervention.

Next, let's explore practical steps for successful integration. Start by assessing compatibility through a review of API documentation for both your no-code platform and existing systems. Most no-code tools come with libraries of connectors that facilitate integration with various applications like Google Sheets, Salesforce, or Slack. A visual tool such as Zapier can serve as a bridge, enabling connections between disparate services without requiring extensive programming knowledge.

Take this example, if you want to set up an automated workflow that triggers an alert whenever a customer submits feedback through your chatbot, you could use Zapier to create a "Zap" connecting your chatbot's API with your email system. This setup allows an automated email notification to be sent to the customer support team upon receiving feedback. Such automation streamlines processes and enhances response times.

Another critical aspect to address is data synchronization. Discrepancies can arise when multiple systems interact with the same data sets, leading to inconsistencies that may confuse users and undermine trust in automated solutions. Implementing webhook technology can mitigate this issue by pushing data changes in real time, rather than relying on periodic polling methods that risk missing updates or creating delays.

It's also vital to consider security vulnerabilities during integration. Each connection point between systems can become a potential entry point for unauthorized access if not properly secured. Utilizing OAuth protocols for authentication ensures secure communication between applications while allowing users to manage their permissions effectively.

Additionally, user training and acceptance of new systems following integration can pose challenges. Employees accustomed to traditional workflows may resist new technologies due to concerns about complexity or disruption of established routines. To address this proactively, provide comprehensive training sessions tailored to different user groups—whether technical staff or everyday users who will interact with the AI agents.

Real-world examples illustrate how companies have successfully navigated these challenges. Take this example, a retail organization integrated its inventory management system with an AI-powered recommendation engine using a no-code platform like Bubble.io alongside Airtable for database management. By visually mapping out their inventory processes within Bubble.io's interface and seamlessly linking it to Airtable's database through pre-built connectors, they achieved real-time stock updates and enhanced personalized shopping experiences online.

While overcoming integration challenges requires foresight and strategic planning, the rewards in operational efficiency and improved user experience are significant when executed effectively. By crafting strategies that include clear identification of integration points, leveraging robust tools like APIs and webhooks, ensuring data security, and fostering user acceptance, you can transform complex integrations into streamlined processes that drive success for your no-code AI initiatives.

Leveraging Cloud Services

Leveraging cloud services can greatly enhance your no-code AI agents, offering benefits like scalability, flexibility, and access to powerful computational resources. These platforms provide a variety of tools and services that streamline the development process while ensuring your AI agents operate efficiently and reliably.

To understand the advantages of cloud infrastructure, consider how it supports the deployment of your no-code applications. Leading platforms such as Amazon Web Services (AWS), Google Cloud Platform (GCP), and Microsoft Azure create a robust environment for hosting your AI agents. By using these services, you can alleviate the challenges of managing physical servers and gain access to advanced computing power tailored to your needs. This allows you to concentrate on developing features instead of worrying about hardware maintenance.

Imagine designing an AI agent that analyzes customer data to generate insights for marketing strategies. Deploying this agent on a cloud platform enables you to utilize auto-scaling features that dynamically adjust resources based on demand. This guarantees that during peak usage periods—like holiday sales—your AI agent remains responsive without requiring manual intervention or pre-provisioning of resources.

Integrating third-party APIs is another crucial aspect of

leveraging cloud services to enhance functionality. Many cloud providers offer machine learning services within their ecosystems, such as AWS SageMaker and Google Cloud AutoML. These tools allow you to implement sophisticated algorithms for predictive analytics or natural language processing with minimal coding effort. For example, if you want your AI agent to classify customer inquiries by sentiment, integrating Google's Natural Language API into your workflow can be done easily without extensive coding.

In addition to computational power and advanced algorithms, security is paramount when utilizing cloud services. Reputable cloud providers implement robust security measures that protect your data through encryption, identity management, and compliance with regulations like GDPR. However, it's essential to configure these settings properly. Make sure that only authorized personnel have access to sensitive information and regularly review the permissions associated with your applications.

Cloud services also promote collaboration among team members who may be working remotely or across different geographic locations. Tools like Microsoft Teams or Slack can be integrated with your no-code platform, facilitating seamless communication while providing real-time access to shared data and project updates. Consider establishing a shared workspace where team members can collaborate on workflows or monitor the performance of deployed AI agents.

For practical implementation, let's walk through a step-by-step example of leveraging cloud functions in a no-code environment. Suppose you're building an AI-driven lead scoring system for your sales team using a no-code tool like Airtable combined with AWS Lambda for processing logic:

1. Set Up Your Airtable Database: Create tables to store lead information—name, email, interaction history, etc.

2. Define Scoring Criteria: Determine parameters that influence lead scores based on interaction frequency or demographic factors.

3. Use AWS Lambda: Write a simple function (in Python or Node.js) hosted on AWS Lambda that calculates scores based on the criteria defined earlier.

4. Integrate via API: Use Airtable's API to send lead data to the AWS Lambda function whenever new leads are added or existing ones are updated.

5. Return Scores: The Lambda function processes the data and sends back calculated scores, which can be automatically updated in Airtable using webhooks.

6. Visualize Results: Use Airtable's built-in features or connect it with visualization tools like Tableau or Google Data Studio for reporting purposes.

This flow not only automates lead scoring but also allows for real-time updates without manual input—a perfect combination of efficiency and accuracy made possible by cloud integration.

embracing cloud services in your no-code AI journey opens up avenues for innovation while simplifying complex processes typically associated with traditional software development methodologies. By taking advantage of scalability, advanced functionalities, enhanced collaboration tools, and robust security measures offered by cloud platforms, you position your projects for success in today's fast-paced digital landscape—allowing creative ideas to flourish without being hindered by technical constraints.

Building a Seamless User Experience

Creating a seamless user experience for your AI agents is crucial for fostering user engagement and satisfaction. A well-designed interface not only improves usability but also builds users' confidence in the technology's capabilities. This endeavor goes beyond aesthetics; it requires a thoughtful integration of functionality, feedback mechanisms, and intuitive design principles.

To start, adopt a user-centric design approach that prioritizes the needs and behaviors of end users. For example, consider the onboarding process for a new AI-driven customer support agent. Users should not be overwhelmed by technical jargon or complex workflows. Instead, a guided tour featuring simple prompts or tooltips can facilitate easy navigation. If the AI agent provides personalized recommendations, visual cues can illustrate how users' preferences shape those suggestions.

Another essential element to enhance user experience is implementing effective feedback loops. Users should feel connected to the system and understand how their inputs lead to actions taken by the AI agent. Incorporating progress indicators during interactions can be invaluable. Take this example, if a user submits a request to generate insights from their data, displaying real-time updates like "Processing your request" ensures they know the system is functioning correctly. This transparency builds trust and encourages further engagement.

To make these concepts more concrete, let's explore an example involving a no-code platform like Bubble for creating a health-tracking app powered by an AI agent. Here's how you might cultivate a seamless user experience:

1. Define User Personas: Identify your target audience —whether health enthusiasts, busy professionals, or healthcare providers—and tailor your app's features to meet their specific needs.

2. Create Wireframes: Sketch out the app layout with a focus on navigation flows that allow users to access information quickly and easily. Take this example, the main dashboard could include large buttons

leading to sections like "Health Data," "Insights," and "Settings.

3. Design Interactive Elements: Use sliders for inputting health metrics (e.g., weight or steps) instead of manual entry fields, as sliders tend to be faster and more engaging.

4. Feedback Mechanisms: After users input data, provide instant visual feedback through graphs showing trends over time, along with brief confirmation messages like "Your weight update has been saved" to enhance clarity.

5. Usability Testing: Involve potential users in testing sessions where they interact with your app while you observe their behaviors and gather feedback on usability issues or desired features.

6. Iterate Based on Feedback: Take advantage of insights gained from testing sessions to refine your interface and workflows continuously, ensuring that you adapt to evolving user needs.

Beyond the immediate interface, consider how the AI agent communicates with users through conversational interfaces like chatbots or voice assistants. These tools should feel natural and intuitive; utilizing natural language processing techniques can enable smoother interactions. Take this example, if a user asks a chatbot about their last workout session, the agent should respond in context—summarizing duration, calories burned, and offering tips based on prior interactions.

Accessibility is another critical factor that ensures all users can benefit from your application, including those with disabilities. Following established guidelines such as the Web Content Accessibility Guidelines (WCAG) will help broaden your audience reach. This may involve incorporating text-to-speech options or ensuring sufficient color contrast for visually impaired users.

Finally, leverage analytics tools integrated into your no-code platform to continuously monitor user behavior. Collect data on common interaction pathways and drop-off points within your application to pinpoint areas requiring improvement. If many users abandon a particular feature midway through usage without completing an action, it highlights an opportunity for enhancement.

Crafting a seamless user experience around your no-code AI agents involves thoughtful design that prioritizes user needs while incorporating effective feedback mechanisms and maintaining accessibility standards. By focusing on these principles throughout your development process, you will not only create more engaging applications but also foster deeper connections between users and technology—making it easier for them to derive value from their interactions without encountering unnecessary friction along the way.

GDPR and Legal Compliance

Navigating the complexities of GDPR and legal compliance is crucial when developing no-code AI agents, particularly in an era where data privacy is of utmost importance. As organizations increasingly leverage AI to process personal data, grasping these regulations is vital—not only to meet legal requirements but also to cultivate trust among users.

The General Data Protection Regulation (GDPR) establishes stringent guidelines regarding the collection, storage, and processing of personal data. At the forefront of these guidelines is the principle of transparency. Users need to be informed about what data is being collected and how it will be utilized. Therefore, when creating your AI agent, it's essential to incorporate clear consent mechanisms. For example, if your AI agent requires user data to deliver personalized recommendations, ensure you have a straightforward opt-in process that allows users to explicitly agree to share their information. Additionally, an easily accessible privacy policy should outline how their data will be managed.

Another fundamental aspect of GDPR compliance is data minimization. This principle advocates for collecting only the information necessary for a specific purpose. Take, for instance, an AI chatbot designed for customer service; rather than asking for extensive details right away, focus on gathering essential information like the user's query or issue. As users interact more with the bot over time, you can gradually collect additional context through these conversations—enhancing the AI's responses while prioritizing user privacy.

Implementing strong security measures is equally important for compliance. Utilize encryption protocols to safeguard sensitive information both in transit and at rest. If you're using a no-code platform like Airtable that integrates with your AI agent, ensure that any personal identifiers are encrypted in the database. Regular audits of your security practices are necessary to adapt to emerging threats and protect against breaches.

Users' rights concerning their data represent another significant component of GDPR. Individuals have the right to access their information and request its deletion. To support this, incorporate features within your application that allow users to view what data has been collected about them easily, along with straightforward options for deleting their accounts or specific data entries. This level of transparency not only meets regulatory standards but also boosts user confidence in your system.

To illustrate these principles in action, consider a scenario where you are developing an AI-driven health application using a no-code platform like Glide Apps. Suppose this app collects health metrics from users for personalized insights:

1. Transparent Consent: During the initial setup, provide users with a clear consent form detailing what health data will be collected (e.g., heart rate and activity levels) and how it will enhance their experience.

2. Data Minimization: At first login, limit the information requested—perhaps only ask for basic metrics such as age or fitness goals instead of comprehensive health histories.

3. Security Protocols: Ensure all health-related data transmitted through the app is encrypted using SSL/ TLS protocols to prevent unauthorized access during transmission.

4. User Rights Management: Include a dedicated section in the app settings where users can review their stored data and offer one-click options for deleting their profiles or individual records if they choose.

5. Regular Updates on Compliance: Keep users informed about any changes in privacy policies or security measures through periodic updates within the app or via email newsletters.

And, training your team on GDPR principles fosters an organizational culture focused on compliance from the ground up. It ensures that everyone involved—from development teams designing algorithms to marketing teams interacting with customers—understands their responsibilities regarding personal data handling.

Integrating legal compliance into your no-code AI project not only meets regulatory demands but also enhances how users perceive your brand's integrity and commitment to their privacy rights. By embedding these practices throughout every stage of development—from initial concept discussions to deployment—you'll create legally compliant solutions while fostering lasting relationships built on trust and respect for user privacy.

Though understanding GDPR and legal compliance may initially seem daunting, embedding these principles into the design and functionality of your no-code AI agents paves the way for ethical technology use while enhancing user experience and confidence in your systems.

CHAPTER 10:
MONITORING AND
MAINTENANCE

Setting Up Monitoring Dashboards

S etting up monitoring dashboards is crucial for managing and optimizing AI agents, offering valuable insights into their performance, user interactions, and overall organizational impact. A well-crafted dashboard allows you to visualize data effectively, enabling quick, informed decision-making.

To start, identify the key metrics that align with your objectives. Common metrics include user engagement levels, error rates, response times, and successful task completions. For example, if you've developed a customer service chatbot, tracking metrics like the average time taken to resolve issues and user satisfaction ratings can reveal opportunities for improvement. Tools like Google Data Studio or Tableau can help you aggregate these data points into meaningful visualizations.

Next, select a no-code platform that facilitates dashboard creation. Options like Airtable or Notion provide easy integration with your AI agent's data sources. If you choose Airtable, you can create a dedicated base for monitoring your agent's performance metrics. By connecting it to your chatbot logs—often stored in spreadsheets or databases—you can automate data collection, ensuring your dashboard reflects real-time information without manual input.

Once you've chosen the right platform and set up your data sources, it's time to design the dashboard. Focus on clarity and simplicity; an overcrowded dashboard can confuse users rather than provide insights. Organize the dashboard into sections tailored to different stakeholders. Take this example, an executive overview might highlight key performance indicators (KPIs) like total user interactions and overall satisfaction ratings, while a detailed section could provide individual session analyses for technical teams troubleshooting specific issues.

Let's walk through a practical example using Airtable as our platform:

1. Data Source Setup: Create an Airtable base with tables representing various aspects of your AI agent's performance—such as User Interactions, Feedback Scores, and Error Logs.

2. Integrate Data: Take advantage of Airtable's integration features to connect this base with external data sources when necessary—like APIs that supply user interaction logs or feedback forms.

3. Visualization Creation: In the base view settings, select "Gallery" or "Grid" view for displaying data summaries. Utilize charts for a visual representation of metrics; for example, create a bar chart illustrating average response times over time.

4. Automate Updates: Set up automations within Airtable to send alerts when specific thresholds are

met—such as notifying the technical team if the error rate exceeds a certain limit.

5. User Access Management: Define roles and permissions in Airtable so that only authorized personnel can access sensitive information or make changes to the dashboard layout.

6. Feedback Loop Establishment: Incorporate a feedback section in the dashboard where team members can note discrepancies in performance or suggest improvements based on their analysis of the data.

Implementing these steps ensures that all team members —from developers to marketing personnel—have access to relevant data while promoting collaboration around actionable insights.

Another important aspect of effective monitoring is real-time updates and alerts. By utilizing tools like Zapier or Integromat (now Make), you can establish triggers that notify team members when specific conditions arise—such as high error rates or significant shifts in user engagement patterns. This immediacy enables teams to respond proactively rather than reactively.

As you continue to refine your dashboards, consider integrating advanced analytics features like predictive modeling using historical performance data to forecast future trends. Tools like Microsoft Power BI facilitate this by allowing you to create predictive models that assess how changes in one metric may influence others down the line.

Always prioritize usability; regularly seek feedback from users interacting with the dashboard. Their insights will guide iterative improvements, ensuring that it remains intuitive and aligned with evolving needs over time.

By establishing robust monitoring dashboards early in

your no-code AI development journey, you equip your team with visibility into system performance and enhance accountability across operations. These dashboards not only act as performance trackers but also serve as strategic assets that inform decision-making processes at all organizational levels—ultimately leading to more refined and effective AI systems capable of efficiently meeting user demands.

Real-Time Performance Analytics

Real-time performance analytics for AI agents fundamentally reshapes our approach to evaluating their effectiveness and enhancing their functionality. By monitoring data in real time, you can gain immediate insights into user interactions, system behavior, and overall performance. This capability is especially vital in fast-paced environments, where timely decisions can significantly influence user satisfaction and operational efficiency.

To begin with, it's essential to define what real-time performance means for your AI agent. For example, if you're working with a virtual assistant or chatbot, you might focus on key performance indicators (KPIs) such as response time, conversation drop-off rates, and user satisfaction scores. Each of these metrics offers valuable insights into how effectively your AI is fulfilling its intended role. Take this example, a spike in drop-off rates during a specific interaction flow can indicate an area that requires redesign or retraining.

Integrating analytics tools into your no-code platform allows for seamless data collection and visualization. Google Analytics is one such tool that can be integrated with your AI systems to monitor user interactions and engagement levels in real time. By embedding tracking codes within your agent's environment or utilizing API integrations, you can funnel engagement data into dashboards that provide a live view of user activity.

Let's explore a practical workflow using Google Analytics:

1. Set Up Tracking: Begin by creating a Google Analytics account and generating the tracking ID for your AI application or website where the agent operates.

2. Integrate with Your Platform: Depending on the no-code platform you're using—such as Webflow or Bubble—you'll need to embed the Google Analytics tracking code directly into the site settings or page configurations to initiate data collection.

3. Configure Event Tracking: Define specific events to capture user interactions with your AI agent. For example, you might set up an event that triggers when a user initiates a chat session or clicks on particular buttons within the interface. This can be done through Google Tag Manager or directly within Google Analytics.

4. Create Dashboards: Use Google Data Studio to build real-time dashboards that effectively visualize this data. Custom reports can highlight metrics like active users, average session duration, and interaction completion rates, providing stakeholders with insights into how users engage with the agent at any moment.

5. Set Up Alert Systems for Anomalies: Establish alerts in Google Analytics to notify you of unusual patterns —such as sudden drops in user engagement or spikes in error responses from the AI agent—enabling prompt responses to potential issues.

While assessing current performance metrics is crucial, predicting future trends is equally important for proactive management. Leveraging predictive analytics enables organizations to anticipate user needs based on historical data patterns—a process streamlined by tools like Microsoft Power BI or Tableau.

To conduct predictive analysis using Power BI:

1. Input Historical Data: Collect historical performance data from your AI agent's interactions stored in databases or spreadsheets.

2. Create Models: Utilize Power BI's analytical features to develop models that forecast user interaction trends based on variables like time of day or specific content types used during engagements.

3. Visualize Predictions: Construct visualizations that display predicted outcomes alongside historical data, allowing decision-makers to understand not only past events but also future possibilities.

4. Continuously Refine Models: Regularly update these predictive models with new data; this will enhance accuracy over time and adapt predictions as user behavior evolves.

User feedback plays a critical role throughout this process —incorporating qualitative insights can further enrich the quantitative findings derived from real-time analytics tools. Encourage team members who engage with these dashboards to share their input on usability and effectiveness regularly; their firsthand experience will guide improvements that align with evolving needs.

In summary, real-time performance analytics serves as a cornerstone of effective AI agent management by delivering actionable insights at key moments while enabling teams to swiftly address issues before they escalate into larger problems. By adeptly harnessing these capabilities within no-code platforms, you can refine your systems—ultimately leading to improved user experiences and heightened satisfaction across all touchpoints of interaction with your intelligent systems.

Diagnosing and Fixing Issues

Diagnosing and fixing issues within AI agents can often feel like searching for a needle in a haystack, particularly when these systems operate autonomously and tackle complex tasks. However, adopting a systematic approach allows you to identify problems efficiently and implement effective solutions. The key is understanding both the technology underpinning your AI agent and the user interactions that shape its performance.

To begin, it's essential to establish a clear methodology for diagnosing issues. Consider the types of problems that may arise: performance lags, incorrect outputs, or user frustration stemming from misunderstood commands. A structured troubleshooting approach involves gathering data, analyzing user feedback, and conducting tests. Each of these steps informs the next, creating a feedback loop that continuously enhances your AI agent's reliability.

Start by collecting data on user interactions. This could involve logging every user query alongside the corresponding AI response. For example, if users frequently ask your chatbot about pricing but receive vague answers, this may indicate a need for better training on keywords related to pricing inquiries. Tools like Firebase or Mixpanel can help you track these interactions effectively without requiring extensive coding.

Once you have gathered sufficient data, analyze it for patterns. Look for recurring issues that may suggest systemic problems within your AI's training set or response logic. If several users drop off after receiving the same response from the AI, it might indicate that the answer is unsatisfactory or unclear. Meticulously documenting these instances will serve as critical evidence when you adjust the AI's training or behavior.

Testing plays an equally essential role in diagnosing problems. Implementing A/B testing with different versions of responses can help you identify which performs better with users. By running tests where half of users receive one version and half another, you can pinpoint strategies that resonate more effectively with your audience. Adjusting responses based on empirical evidence rather than intuition ensures that your modifications lead to measurable improvements.

When issues arise, engaging directly with users through surveys or feedback forms can yield valuable insights beyond automated data collection. Targeted questions about their experiences may reveal confusion about how to initiate tasks with your AI agent, prompting you to simplify or clarify the onboarding process.

After identifying specific problems and gathering relevant feedback, it's time to implement fixes. This may involve retraining your AI model with additional data or refining existing algorithms to improve accuracy and efficiency. Take this example, if your virtual assistant struggles with natural language processing (NLP) tasks—such as understanding variations in phrasing—consider employing transfer learning techniques using larger datasets tailored for conversational contexts.

Throughout this process, documentation is crucial—not only for tracking changes but also for future reference as new team members join or as the project evolves. Create detailed logs of identified issues, proposed solutions, testing outcomes, and implemented changes so that everyone involved can learn from past experiences.

And, establish a monitoring system that alerts you when certain thresholds are breached—such as unusually high error rates in responses or significant drops in user engagement metrics. Automated alerts enable swift action before minor glitches escalate into larger setbacks.

Sometimes, integrating external support from community forums or expert consultations can provide fresh perspectives on persistent issues. The collective wisdom available online often reveals solutions that might have been overlooked and helps streamline troubleshooting processes.

diagnosing and fixing issues within AI agents is not just about addressing current challenges; it's also about building resilience into your systems for the future. By fostering a culture of continuous improvement and leveraging both quantitative data and qualitative insights from users, you establish an adaptive framework capable of evolving alongside changing needs and technologies.

Each step taken to refine your AI agent contributes not only to enhanced performance but also to building trust among users who increasingly rely on these systems for their daily tasks. As issues are resolved systematically and communicated transparently to end-users, confidence in AI technology grows —a vital ingredient for sustainable growth in any organization leveraging no-code solutions.

Regular Updates and Upgrades

Regular updates and upgrades are essential for any successful AI agent, enabling it to adapt to changing user needs and technological advancements. Given the ever-evolving landscape of artificial intelligence, a proactive approach to enhancing your AI agent is crucial for maintaining its effectiveness and relevance.

To start, establish a regular update schedule—be it monthly, quarterly, or aligned with specific project milestones. During each update cycle, review performance metrics gathered from user interactions. Are users satisfied with the AI's responses? Is it meeting their needs effectively? If the answers are not reassuring, it's time to delve deeper into the analytics. Tools like Google Analytics can provide valuable insights into user engagement with your AI system, helping you identify patterns that guide necessary changes.

For example, if feedback reveals that users often abandon tasks after interacting with the AI agent, this may indicate a need for enhancements in either its capabilities or user interface. By analyzing session durations and identifying drop-off points, you can pinpoint where users lose interest or encounter difficulties, allowing you to address these pain points in your next update.

User feedback should play a pivotal role in shaping your upgrade strategy. Implement structured feedback mechanisms—such as post-interaction surveys—to gather insights on which features or functionalities require enhancement. If several users express confusion over a specific feature, prioritize its redesign to improve clarity and usability.

Additionally, keep an eye on emerging technologies during your updates. As new algorithms and methodologies develop within the AI field, consider how they can enhance your existing systems. Take this example, advancements in machine learning might offer improved natural language processing capabilities; incorporating such technologies could significantly enhance your AI agent's ability to understand and respond to complex queries.

Testing new features before full deployment is crucial for minimizing risk. Create a beta testing group composed of select users who can trial new functionalities and provide immediate feedback. This approach not only ensures that updates are beneficial but also fosters a sense of community among users who feel their input shapes the evolution of the AI agent.

Meticulous documentation should accompany every update. Clearly log each change—whether minor tweaks or major overhauls—for future reference. This practice aids current team members in understanding past decisions and helps onboard new contributors who may join later in the project lifecycle.

It's also important to stay informed about industry trends and competitor innovations. Observing what others are doing can inspire enhancements within your own systems. If competitors introduce successful features that resonate with users, explore how similar adaptations could be implemented in your AI agents while maintaining your unique value proposition.

Encouraging a culture of experimentation within your team can drive continuous improvement. Invite team members to propose new ideas for functionalities or enhancements based on their experiences and observations. This collaborative approach often leads to innovative solutions that might not arise through formal processes alone.

Monitoring tools can facilitate ongoing performance evaluations between scheduled updates. Consider implementing real-time analytics dashboards that continuously track user engagement and satisfaction metrics rather than relying solely on fixed intervals. This lets you swift responses to emerging issues before they escalate into larger problems.

Integrating external resources such as community forums or expert consultations during your upgrade process can bring fresh perspectives and expertise into play. The wealth of knowledge available online can offer creative solutions or highlight potential pitfalls based on similar experiences faced by others in the field.

regular updates and upgrades go beyond keeping pace with technology; they represent an opportunity to build trust with users through transparency and responsiveness. By actively engaging with user feedback and remaining adaptable to changing circumstances, you cultivate an environment where both the AI agent and its users thrive together.

As you implement these practices, keep in mind that each update enhances functionality while also strengthening user confidence in your system's reliability—a crucial factor as more individuals turn toward no-code solutions for their operational needs. Embracing this iterative approach ensures that your AI agent remains an invaluable asset tailored to effectively meet the demands of its users over time.

Scaling Your AI Agent

Scaling your AI agent effectively is crucial for maximizing its potential as user demands evolve and business environments change. Building on the foundation of regular updates and feedback integration, which support continuous improvement, scaling presents the challenge of maintaining performance while expanding capabilities.

To begin scaling your AI agent, assess your existing architecture. A well-structured system is vital for managing increased loads while ensuring responsiveness. If your agent operates on a microservices model, each service can be scaled independently based on demand, which helps prevent bottlenecks during peak usage. Take this example, if data processing becomes a limiting factor due to a surge in user interactions, you can scale that specific service without making extensive changes across the entire system.

Another essential consideration in scaling is load balancing. By evenly distributing incoming requests across multiple instances of your AI agent, you can enhance performance and reduce latency for users. Utilizing cloud services such as AWS or Google Cloud, which offer built-in load balancing features, allows resources to adjust automatically based on current traffic levels. This guarantees that no single instance becomes overwhelmed while others remain underutilized.

As you scale, think about how additional integrations could enhance your AI agent's functionality. For example, incorporating third-party APIs can significantly broaden its capabilities. If you operate an e-commerce platform and aim to improve customer experience, integrating a payment processing API can streamline transactions directly through your AI assistant's interface. This not only enriches the user experience but also adds functionality tailored to their specific needs.

Data management is another critical factor in the scaling process. Increased interactions often result in larger datasets that require effective handling for real-time processing and analysis. Implementing efficient data pipelines will help you manage these growing datasets seamlessly. Tools like Apache Kafka or Amazon Kinesis facilitate real-time data streaming into your AI systems, ensuring timely insights and responses from the agent.

Also, optimizing the machine learning models that power your AI agent is essential as user interactions increase. Continuously training these models with new data is vital for improving accuracy and relevance over time. A robust retraining strategy should be part of your scaling plan, involving periodic updates to the system with fresh datasets that refine algorithms based on recent patterns and trends in user behavior.

Monitoring performance metrics is also key to effective scaling strategies. Utilize comprehensive analytics tools to gain insights into how well your AI agent performs under increased load conditions. Metrics such as response times, failure rates, and user satisfaction scores can help identify potential issues before they negatively impact users.

Building a scalable support structure is equally important as technology evolves alongside your AI agent's capabilities. Customer support teams should be equipped to handle an influx of inquiries as new features are rolled out; training them on these functionalities ensures users receive accurate guidance promptly.

In addition to internal scaling efforts, collaborating with external partners can create further growth opportunities.

Partnering with complementary businesses or tech providers may unlock synergies that benefit all parties involved—whether through shared technology stacks or co-developing features based on mutual customer needs.

successful scaling depends on maintaining flexibility while prioritizing user experience throughout expansion efforts. Regularly revisiting existing processes for optimization keeps systems agile enough to adapt quickly without sacrificing quality or reliability—a critical balance every no-code AI developer must strive for as their projects grow beyond initial expectations.

Emphasizing adaptability not only positions your AI agent favorably within its marketplace but also fosters a culture of trust among users who witness consistent improvements reflecting their evolving requirements. This adaptability is a key driver in cultivating long-term engagement and satisfaction with your solution.

User Feedback Systems

Effective user feedback systems are fundamental to the success of any AI agent. By implementing mechanisms for collecting, analyzing, and responding to user insights, you foster a dynamic relationship between your AI and its users. This ongoing dialogue enhances user satisfaction and drives innovation within your solution.

To start, integrate multiple channels for feedback collection. Tools such as surveys, direct feedback forms, and social media engagement are essential. For example, after a user interacts with your AI agent, you can prompt them with a brief survey asking how well their needs were met or if they encountered any issues. Platforms like Typeform or Google Forms can streamline this process. The goal is to make providing feedback as easy as possible; lengthy forms may discourage users from completing them.

After gathering feedback, the next step is analysis. Utilize tools like sentiment analysis algorithms to sift through qualitative data and extract meaningful insights. Techniques from Natural Language Processing (NLP) can help identify common themes or issues raised by users. If a significant number of users express frustration over a particular feature, this serves as a clear signal that improvements are necessary.

Incorporating user feedback into your development cycle should be systematic. Establish a feedback loop where insights lead to tangible changes in the AI's functionality. If users consistently request certain features or report difficulties with existing ones, prioritize these adjustments in your project roadmap. Project management tools like Trello or Asana can help visualize this process and keep your team aligned on priorities.

Communication is vital after implementing changes based on feedback. Informing users about updates not only demonstrates that their input is valued but also fosters trust in your AI agent's capabilities. Consider sending newsletters or platform updates to highlight new features or improvements that result from user suggestions.

To maintain engagement and encourage further feedback, think about gamifying the experience. Reward users who provide valuable insights with incentives such as discounts, exclusive access to new features, or recognition within your community. This approach motivates participation and helps build a loyal user base invested in the success of your AI solution.

As your AI system grows in complexity, tracking user engagement metrics becomes increasingly important. Tools like Mixpanel or Google Analytics offer invaluable data on user interactions with your AI agent, highlighting areas that need attention and improvement. Regularly reviewing these metrics enables you to adapt swiftly to shifting user expectations.

And, cultivating a culture of open communication goes beyond immediate feedback collection; it involves creating a community around your AI agent where users feel comfortable sharing experiences and suggestions. Platforms such as Discord or Slack can facilitate ongoing discussions among users, allowing them to exchange ideas and support one another while providing you with additional channels for real-time feedback.

When implementing user feedback systems, also consider accessibility. Ensure that all users have equal opportunities to provide insights, regardless of their technical expertise or preferred communication style. Incorporating voice-to-text options or multilingual support can help reach a broader audience.

Finally, don't underestimate the value of case studies and success stories drawn from user experiences. Highlighting how specific features have solved real-world problems for users not only serves as an effective marketing tool but also reinforces the practical benefits of integrating feedback into your development processes.

By creating robust user feedback systems that prioritize both the collection and action on received insights, you're not just enhancing an AI agent; you're nurturing an ecosystem that continuously evolves based on user needs. The result is an intelligent system that exceeds expectations—a crucial factor in sustaining long-term engagement and satisfaction in an increasingly competitive landscape.

Building a Knowledge Base for Users

Creating a comprehensive knowledge base is essential for enhancing user experience and ensuring the longevity of your AI agent. It serves as a critical resource that empowers users to troubleshoot issues independently, discover new features, and build confidence in using the system effectively.

Begin by identifying the core topics your knowledge base should cover. Focus on foundational information, such as effective usage of the AI agent, common troubleshooting tips, and explanations of advanced features. Take this example, if your AI agent utilizes natural language processing, provide detailed guides on optimal user interactions. Including FAQs that address common queries can save time for both users and support staff while fostering trust.

As you compile content, prioritize clarity and conciseness. Avoid jargon whenever possible; when technical terms are necessary, ensure they are clearly defined within the context. For example, when discussing machine learning concepts, provide simplified explanations and relatable analogies to everyday experiences. The aim is accessibility—make sure even users with limited technical backgrounds can grasp and apply the information.

Incorporating diverse formats can also cater to varying learning preferences. Some users may favor written instructions, while others might find video tutorials or interactive demonstrations more effective. Consider creating step-by-step guides with screenshots alongside short video clips that highlight specific functionalities. Tools like Loom or Camtasia can help you produce high-quality video content with ease.

Logical categorization of your knowledge base is vital for user navigation. Organizing content in a structured manner allows users to find what they need without frustration. Implementing a search function further enhances usability—users should be able to type keywords into a search bar and quickly locate relevant articles or resources.

Encouraging community contributions can significantly enrich your knowledge base over time. Users who navigate challenges successfully often have valuable insights to share. Consider creating a forum or discussion board where users can post solutions they've discovered or suggest additional topics for coverage. This not only fosters community engagement but also transforms your knowledge repository into a living document that evolves based on user input.

Maintaining your knowledge base requires ongoing effort. Regularly review content for relevance and accuracy; this may involve updating articles to reflect new features or revising outdated information based on user feedback received through support channels. Establishing a schedule for audits helps ensure that your knowledge base remains a reliable resource.

Integrate analytics tools into your knowledge base system to track which articles are most viewed and identify where users tend to disengage. This data reveals gaps in information and highlights areas needing further focus or clarification. If you notice high traffic around certain topics but low engagement with existing articles, consider revisiting those subjects to improve detail or presentation.

To maximize the effectiveness of your knowledge base, ensure it is easily accessible across various interaction points with your AI agent—whether through an app interface or embedded within email communications following user interactions. Consistency across platforms reinforces familiarity and encourages users to seek help when needed.

Finally, remember that creating an engaging onboarding experience is part of building a robust knowledge ecosystem. When new users first encounter your AI agent, offer immediate access to curated introductory materials tailored specifically for beginners. This approach provides instant value while alleviating initial confusion or hesitation about how best to utilize the tool.

By establishing a thorough and dynamic knowledge base enriched by community insights, clear communication styles, diverse content formats, and systematic updates, you create an invaluable resource not only for troubleshooting but also for enhancing overall user competence with your AI solution. This proactive approach fosters loyalty among users who feel valued—an essential ingredient in cultivating long-term relationships in today's competitive technology landscape.

Dealing with Downtime and Outages

Downtime and outages can significantly disrupt the seamless experience you strive to deliver with your AI agent. Whether these interruptions stem from server issues, software bugs, or unexpected spikes in user traffic, they pose challenges to both user satisfaction and operational efficiency. To maintain trust and ensure continuity, it's essential to understand how to navigate these situations effectively.

Start by developing a robust incident response plan that clearly outlines the steps your team will take during downtime. This plan should include communication protocols and escalation procedures. Designating a specific team member or group to manage outages can streamline the process. This designated team would monitor systems, analyze root causes, and coordinate efforts to restore services promptly.

Transparency plays a crucial role during outages. Keeping users informed through various channels—such as email notifications, social media updates, or in-app alerts—about the status of the situation is vital. Even if immediate solutions are not available, acknowledging the issue shows users that you recognize their concerns and are actively working to resolve them. A simple message like, "We're currently experiencing technical difficulties and are working to resolve them as quickly as possible," can reassure users that they are not alone in their frustration.

Implementing monitoring tools can greatly enhance your ability to identify potential issues before they escalate into major outages. Services like New Relic or Datadog offer real-time insights into application performance metrics, server health, and user activity patterns. By regularly analyzing these metrics, you can spot anomalies or trends that may signal an impending failure.

Additionally, having backup systems in place ensures business continuity even during significant downtimes. This might involve redundant servers that automatically take over if one fails or cloud-based solutions that can scale according to demand. For example, Netflix utilizes Amazon Web Services (AWS) for its cloud infrastructure; when problems occur in one region, traffic can seamlessly reroute to other regions without noticeable interruption for users.

Once the immediate issue is resolved, conducting a post-mortem analysis is essential. Gather your team to discuss what went wrong, how it was handled, and how future responses could be improved. Documenting these findings serves not only as a valuable learning opportunity but also helps refine your incident response strategy over time.

After resolving an outage, consider leveraging user feedback to understand their experiences during the incident. Surveys or follow-up emails asking for input on how well the situation was communicated can provide valuable insights into user sentiment and highlight areas for improvement in future communications.

Establishing a service-level agreement (SLA) is another effective way to set clear expectations regarding uptime commitments and incident management. An SLA not only instills confidence in users regarding your service reliability but also serves as a benchmark for your team's performance during outages.

Training your support staff is equally important. Ensure they are equipped to handle outage-related inquiries with both efficiency and empathy. A knowledgeable support team can alleviate user anxiety by providing prompt assistance based on established protocols while reinforcing trust through their expertise.

Finally, periodically reviewing your AI agent's architecture allows you to identify potential vulnerabilities that could lead to future outages. A proactive approach includes upgrading software components and stress-testing your system under simulated high-load conditions to prepare for unexpected traffic spikes.

By integrating structured incident management processes with effective communication strategies and proactive monitoring tools, you create an environment resilient enough to gracefully handle downtime. This level of preparedness not only mitigates disruptions but also fosters a culture of trust among users who know they can rely on you—regardless of the challenges that may arise.

CHAPTER 11:
ENHANCING USER
EXPERIENCE

Personalization Techniques

P ersonalization plays a crucial role in enhancing user experience, particularly when integrating AI agents into various applications. By understanding user needs and tailoring interactions to match individual preferences, businesses can significantly boost engagement and satisfaction. Take platforms like Netflix or Spotify, for example; they analyze user behavior to recommend content that aligns closely with individual tastes. This degree of customization not only captivates users but also builds loyalty —a vital asset in any competitive landscape.

To effectively implement personalization techniques, begin by gathering user data through multiple channels. This can include direct feedback, tracking user activity, and collecting demographic information. Each piece of data helps build a comprehensive profile for each user, which serves as the foundation for personalized experiences. Take this example, an e-commerce website may monitor past purchases and browsing habits to provide tailored product recommendations. It's imperative that this data collection is transparent and compliant with privacy regulations, as trust is essential for maintaining strong user relationships.

Once you have collected relevant data, the next step is to segment your users based on shared characteristics or behaviors. For example, an online education platform could categorize users as 'new learners,' 'advanced users,' or 'course completers.' This segmentation allows you to deliver customized content that directly addresses their current needs and knowledge levels. Such a targeted approach enhances engagement by making users feel recognized and valued.

Incorporating dynamic content into your AI agents can further enhance personalization. This means adjusting the information presented to users based on their profiles and interactions. Take this example, if a user has expressed interest in digital marketing courses, the AI could prioritize suggestions for relevant courses or articles on that topic. This immediate value not only keeps users engaged but also encourages them to explore additional offerings.

Machine learning models also play a significant role in enhancing personalization efforts by predicting user preferences and behaviors. By analyzing historical data, these models can identify patterns that inform intelligent recommendations. For example, if a user frequently reads articles about technology trends, the system might prioritize similar content in their feed or alert them to new articles on that subject. These predictive capabilities are essential for creating intuitive and personalized interactions.

Beyond the analytical aspects of personalization, it's important to foster an emotional connection with your users. Personalization should extend beyond mere data; it involves crafting narratives that resonate with individual values and aspirations. Incorporating elements like customizable avatars or personalized greetings can humanize interactions, making users feel valued beyond just their data points. For example, a fitness app might use a user's name in motivational messages or congratulate them on achieving milestones—adding a personal touch that strengthens loyalty.

Feedback mechanisms are also vital in this personalization journey. Provide opportunities for users to share their insights about their experiences—what they enjoyed and what didn't meet their expectations. Tools such as quick surveys or feedback forms embedded within your AI agent's interface can help you continuously refine your understanding of user preferences. The iterative nature of these feedback loops ensures that your offerings remain relevant and adapt to evolving user needs over time.

Consider a practical example: imagine a travel planning AI agent designed for frequent travelers. Initially, it gathers data about past trips—destinations visited, preferred airlines, types of accommodations (like hotels vs. hostels), and enjoyed activities (such as sightseeing vs. culinary experiences). With this information, the agent can curate personalized travel itineraries for future trips—suggesting destinations based on seasonal trends or offering exclusive deals from airlines previously flown.

Another aspect worth exploring is multi-channel integration for personalization. Users often engage with businesses across various platforms—websites, mobile apps, social media—and ensuring a seamless experience across these channels enhances their overall journey. Take this example, if a customer browses items on an online store app but doesn't complete their purchase, sending a personalized email reminder about those items can encourage conversions without feeling intrusive.

In summary, effective personalization techniques hinge on understanding user preferences through robust data collection methods and segmentation strategies. Utilizing dynamic content delivery alongside machine learning predictions fosters intuitive interactions that resonate emotionally with users while significantly enhancing engagement levels. As organizations adopt these strategies, they must remain vigilant about upholding ethical standards concerning data usage—an increasingly important consideration in today's privacy-conscious world.

By weaving together these elements—data-driven insights, emotional connections, ongoing feedback mechanisms, and cross-platform coherence—businesses can elevate their AI agents from mere tools to trusted companions that genuinely cater to user needs. Personalization is not just an add-on; it is woven into the fabric of modern digital interactions and has the power to transform casual users into loyal advocates when executed thoughtfully and strategically.

UI/UX Best Practices

Crafting an intuitive user interface (UI) and experience (UX) is crucial for the success of any application, especially when integrating AI agents. A well-designed UI/UX not only attracts users but also fosters their comfort and confidence while interacting with the system. This journey begins with a thorough understanding of user expectations and behaviors, which lays the groundwork for seamless interactions.

To start, prioritize clarity in your design. Users should be able to navigate your application effortlessly, without confusion or frustration. Clear labeling, consistent layouts, and logical pathways guide users toward their goals. For example, consider a no-code platform that allows users to create chatbots. If the creation process is broken down into easy-to-understand steps, users are more likely to engage fully and successfully build their chatbots without feeling overwhelmed.

Next, responsiveness is key to a positive user experience. Your application should behave predictably across various devices and screen sizes. A responsive design not only enhances usability but also improves accessibility for diverse audiences. Adopting a mobile-first approach can be particularly effective; if an online service offers both web and mobile interfaces, optimizing features for smaller screens can significantly elevate user satisfaction.

Visual elements are also pivotal in UI/UX design. Appropriate colors, typography, and icons enhance comprehension and engagement. Consistency in these visual components fosters familiarity over time; for instance, Google's design language uses a cohesive color palette and iconography across its applications, building trust and making technology feel less intimidating.

Incorporating feedback mechanisms into your AI agent can greatly enhance user interactions. After users complete tasks within the application, prompting them for feedback invites engagement and highlights areas for improvement. Simple thumbs up/thumbs down ratings or quick surveys can provide invaluable insights into user satisfaction without overwhelming them with lengthy forms.

Micro-interactions—small animations or visual cues that offer subtle feedback—can further enrich the user experience. These interactions inform users that their actions have been recognized by the system, instilling a sense of control. For example, when a user selects an option or completes a form field, brief animations can affirm the action taken without distracting from the primary function of the interface.

Accessibility is another vital aspect of UI/UX design. Creating an inclusive environment ensures that all users can effectively engage with your application, regardless of their abilities or disabilities. This may involve providing text alternatives for images or ensuring sufficient contrast between text and background colors to enhance readability for individuals with visual impairments.

To illustrate these principles in action, consider an AI-driven scheduling assistant designed for busy professionals. The app should clearly display upcoming meetings while allowing users to effortlessly add new appointments using natural language input—such as typing "lunch with Sarah next Thursday." By designing an interface that instantly interprets this input and suggests available times based on previously set preferences, you streamline functionality and enhance engagement through intuitive interaction.

Usability testing is another cornerstone of effective UI/UX development. Iteratively testing your design with real users helps identify pain points before a full-scale launch. Observing how individuals interact with your AI agent reveals invaluable insights; certain features may be too hidden or the navigation could be confusingly structured. This iterative process allows you to refine your design based on actual feedback rather than assumptions.

Building emotional resonance into interactions transforms mere utility into memorable experiences. When users feel understood by an AI agent—through personalized greetings or relevant suggestions—it fosters loyalty beyond mere functionality. Take this example, if an AI health app congratulates users on reaching fitness milestones by name ("Great job today, Alex!"), it cultivates motivation alongside usability.

embracing best practices in UI/UX is not just about aesthetics; it's about creating an environment where users feel empowered to explore and utilize technology effectively without intimidation or confusion. By prioritizing clarity, responsiveness, visual consistency, accessibility, feedback mechanisms, emotional connections through micro-interactions, usability testing, and human-centered design, you pave the way for engaging AI agents that resonate deeply with users.

Enhancing UI/UX involves weaving these diverse threads into a cohesive narrative where every element contributes meaningfully to overall functionality and experience. This meticulous attention transforms interactions from mere transactions into lasting relationships between technology and its users.

Gathering User Feedback

Gathering user feedback is a crucial aspect of the AI agent lifecycle. This process not only refines the product but also deepens the connection between users and the technology they engage with. By actively seeking feedback, you create open channels for dialogue that yield valuable insights, enabling continuous improvement of your AI solutions based on real-world experiences.

To start, establish clear channels for users to share their feedback. This could be as simple as integrating a feedback form within your application or providing a dedicated email address for suggestions. However, it's not enough to just offer a means of communication; you must also foster an inviting atmosphere that encourages users to express their thoughts and experiences. Take this example, consider using prompts after specific tasks—like "How was your experience creating a new task?"—to facilitate immediate feedback while the interaction is still fresh in their minds.

In addition to qualitative insights, quantitative metrics such as Net Promoter Score (NPS) or Customer Satisfaction Score (CSAT) can provide measurable data reflecting overall user satisfaction and loyalty. Regularly tracking these metrics helps identify trends over time and assess the impact of any changes made within the application. For example, if you introduce a new feature and notice a decline in NPS, it may indicate that this change negatively affected user experience.

Exploring qualitative feedback can unveil even richer

narratives about user experiences. Conducting interviews or focus groups allows for open-ended discussions where users can share their thoughts without constraints. This direct engagement often uncovers pain points that surveys might overlook. Imagine hosting a focus group where participants discuss their interactions with an AI-driven customer support agent; their stories could reveal frustrations with response times or feature limitations that need addressing.

Incorporating analytics tools into your application can further enhance your understanding of user behavior. Tools like Google Analytics or Hotjar enable you to track how users navigate your platform, identifying drop-off points where they lose interest or encounter difficulties. Take this example, if analytics reveal a high abandonment rate during the onboarding process of your AI agent, it may suggest that users find it overwhelming or unclear—an insight crucial for refining that experience.

Collecting feedback goes beyond data gathering; it's about demonstrating responsiveness to user needs. When users see that their suggestions lead to tangible improvements, it builds trust and encourages future engagement. For example, if several users recommend simplifying a complex feature and you act on this by streamlining the interface, communicate these changes back to them: "Thanks to your feedback, we've made it easier for you to manage your tasks!" This transparency not only validates their input but also strengthens community engagement.

To maintain a cycle of continuous improvement, regularly reviewing feedback is essential. Establish routine intervals for evaluating collected data to ensure no valuable insights are overlooked. Consider forming an internal team tasked with analyzing user feedback weekly or monthly; they can prioritize issues based on frequency and severity before planning development sprints focused on addressing them.

Additionally, incorporating A/B testing into your feedback strategy can provide comparative insights into user preferences. By presenting different versions of features or interfaces to subsets of users, you can determine which design resonates better with them. If one version leads to higher engagement rates during testing phases, it offers concrete evidence for making informed decisions about final implementations.

A strong emphasis on user feedback is not merely about creating functional AI agents; it's about building relationships founded on trust and understanding between technology and its users. By actively soliciting opinions and adapting accordingly, you cultivate an environment where innovation flourishes alongside user satisfaction.

gathering user feedback transcends simple data collection; it becomes a collaborative journey toward refining AI agents that align closely with user expectations and desires. Embracing this approach ensures that each interaction evolves from a mere transaction into an engaging experience that resonates deeply with those who choose to interact with your technology.

User-Centric Design Approaches

Creating user-centric design approaches is essential for developing AI agents that truly resonate with users, ensuring not just functionality but also a meaningful experience. This perspective shifts the focus from merely building a product to comprehending the nuances of user interactions and preferences. When user needs take precedence, the resulting design fosters greater satisfaction and engagement, ultimately strengthening the relationship between technology and its users.

To begin, immerse yourself in your users' world. Conduct empathy-driven research to lay the groundwork for understanding their motivations, frustrations, and aspirations. Techniques like user personas prove invaluable in this process. These personas synthesize data collected from interviews and observations into representative profiles of your target audience. Take this example, if you are designing an AI assistant for small business owners, develop personas that capture various user types—such as a tech-savvy entrepreneur versus someone less familiar with technology—allowing you to tailor your design strategies to their distinct needs.

Once you have a clear understanding of who your users are, consider mapping out their journey through your AI agent's ecosystem. A customer journey map visually illustrates each interaction point—from initial engagement to ongoing use—highlighting critical moments that can significantly impact their experience. If users struggle during onboarding or find certain features unintuitive, these insights reveal areas for improvement. As you refine this journey, focus on moments that add value or delight; for example, integrating helpful tips at various stages can guide new users smoothly through the experience.

Prototyping becomes an indispensable tool in user-centric design. Start by creating low-fidelity prototypes using tools like Figma or Sketch to visualize ideas before they evolve into fully developed products. Present these prototypes to real users for feedback; their reactions will provide early indicators of whether your designs resonate with them or require adjustments. Embrace rapid iteration based on user input; even simple modifications can lead to significantly enhanced experiences.

When designing interactive elements of your AI agent, prioritize simplicity. Users appreciate intuitive interfaces that minimize cognitive load—this involves reducing clutter and clearly guiding them toward desired actions. For example, consider how simplifying language and visuals in the onboarding process could replace jargon-heavy instructions that might alienate some users.

Additionally, implementing iterative testing rounds throughout the design process ensures continuous refinement based on actual user behavior rather than assumptions. Conduct usability testing sessions where participants navigate tasks while vocalizing their thoughts; this method often uncovers unexpected challenges they encounter while interacting with your AI agent. Observing real users navigate complex paths can provide clearer insights than theoretical planning ever could.

Incorporating personalization features within your AI agent can further enhance user satisfaction. By leveraging data analytics to understand individual preferences and behaviors, you can tailor interactions accordingly—such as offering personalized recommendations based on previous interactions or adapting responses based on detected sentiment during conversations.

Collaboration also plays an integral role in successful user-centric design. Bringing together diverse perspectives fosters innovative solutions that might not emerge in isolation. Engaging cross-functional teams—from designers and developers to marketers—creates a richer dialogue about what truly serves the end-user well.

Finally, maintain open communication even after launching your AI agent into the world; actively engaging with users post-launch is crucial for sustaining relevance over time. Use surveys or check-in emails to ask about their experiences after several weeks of use; this ongoing dialogue signals to users that their feedback is valued beyond the initial deployment.

Adopting a user-centric design approach transforms how you conceive and develop AI agents from start to finish— ensuring they not only meet functional expectations but also genuinely resonate with those who interact with them daily. By weaving empathy into every stage of development—from understanding user journeys to embracing feedback loops— you create systems that serve not just as tools but as valuable partners in achieving goals and solving problems effectively together.

Improving Interaction Quality

Enhancing the quality of interactions with AI agents involves refining how these systems communicate and engage with users. When an AI agent responds fluidly to user input, provides relevant suggestions, and anticipates needs, it creates a more enriching experience. Such high-quality interactions elevate the technology from being viewed merely as a tool to becoming a responsive partner in problem-solving.

One effective way to improve interaction quality is by implementing adaptive learning algorithms. These algorithms analyze past user behavior and tailor responses accordingly. Take this example, if an AI agent recognizes that a user frequently requests specific types of information—such as sales data or marketing insights—it can prioritize these requests or present them in an easily accessible format. This anticipatory design not only saves time but also fosters trust between the user and the system.

Natural language processing (NLP) is another crucial aspect of enhancing interaction quality. By enabling AI agents to interpret and generate human-like responses, NLP helps bridge the gap between technology and users. The more naturally an AI can communicate, the less users feel they are interacting with a rigid machine. To achieve this, it's essential to train your agent on diverse datasets that encompass various dialects, colloquialisms, and emotional nuances. When users feel understood and their subtleties acknowledged, their satisfaction significantly increases.

Context plays a powerful role in communication as well. An AI agent that retains context from previous interactions can provide more cohesive experiences. For example, if a customer has previously inquired about a specific product line, an effective AI should remember that inquiry in future conversations. This continuity allows the agent to build on past discussions rather than starting from scratch, demonstrating an understanding that enriches the overall experience.

Incorporating user feedback is equally important for refining interactions. When users share their experiences—both positive and negative—they contribute to the ongoing improvement of the AI system. Implementing mechanisms for gathering this feedback actively within your AI environment is essential. A simple prompt at the end of a conversation asking users to rate their interaction or suggest improvements can yield invaluable insights for continuous enhancement.

Creating clear feedback channels not only empowers users but also makes them feel valued as contributors to your AI's evolution. Take this example, during rollout phases, companies might introduce features that allow users to submit suggestions for new functionalities directly through the agent interface. This approach enhances user engagement and opens avenues for innovation based on actual user needs.

Visual elements also play a significant role in interaction quality. A well-designed interface that utilizes consistent icons and intuitive layouts helps guide users smoothly through processes without overwhelming them with information. If users find it easy to navigate your agent—whether through voice commands or graphical interfaces—they are more likely to return.

Beyond basic interactions, personalization is another critical dimension to consider. By integrating behavioral insights into the design process, you can tailor communication styles based on user preferences or provide customized suggestions based on previous interactions. For example, an educational AI that assists students with math homework could learn which types of problems they struggle with and offer targeted practice questions accordingly.

Also, incorporating gamification elements into your AI framework can enhance user engagement while improving interaction quality. Features like achievements, rewards for frequent use, or mini-challenges create a more interactive environment that motivates users to continue engaging with the system.

Finally, it's essential to monitor interaction outcomes after launch continuously. Establish key performance indicators (KPIs) that reflect user satisfaction and engagement levels—such as response accuracy and the frequency of returning users—and use this data to inform future updates and enhancements. Keeping track of these metrics will highlight both successful areas and those requiring attention.

In summary, improving interaction quality is a multifaceted endeavor focused on understanding user needs through adaptive learning and NLP while embracing feedback loops and personalized experiences. By weaving these elements together, you can create engaging AI agents that foster lasting relationships built on trust and reliability—a partnership poised for continuous growth and innovation.

Multilingual Support

In today's interconnected world, the ability to communicate across languages is essential for both businesses and individuals. This emphasizes the importance of multilingual support in AI agents. As organizations aim to connect with diverse audiences, an AI agent's capability to engage in multiple languages becomes transformative. Effective communication across linguistic barriers not only expands an AI's reach but also fosters inclusivity, making users feel valued regardless of their language skills.

To successfully implement multilingual support, organizations should start by selecting appropriate natural language processing (NLP) tools that can handle a variety of languages. Many modern platforms come equipped with built-in translation and comprehension capabilities, enabling developers to create AI agents that understand and respond in multiple languages. Take this example, Google's Dialogflow offers multilingual configurations that allow developers to build agents capable of switching seamlessly between languages based on user preferences.

However, it is not sufficient to merely add translation features. The subtleties of language—including dialects, idioms, and cultural references—are crucial for effective communication. A phrase that works well in English may lack a direct translation in Spanish or carry a different connotation in French. To address these complexities, localization is key; this involves adapting the language used by the AI agent to suit the cultural context of its target audience. Engaging native speakers during development ensures that translations are authentic and resonate with users.

Training the AI agent on diverse datasets is equally important. By providing examples of conversational data from different linguistic backgrounds, developers can enhance the agent's ability to generate contextually relevant responses. Utilizing public datasets that include multilingual interactions or creating custom datasets through user interactions during beta testing can significantly enrich the AI's vocabulary and improve its understanding of various phrasings.

User interface design must also cater to multilingual needs. This includes creating layouts that can dynamically adjust text based on language length—some languages may require more space for the same message than others. Incorporating visual elements like flags or language selectors allows users to easily navigate between different language options.

Testing is critical when rolling out multilingual features. Conducting thorough user acceptance testing (UAT) with speakers of various languages helps ensure that the AI agent performs effectively across all supported languages. Observing real interactions can uncover potential issues stemming from cultural differences or translation inaccuracies.

And, establishing feedback mechanisms specifically for multilingual interactions is essential. Providing users with opportunities to report misunderstandings or inaccuracies related to language enhances continuous improvement efforts. For example, including a simple feedback form at the end of a conversation can help gather insights into how well the agent addresses language-specific inquiries.

Integrating voice recognition capabilities further enhances multilingual support by allowing users to communicate verbally in their preferred language. Platforms like Amazon Alexa offer tools for developers to create voice applications that understand multiple languages and dialects, improving accessibility for users who may find written communication challenging.

As organizations continue to expand globally, embracing multilingual support becomes crucial for building relationships and enhancing customer experiences. By investing time and resources into developing a robust multilingual strategy within your AI agents, you can create systems that effectively engage users from diverse linguistic backgrounds.

multilingual support goes beyond mere translation; it requires an understanding of cultural nuances and ensuring that communication feels natural and authentic for all users. By thoughtfully integrating these practices into your no-code AI solutions, you position yourself at the forefront of global communication—ready to engage with an increasingly interconnected world seamlessly.

Adapting to Diverse Audiences

User interaction is inherently diverse, influenced by a variety of cultural nuances, communication styles, and preferences that span different demographics. To create meaningful and effective user experiences, adapting AI agents to address this diversity is not just advantageous; it's essential. In today's landscape, where personalization is paramount, a one-size-fits-all strategy falls short. By customizing AI agents to meet the unique needs of various audiences, you can enhance engagement, build trust, and ultimately drive better outcomes.

The first step in tailoring AI agents for different audiences is to grasp their specific needs and preferences. Conducting thorough audience research will yield insights into language use, cultural references, and behavioral patterns. Take this example, consider an e-commerce platform catering to both North American and Asian markets. Shopping behaviors, preferred payment methods, and customer service expectations can vary significantly between these groups. Recognizing these differences allows for the customization of AI interactions to better suit each audience.

Once you understand your audiences, the next task is designing dialogue flows that resonate with them. This involves selecting not only appropriate language but also the right tone and style of communication. A formal tone might be ideal for business users seeking technical support, while a casual approach could appeal more to younger consumers in search of product recommendations. By crafting multiple dialogue paths within your no-code platform, you can implement these tailored interactions without requiring extensive coding expertise.

Incorporating user feedback throughout this process is crucial. Engaging users from diverse backgrounds offers valuable insights into what resonates and what does not. Setting up beta testing groups with individuals from your target demographics allows their feedback to guide necessary adjustments before a full launch. Continuous iteration based on real-world interactions ensures that your AI agent remains relevant and effective over time.

Another essential consideration is ensuring accessibility across the various devices and platforms where your audience interacts with the AI agent. Some users may prefer mobile app interactions while others might engage through web interfaces or smart devices. Evaluating UI/UX designs to maintain consistent functionality across these platforms enhances usability for all users.

Real-world examples illustrate the effectiveness of this adaptive approach. A global news organization might deploy an AI-driven chatbot that discusses current events with users from different countries. By programming the bot with localized content—addressing not only language differences but also regional interests—it can facilitate conversations that feel relevant and engaging for each audience segment.

Visual elements also play a significant role in enhancing accessibility for diverse audiences. Utilizing culturally resonant icons or images can strengthen user connections while providing intuitive navigation cues across interfaces. For example, a healthcare chatbot should be sensitive to culturally specific health practices or beliefs when interacting with patients from varied backgrounds.

Training your AI agent on diverse datasets enriches its understanding and responsiveness to different audience segments. By integrating input from varied linguistic sources, you equip the agent with a broader vocabulary and greater contextual awareness—allowing it to respond appropriately regardless of cultural context or user background.

And, incorporating emotional intelligence features enhances user engagement across diverse populations. With sentiment analysis capabilities, the AI agent can recognize emotional cues in text inputs or voice commands; responding in ways that acknowledge user sentiments fosters deeper connections.

adapting AI agents for diverse audiences requires ongoing commitment—a continuous evolution rather than a one-time effort. As demographic trends shift and new cultures emerge within digital spaces, consistently refining your approach will ensure relevance in an ever-changing landscape.

By embedding flexibility into your no-code strategies while remaining attuned to audience dynamics, you position your AI solutions as not only functional but also deeply resonant with users worldwide—taking significant strides toward fostering inclusive technology that embraces diversity at every level.

Prototyping and Testing

Creating a robust prototype for your AI agent is a crucial step in the development process, as it allows you to visualize user interactions with the system. This prototyping phase transforms abstract ideas into tangible experiences, enabling you to test functionalities before full-scale implementation. The iterative cycle of building, testing, and refining is essential to ensure that the final product meets user expectations.

Start by outlining the core functionalities your AI agent will offer. This can involve sketching user journeys or flowcharts to map out interactions. Take this example, if you're developing a virtual customer service assistant, consider the steps a user would take when inquiring about order status, troubleshooting an issue, or seeking product recommendations. Visual aids can simplify this process; tools like Figma or Miro are excellent for creating interactive wireframes that illustrate the flow of conversation and decision-making.

With a clear picture of these interactions in mind, choose the features of your no-code platform that best suit your needs. Most no-code tools provide intuitive drag-and-drop interfaces for creating workflows without writing code. For example, if you're using a platform like Bubble or Adalo to build your AI agent, you can easily design screens that represent different stages of user interaction.

When building the initial chatbot interface for customer inquiries, start by dragging text boxes for user inputs and response fields for the AI's outputs. Incorporate buttons that guide users to specific actions—such as checking order status or initiating returns—ensuring these elements align with your designed user journey. Each button click should trigger corresponding workflows defined earlier in your prototyping phase.

Testing is a pivotal part of this process; it provides immediate feedback on how well your design performs in real-world scenarios. Conduct usability tests with potential users to gather their impressions on the interaction flow and overall experience. Engaging participants from diverse backgrounds is vital, as this diversity can uncover unexpected issues or highlight features that resonate particularly well with certain groups.

During testing sessions, pay close attention to how users navigate through the AI agent's interface. Are they able to find information easily? Do they understand how to initiate conversations? Observations from these sessions can yield valuable insights for further refining your design. If users encounter difficulties at any point, it indicates areas needing adjustment—whether that means simplifying language or redesigning specific elements for clarity.

After gathering feedback, iterate on your prototype based on users' suggestions and observations. This could involve revisiting dialogue flows or modifying response types based on common questions raised during testing sessions. For example, if many users express confusion about resetting their passwords, adding a dedicated button for this function could significantly enhance user satisfaction.

Another effective strategy during this phase is A/B testing— creating two versions of certain features to determine which resonates more with users. Take this example, you might present two different styles of responses from your AI agent: one formal and technical versus another casual and friendly. Analyzing which version garners better engagement can help fine-tune voice and tone while optimizing communication effectiveness.

Once you've refined your prototype based on real-world interactions and feedback loops, it's essential to document everything learned throughout the process. Comprehensive documentation not only tracks changes made but also serves as an invaluable resource for future development cycles or onboarding new team members involved in ongoing enhancements.

As you approach the launch phase of your AI agent, remember that prototyping is not just a step but an ongoing practice within your development lifecycle. Continuous evaluation post-launch will enable you to adapt and improve your system based on real-time user data and interactions.

By embracing an iterative prototyping approach combined with thorough testing practices within no-code frameworks, you are setting yourself up for success in deploying an intelligent system that genuinely meets user needs—one that is responsive and tailored rather than rigidly predefined. this commitment to refinement fosters not only functionality but also an engaging experience that stands out in today's digital landscape.

CHAPTER 12:
AI ETHICS AND
RESPONSIBLE AI

Understanding AI Ethics Principles

U nderstanding AI ethics is essential for anyone entering the field of artificial intelligence. As this domain rapidly evolves, it becomes increasingly important to navigate the ethical landscape with care. The principles of AI ethics provide a framework for addressing potential challenges and aligning technological advancements with societal values.

At the heart of AI ethics is the principle of fairness. As AI systems play a growing role in decisions that impact people's lives—such as hiring, lending, and law enforcement—it is vital that their algorithms do not reinforce existing societal biases. For example, if an AI system is trained on historical data that reflects discriminatory hiring practices, it may unintentionally favor certain demographics over others. To combat this, it is crucial to ensure that training datasets are diverse and representative. Additionally, conducting regular audits of these systems can help identify and rectify biases before they lead to harm.

Another key principle is transparency. Users should have a clear understanding of how AI systems function and make decisions. This need for transparency has spurred interest in explainable AI (XAI), which seeks to provide insights into the decision-making processes of algorithms. Take this example, a loan approval algorithm might clarify why an application was denied by outlining specific factors—such as income level or credit score—that influenced its decision. This approach not only helps applicants understand the outcomes but also enables them to seek redress when necessary.

Accountability is equally critical in the ethical use of AI. As organizations deploy more autonomous systems, establishing clear accountability mechanisms becomes essential. Questions arise regarding who is responsible when an AI agent makes an error—should it be the developers, the organization using the technology, or both? By clearly delineating responsibility, companies can proactively address mistakes rather than responding reactively after damage occurs.

Privacy concerns are inherently linked to these ethical principles. Data collection practices must honor individuals' privacy rights while still providing valuable insights for system improvement. Implementing strong data protection measures—such as anonymization techniques and stringent access controls—helps safeguard personal information from misuse or breaches. For example, when deploying an AI agent for customer service inquiries, organizations must comply with regulations like GDPR by obtaining user consent before collecting data.

And, ethical considerations must extend to sustainability in AI development. As technology advances, so does its environmental impact. The energy consumption associated with training large models significantly contributes to carbon emissions; thus, promoting efficient algorithms can help mitigate this issue. Adopting green computing strategies—such as optimizing resource allocation during model training or using cloud solutions powered by renewable energy sources—can align technological progress with ecological responsibility.

While ethical frameworks offer valuable guidance, applying them in real-world scenarios can be challenging due to varying cultural contexts and perspectives on technology use. Organizations should engage stakeholders from diverse backgrounds—including ethicists, technologists, and affected communities—to foster inclusive dialogue about AI deployment strategies. This collaborative approach not only enriches understanding but also empowers organizations to develop more comprehensive policies that resonate across different viewpoints.

As we delve deeper into these principles throughout our discussion on responsible AI use, it's important to remember that ethical considerations are not merely checkboxes—they are fundamental to building trust between technology providers and users alike. Stakeholders who prioritize ethical standards create not only more effective AI solutions but also contribute positively to societal progress.

In summary, grounding your work in ethical principles ensures that your contributions to artificial intelligence reflect not just technical expertise but also a commitment to improving lives through responsible innovation—a mission that resonates profoundly in today's interconnected world.

Bias and Fairness in AI

Artificial intelligence is transforming our interactions with technology, but this shift brings its own set of complexities. As AI systems increasingly influence everyday decisions, issues of bias and fairness demand our attention. Each algorithm we implement has the potential to significantly impact lives, underscoring the necessity for careful examination of their inner workings and the data that drives them.

Bias in AI primarily stems from the datasets used to train these systems. When historical data reflects societal inequities— such as those found in hiring practices, loan approvals, or law enforcement—algorithms built on this data can perpetuate those biases. A notable instance of this occurred with a facial recognition system that exhibited racial bias due to insufficient representation in its training dataset. That's why, it misidentified individuals from underrepresented groups at disproportionately high rates. This example starkly illustrates how bias can be inadvertently ingrained in AI models, leading to tangible consequences in the real world.

To mitigate bias, it is essential to prioritize conscious efforts during the data collection phase. Gathering diverse datasets that accurately represent various demographics is crucial. For example, when developing an AI model for hiring, organizations should ensure that their training data encompasses a wide array of backgrounds and experiences. This approach not only fosters a more equitable system but also enhances the model's overall effectiveness by allowing it to grasp different contexts and nuances.

Transparency is another vital aspect of addressing bias and fairness concerns. Stakeholders must have insights into how AI systems operate and make decisions. The movement towards explainable AI (XAI) supports this transparency by clarifying the often opaque nature of algorithmic decision-making. Take this example, if an AI denies a loan application, providing clear explanations about the factors influencing this decision empowers applicants to understand their situations better and take necessary actions.

Accountability also plays a crucial role in this conversation. As our reliance on AI grows, we must clearly define who is responsible when errors occur. This becomes particularly complex when multiple parties are involved—developers, organizations deploying the technology, and end-users all contribute to the outcomes produced by these systems. Establishing explicit guidelines around accountability ensures that when mistakes happen—such as discriminatory decisions —the responsible party can be identified, leading to corrective measures rather than mere blame-shifting.

Privacy concerns intersect with discussions about bias and accountability as well. With data becoming an increasingly valuable asset for training AI systems, protecting user privacy is paramount. Organizations need robust data governance policies that prioritize consent and respect user rights while still enabling effective system performance. Techniques such as anonymization can help safeguard personal information during data analysis processes, striking a balance between operational needs and ethical considerations.

In addition to these ethical principles, we must incorporate sustainability into our discussions around AI deployment. The environmental impact of training large-scale AI models raises questions about our commitment to ecological responsibility. By adopting energy-efficient algorithms and sustainable practices in technology development, we can significantly reduce carbon footprints while advancing technological capabilities.

Real-world applications often reveal challenges related to bias and fairness influenced by diverse cultural contexts affecting perceptions of technology use. Engaging with stakeholders— including ethicists, technologists, and affected communities —deepens our understanding of how AI should evolve responsibly across different environments. Creating platforms for open dialogue enables organizations to formulate more nuanced policies that resonate across varied perspectives.

As we explore responsible AI practices throughout this discussion, it becomes clear that embedding ethical considerations within our work is essential—not only for compliance but also for fostering trust between technology providers and users alike. By prioritizing fairness and accountability alongside technical excellence, we can advance progress that benefits society while ensuring our innovations uplift rather than undermine those they touch.

understanding bias and striving for fairness is not just an academic exercise; it is foundational for building technologies that reflect our societal values. Embracing these principles paves the way for a future where AI serves humanity equitably and responsibly—reinforcing our commitment to improving lives through innovation rather than exacerbating existing disparities or introducing new ones.

Transparency and Explainability

Transparency and explainability in AI systems are essential for fostering trust and accountability. As AI becomes more embedded in our everyday lives, the urgency for a clear understanding of how these systems function increases. Stakeholders—including users, developers, and regulators—need insight into the mechanisms driving AI decisions to ensure they uphold ethical standards and reflect societal values.

Essentially of transparency is the ability to clarify the decision-making processes of AI algorithms. Take this example, consider an AI system designed to recommend treatments in healthcare. When a doctor receives a suggestion from such an algorithm, understanding how that recommendation was generated can significantly influence their trust in the system. Providing clear explanations about the factors considered—such as patient history, demographics, and relevant medical literature—empowers healthcare professionals to make informed choices that ultimately enhance patient care.

Explainable AI (XAI) techniques are pivotal in achieving

this level of transparency. XAI includes methods that elucidate how models arrive at specific outputs without revealing proprietary algorithms. Techniques like LIME (Local Interpretable Model-agnostic Explanations) and SHAP (SHapley Additive exPlanations) help generate insights into model behavior, making it easier for users to understand the rationale behind predictions. For example, when applying LIME to a machine learning model predicting loan defaults, it may highlight key features such as income level or previous credit history as significant factors influencing its decisions.

Beyond technical solutions, organizations must cultivate a culture of openness regarding their AI practices. This means not only sharing performance metrics but also actively engaging with communities impacted by these technologies. Take this example, if a city adopts an AI-driven traffic management system, involving local residents in discussions about data collection and usage can help clarify the technology while addressing potential concerns related to surveillance or data misuse.

Regulatory frameworks also play a crucial role in promoting transparency in AI systems. As governments worldwide establish guidelines for ethical AI use, ensuring clarity about data utilization and algorithmic decision-making becomes vital. The European Union's General Data Protection Regulation (GDPR) grants individuals the right to obtain meaningful information about the logic involved in automated decision-making processes that affect them. This legal requirement encourages organizations to enhance transparency and bolsters public trust.

However, simply providing explanations is insufficient; they must be understandable and relevant to end-users. Technical jargon can alienate non-expert audiences and lead to confusion rather than clarity. Therefore, prioritizing user-friendly explanations is essential—using relatable language and visual aids can effectively bridge this gap. For example, an online platform offering personalized financial advice through an AI assistant should break down complex recommendations into digestible insights, enabling users from diverse backgrounds to engage meaningfully with their financial health.

Engaging various stakeholders also involves incorporating feedback mechanisms into AI systems themselves. When users have opportunities to share their experiences—whether through surveys or direct reporting channels—it helps refine algorithms while enhancing accountability. Take this example, if users consistently express dissatisfaction with decisions made by a customer service chatbot due to lack of clarity or perceived unfairness, developers can iteratively improve the model based on this real-world feedback.

Ethical considerations surrounding transparency extend beyond merely explaining algorithms; they involve fostering trust by aligning technology with human values. The implications are significant: if individuals feel excluded from understanding how decisions impact their lives or perceive biases within those decisions, it may undermine confidence in technological advancements altogether.

As we navigate this evolving landscape of transparency and explainability in AI applications, we encounter both challenges and opportunities. The challenge lies in balancing technical complexity with user comprehension while ensuring accountability at all levels—from design through deployment.

fostering transparent practices isn't merely about compliance; it's about cultivating relationships grounded in mutual respect between technology providers and society at large. By committing ourselves not only to building effective systems but also to clarifying their workings, we create pathways toward responsible innovation—where artificial intelligence enhances lives rather than complicating them further.

In summary, transparency is not just an accessory; it's a cornerstone of responsible AI deployment that requires ongoing commitment from all parties involved—from developers striving for clarity in their models' operations to users advocating for understandable explanations regarding automated decisions that directly affect their lives.

AI and Privacy Concerns

The discussion surrounding AI inevitably brings us to the crucial intersection of technology and privacy. As AI systems become more sophisticated, they increasingly handle vast amounts of personal data, prompting essential questions about how this information is collected, utilized, and protected. Understanding the complexities of AI in relation to privacy isn't just about adhering to regulations; it's an ethical imperative that directly influences public trust in technology.

When AI systems process data, they often rely on sensitive information such as health records, financial details, or personal identifiers. Take, for example, a healthcare chatbot designed to provide personalized medical advice. To deliver tailored recommendations, it must analyze patient data. However, without robust privacy safeguards in place, this sensitive information can become vulnerable to breaches or misuse. The potential for exploitation—whether by external attackers or insiders—underscores the urgent need for comprehensive privacy protocols.

Implementing strong data protection measures is one effective way to address these issues. Techniques like data anonymization help mitigate risks by ensuring that personal identifiers are removed before analysis. Take this example, when creating datasets for training machine learning models in finance, anonymizing client information allows institutions to gain insights without compromising individuals' identities. This not only protects user privacy but also builds trust among clients who may be apprehensive about how their data is being used.

Yet, relying solely on technical safeguards is not enough. Organizations must foster transparency regarding their data practices. Users should have a clear understanding of what data is being collected and how it will be used. This necessitates clear communication policies that articulate data handling in straightforward terms—essential for demystifying AI processes. Take this example, if a retail AI system tracks customer preferences to enhance shopping experiences, consumers should be informed about the specific information being gathered and its purpose.

The conversation around privacy must also address user consent, which is a critical aspect of ethical AI deployment. Organizations should ensure that consent processes are clear and simple, enabling users to make informed decisions about their data usage. Adopting opt-in models rather than opt-out ones can be an effective strategy; this approach allows users to actively agree to share their information rather than having their consent assumed by default.

Regulatory frameworks are increasingly shaping how companies respond to privacy concerns. The General Data Protection Regulation (GDPR) in Europe has established rigorous guidelines that require businesses to manage personal data responsibly and transparently. This regulation empowers individuals with rights such as accessing their data and requesting its deletion, reinforcing the principle that users should retain control over their personal information. As similar laws emerge globally, organizations must adapt their practices to ensure compliance while nurturing a culture of respect for user privacy.

Addressing privacy challenges also calls for ongoing education about responsible AI use among developers and users alike. Training sessions on ethical considerations in AI development can equip teams with the knowledge needed to integrate privacy features from the start. For example, involving diverse stakeholders—including employees—in the development of an AI tool for monitoring performance can help identify potential privacy pitfalls and encourage practices that uphold individual rights.

And, organizations should actively seek user feedback through mechanisms designed to gather insights about their experiences with AI systems. When users voice concerns or highlight issues related to privacy—such as unintended data sharing—this feedback can drive continuous improvements in systems that prioritize user rights.

As we navigate the complexities of AI and privacy, one fundamental truth stands out: building trust requires more than just technological innovation; it demands a genuine commitment to ethical principles that prioritize individual autonomy and security. Companies that take proactive steps toward transparency are likely to cultivate stronger relationships with their users—turning skepticism into trust.

navigating the intersection of AI and privacy challenges everyone involved—developers must critically consider how their creations impact society as a whole while users demand accountability from those who wield powerful technologies. Embracing this shared responsibility will help shape a future where innovation flourishes alongside respect for individual rights—a delicate balance as we leverage the transformative potential of artificial intelligence while safeguarding our collective privacy.

Regulatory Compliance

Navigating the regulatory compliance landscape is crucial for any organization utilizing AI technologies, especially as these solutions become increasingly embedded in everyday business operations. A solid understanding of the regulatory environment helps mitigate risks related to data privacy, security, and ethical considerations. The challenge lies not only in adhering to national laws but also in managing a patchwork of international regulations that can differ significantly. That's why, organizations must remain vigilant and proactive to ensure compliance.

At the forefront of these regulatory frameworks is the General Data Protection Regulation (GDPR), which imposes stringent guidelines on data handling across Europe. This regulation mandates transparency regarding how personal data is collected, processed, and stored. Take this example, if your AI system gathers user data to personalize experiences, you must obtain explicit consent from users. And, businesses are required to clearly communicate their data practices and ensure that users can easily access or delete their personal information. Non-compliance can lead to substantial fines— up to 4% of a company's global annual revenue—highlighting the necessity for organizations to adopt comprehensive compliance strategies.

In addition to GDPR, other regulations such as the California Consumer Privacy Act (CCPA) also have significant implications. The CCPA offers similar protections for California residents and emphasizes consumer rights concerning their personal information. Under this act, businesses must disclose what personal data they collect and grant users the right to opt out of its sale. To comply with such laws, organizations must maintain diligent records and possess a thorough understanding of what constitutes personal information within their AI systems.

This regulatory landscape often drives organizations to embrace privacy-by-design principles when developing AI solutions. This approach involves integrating data protection measures from the very beginning of an AI project rather than treating them as an afterthought. For example, when creating an AI chatbot for customer inquiries, incorporating features that anonymize user interactions can safeguard sensitive information while still providing valuable insights into customer behavior.

Regular audits are essential for maintaining compliance amid evolving regulations. Establishing a routine process for reviewing your AI systems helps ensure that you meet current legal standards while preparing for potential legislative changes. By monitoring updates related to regulations like GDPR or CCPA, organizations can adapt swiftly without disrupting operations or incurring penalties.

It's important to understand that regulatory compliance extends beyond mere adherence to laws; it also involves building trust among users. Transparency in how AI systems operate and manage data fosters confidence among consumers and stakeholders alike. Engaging users with clear privacy policies and regular updates about their rights further enhances this trust.

Collaboration with legal experts is invaluable as businesses navigate this complex regulatory terrain effectively. A legal team well-versed in both technology and compliance can provide guidance during development phases—ensuring that all aspects of AI deployment align with regulatory expectations.

The stakes are particularly high in sectors like healthcare and finance, where non-compliance could result not only in financial penalties but also in significant harm to individuals' well-being or privacy. In healthcare applications that utilize AI for patient diagnostics or treatment recommendations, adherence to the Health Insurance Portability and Accountability Act (HIPAA) is vital for protecting patient information while leveraging AI's capabilities.

In summary, effectively navigating regulatory compliance is integral when deploying no-code AI solutions. Organizations must proactively understand relevant laws such as GDPR and CCPA while embedding privacy-by-design principles throughout their development processes. Regular audits, transparency initiatives, and collaboration with legal experts form the foundation of successful compliance strategies —ultimately enabling businesses to innovate responsibly without compromising user trust or facing severe penalties.

Managing AI Risks

The landscape of artificial intelligence is evolving rapidly, introducing a range of potential risks that organizations must navigate with care. As AI systems become increasingly integrated into decision-making processes, these risks can manifest in various ways, including data breaches, ethical dilemmas, and operational failures. To foster trust and ensure the responsible use of AI technologies, a proactive approach to risk management is essential.

One of the most significant concerns is data security. Organizations leveraging AI often handle vast amounts of sensitive information, making them prime targets for cyberattacks. When personal data is compromised—whether through hacking, inadequate encryption practices, or other vulnerabilities—the repercussions can be severe. A data breach can erode customer trust and lead to substantial regulatory fines. Take this example, if a company employing an AI-driven customer service platform experiences a breach, it not only jeopardizes customer confidence but also risks financial penalties.

To mitigate these risks, establishing robust security measures is imperative. This includes implementing strong encryption protocols to safeguard data both in transit and at rest. Additionally, regularly updating software and conducting security audits can help organizations identify vulnerabilities before they are exploited. Techniques such as penetration testing allow businesses to simulate attacks on their systems to uncover weaknesses that require attention.

In addition to technical vulnerabilities, ethical considerations play a crucial role in the deployment of AI solutions.

Organizations must confront biases that may inadvertently infiltrate their algorithms, leading to unfair treatment of individuals or groups. For example, an AI system used for hiring decisions that relies on historical data reflecting past biases may perpetuate discriminatory practices by favoring certain demographics over others. To address this issue, organizations should prioritize fairness by continuously auditing their models for bias and recalibrating them as necessary.

Another risk arises from the opacity of AI decision-making processes. Many AI systems operate as "black boxes," leaving even their developers unsure about how decisions are made. This lack of transparency can impede accountability, especially in sectors like finance or healthcare where decisions significantly impact individuals' lives. Implementing explainable AI techniques can shed light on how models arrive at conclusions, thereby enhancing user trust and ensuring compliance with regulations.

Training employees about the capabilities and limitations of AI technologies is also vital for effective risk management. By fostering a culture of awareness regarding potential pitfalls, organizations empower their teams to proactively identify and address risks rather than reacting after the fact. Take this example, conducting workshops on recognizing bias in algorithms helps team members understand how their choices influence outcomes.

Also, developing clear protocols for incident response is critical for managing risks effectively. An established incident response plan enables organizations to act swiftly when breaches or failures occur, mitigating damage and ensuring transparent communication with affected parties. Regular updates to these plans are essential to address new threats and adapt to changes within the organization.

Collaboration with external partners further enhances

effective risk management. Organizations should engage with academic institutions and industry groups focused on AI safety and ethics. Staying informed about emerging trends and best practices allows businesses to adapt more readily to evolving challenges.

viewing risk management as an ongoing process rather than a one-time effort is crucial. As technologies advance and new regulations emerge, organizations must remain agile in their approach to risk management strategies. Regular assessments of the risk landscape enable businesses to adjust their practices accordingly, fostering an environment where innovation can thrive without compromising accountability or safety.

Managing the risks associated with AI is multifaceted but achievable through a comprehensive strategy that emphasizes security measures, ethical considerations, transparency in decision-making processes, employee training, incident response planning, collaboration with external experts, and continuous assessment of evolving challenges. By adopting this holistic approach, organizations can harness the vast potential of AI while safeguarding against its inherent risks —building intelligent systems that inspire confidence among users and stakeholders alike.

Building Trust with Users

The relationship between technology and trust is intricate, particularly in the realm of artificial intelligence. Establishing trust with users goes beyond simply ensuring that a system operates correctly; it involves creating an environment where users feel secure, informed, and respected. This foundation of trust is essential for the effective deployment of AI agents, especially as they become increasingly woven into our daily lives.

At the heart of building this trust is transparency. Users want clarity not just on how an AI agent functions but also on how it arrives at its decisions. When organizations offer straightforward explanations of the algorithms and processes behind their technologies, they help demystify AI. Take this example, take a health app that uses AI to recommend dietary changes. If users understand that their data is processed with their consent and can trace how specific recommendations are derived from their inputs, they are more likely to accept and act on those suggestions.

In addition to transparency, empowering users with control over their personal data reinforces trust. Users should have the ability to manage what information they share with AI systems and dictate how it is utilized. Features that allow for data visibility—such as logs of interactions or options for data deletion—can enhance users' confidence in the system's integrity. Companies like Apple exemplify this approach by emphasizing user privacy in their marketing and design strategies. By enabling users to control their data through features like app tracking transparency, Apple not only adheres to regulations but also cultivates a strong foundation of trust.

Consistency in performance is another critical factor in building user trust. When AI agents reliably make accurate predictions or fulfill requests promptly, users feel more assured in their interactions. Conversely, frequent misunderstandings or inaccuracies can quickly lead to frustration and skepticism about an AI's capabilities. Therefore, regular updates and maintenance are vital to ensure these systems continue to function effectively over time.

User engagement further enhances trust between AI agents and their users. Providing easy channels for feedback demonstrates that organizations value user input and are committed to continuous improvement. For example, consider a customer support chatbot that collects feedback after each interaction; the insights gained can refine its responses and increase its utility over time. By responding to user suggestions, companies show that they listen—a practice that significantly bolsters trust.

Ethical considerations must also underpin every interaction between AI agents and users. Implementing principles that prioritize fairness and equality helps mitigate biases in AI responses or decisions. Organizations can conduct regular audits of their AI models to identify potential biases related to demographic factors such as race or gender, making necessary adjustments to ensure equitable treatment across all user interactions.

Educational initiatives aimed at informing users about AI capabilities contribute to a deeper understanding of what these technologies can achieve—and where their limitations lie. Businesses might host informational webinars or create content-rich resources that explain the rationale behind specific algorithms used within their systems, highlighting both strengths and limitations.

As organizations navigate the evolving landscape of AI development and deployment, accountability remains crucial for maintaining user trust. Establishing clear ethical guidelines—including mechanisms for redress when issues arise—demonstrates a commitment to responsible practices. This could involve forming dedicated teams responsible for addressing ethical concerns or developing policies for the responsible use of sensitive data.

Finally, continuously monitoring user experiences allows organizations to effectively gauge sentiment towards their AI agents. Metrics such as user satisfaction scores and net promoter scores (NPS) serve as powerful tools for assessing success over time while pinpointing areas needing improvement.

Building trust with users encompasses a variety of strategies—from transparency and data control to consistent performance and engagement through feedback—all intertwined with ethical principles guiding organizational actions in deploying AI technologies. By adopting these practices holistically rather than piecemeal, businesses can leverage advanced technologies while fostering enduring relationships based on mutual respect between machines designed for assistance and humans seeking support from them.

Promoting Sustainability with AI

In a world increasingly focused on environmental concerns, the convergence of artificial intelligence and sustainability stands out as a promising frontier. Organizations are recognizing their environmental responsibilities, and AI offers opportunities to enhance efficiency while reducing ecological footprints. By harnessing AI's capabilities, businesses can streamline operations and spearhead significant sustainability initiatives that contribute to a healthier planet.

One clear illustration of AI's role in promoting sustainability can be found in energy management. Smart grids powered by AI algorithms optimize electricity distribution, cutting waste and improving the use of renewable resources. For example, these systems analyze consumption patterns in real time, predicting peak usage times and adjusting energy flow accordingly. This dynamic approach not only integrates renewable energy sources like solar and wind more effectively into the grid but also leads to lower carbon emissions.

Agriculture also reaps substantial benefits from AI technologies that promote sustainable practices. Precision farming employs machine learning algorithms to process data from sensors and drones, determining the best times for planting, watering, and harvesting crops. A notable startup utilizes AI to monitor soil health and moisture levels, providing farmers with tailored insights that help reduce water usage while maximizing crop yields. This approach conserves vital resources and bolsters food security in a world with a growing population.

Transportation is another sector ripe for transformation through AI-driven sustainability efforts. Autonomous vehicles are being outfitted with algorithms that optimize routes based on traffic patterns, weather conditions, and energy consumption metrics. By minimizing idling time and improving overall route efficiency, these vehicles can significantly reduce fuel usage. Take this example, a logistics company that implemented AI routing software not only decreased delivery times but also reduced its carbon footprint, demonstrating that profitability and environmental responsibility can go hand in hand.

Waste management is evolving as well, thanks to intelligent systems capable of analyzing waste patterns. AI can predict trends in waste generation and inform better resource allocation strategies for collection services. Smart bins equipped with sensors alert collection teams when they are full and analyze the types of waste being discarded. This insight enables municipalities to tailor recycling programs to community needs while cutting costs associated with waste disposal.

On a broader scale, companies are utilizing AI analytics for sustainability reporting and compliance tracking. By leveraging machine learning models to analyze large datasets related to emissions and resource consumption, organizations gain valuable insights into their environmental impact. These insights not only help businesses meet regulatory requirements but also empower them to adopt more proactive sustainable practices.

Engaging stakeholders in sustainability initiatives is crucial for fostering acceptance of these technologies. Education plays a significant role; companies must communicate the benefits of AI in achieving sustainable outcomes transparently. Hosting workshops or creating informational content about AI's positive impacts can demystify these technologies for both employees and consumers.

As organizations embrace these innovations, ethical considerations must remain at the forefront to ensure that sustainability efforts do not inadvertently reinforce existing inequities or biases. Responsible data use and transparent communication about decision-making processes will be vital as businesses navigate this landscape.

promoting sustainability through AI is not just about implementing new technologies; it involves a cultural shift within organizations toward prioritizing ecological responsibility alongside economic growth. This dual focus can lead to innovative solutions that benefit both business objectives and the environment—creating a win-win scenario for all stakeholders involved.

The journey toward sustainable practices through AI is ongoing; continuous adaptation and improvement are essential as technology evolves and environmental challenges persist. By responsibly harnessing AI's potential, organizations can make significant strides toward a more sustainable future while setting industry standards that others may follow—a testament to how technology can serve as an ally in the quest for planetary health.

Case Studies of Ethical AI Implementation

The implementation of ethical AI is not just an aspiration; it is essential for organizations dedicated to sustainable and responsible practices. As businesses increasingly adopt AI technologies, real-world case studies reveal how ethical considerations can be seamlessly integrated into AI development and deployment. These examples illustrate that prioritizing ethics can lead to improved societal outcomes and enhanced business performance.

Take, for instance, a prominent healthcare provider that came under scrutiny for its use of AI in patient diagnosis. Recognizing the potential for bias in algorithmic decision-making, the organization proactively established a diverse ethics committee tasked with reviewing the AI models utilized in clinical settings. This committee meticulously evaluated data sources for biases and ensured that training datasets included a wide range of demographics, ultimately improving diagnostic accuracy across diverse populations. By committing to ethical AI, the provider not only mitigated risks but also built trust among patients and stakeholders, demonstrating how ethical practices can enhance brand reputation.

In a similar vein, a leading tech company developed an AI-driven hiring tool designed to streamline recruitment processes. However, initial testing revealed that the algorithm disproportionately favored candidates from specific backgrounds, exposing inherent biases in the training data. Rather than pushing forward with technology without addressing these concerns, the company decided to pause its deployment and reassess its approach. Through extensive audits and consultations with external experts on fairness and diversity, they re-engineered their algorithm to promote equitable hiring practices. This strategic pivot not only avoided potential legal challenges but also attracted talent eager to join a socially responsible employer.

In the finance sector, a fintech startup employed machine learning models to evaluate creditworthiness. Aware of the sensitivity surrounding financial decisions that profoundly impact individuals' lives, the company established a framework for transparency that included clear communication about decision-making processes. They empowered consumers by providing access to explanations regarding their credit scores and the AI algorithms influencing those decisions. This commitment to transparency fostered trust and demonstrated that ethical practices can serve as both an imperative and a competitive advantage.

Organizations are also harnessing AI systems designed

with ethics at their core to tackle climate change challenges. For example, an environmental NGO utilized machine learning algorithms to analyze satellite imagery for deforestation patterns in vulnerable regions. Their initiative focused on ensuring that data collection processes respected local communities' rights while offering valuable insights into conservation strategies. By maintaining a transparent methodology, the organization effectively collaborated with local stakeholders, strengthening community ties as they worked toward shared sustainability goals.

Education plays a crucial role in nurturing ethical AI practices within organizations. Companies must raise awareness among employees about potential biases and ethical dilemmas associated with AI applications. Regular training sessions can empower staff at all levels—from developers who create algorithms to executives making strategic decisions —to appreciate the importance of ethics in technology deployment. One notable retailer launched an internal campaign emphasizing "ethics by design," encouraging all teams to consider potential societal impacts throughout every phase of product development.

While these case studies showcase positive outcomes from ethical considerations in AI implementation, challenges remain in achieving widespread adherence to best practices. A significant barrier is the resistance from stakeholders who may prioritize profitability or efficiency over ethics. Bridging this gap requires compelling narratives that illustrate the business value of ethical behavior—such as increased customer loyalty or reduced litigation risks.

Examining these case studies collectively reveals that integrating ethics into AI frameworks transcends compliance or risk avoidance; it signifies a commitment to responsible stewardship of technology for societal benefit. Businesses that champion ethical practices position themselves as industry leaders—catalysts for change that others aspire to emulate.

pursuing ethical AI implementation is an ongoing journey that demands vigilance and adaptability as new challenges emerge within rapidly evolving technological landscapes. By embedding ethics into every aspect of AI development and deployment—from conception through monitoring—organizations can responsibly harness technology's full potential while positively contributing to society at large. This holistic approach serves as a powerful reminder that innovation must always be coupled with responsibility—a principle essential for navigating today's complex world where technology deeply intersects with human lives.

CHAPTER 13:
SCALING YOUR
AI SOLUTIONS

Identifying Growth Opportunities

I dentifying growth opportunities in the no-code AI solutions space necessitates a multifaceted approach that combines strategic insight with a deep understanding of emerging trends. Today's businesses are navigating a rapidly evolving landscape filled with potential, where technology advances swiftly and customer needs change unpredictably. To seize these opportunities, adopting a mindset centered on adaptability and foresight is crucial.

The first step is to analyze market trends and consumer behaviors that signal shifting demands. For example, the normalization of remote work has created a surge in demand for tools that enable collaboration and productivity without requiring technical expertise. By recognizing such trends, companies can develop AI solutions specifically designed for this new normal. A focus on creating no-code platforms that streamline communication or project management, while leveraging AI to enhance efficiency and user experience, can be particularly fruitful.

Engaging with your existing customer base also reveals untapped opportunities for growth. Implementing feedback mechanisms—like surveys or interactive forums—can highlight pain points and desires that customers may not explicitly share. Take this example, if a small business owner using a no-code platform for customer relationship management finds tracking engagement data cumbersome, a responsive organization could respond by creating an AI-driven feature to automate this process. Such initiatives transform feedback into actionable improvements, enhancing user satisfaction and retention.

Competition analysis is another key aspect of identifying growth opportunities. By studying successful players in the no-code AI realm, businesses can gain insights into features and functionalities that resonate with users. If competitors prioritize integration capabilities with popular applications, companies should consider bolstering their own integrations to match or exceed these offerings. Additionally, if certain market segments—such as non-profits—remain underserved in terms of cost-effective AI solutions, focusing on these niches can help establish a company as a leader in an emerging sector.

Networking within industry circles can provide invaluable insights as well. Attending conferences or participating in online communities enables innovators to connect with peers facing similar challenges and successes. These interactions can spark fresh ideas, encouraging companies to adapt their offerings or explore collaborations that broaden their reach. For example, an emerging startup might partner with established organizations to co-develop no-code AI tools tailored to specific industries, thereby leveraging their combined strengths for greater impact.

Conducting pilot programs is also an effective strategy for

testing new ideas while mitigating risk. By launching limited-scale initiatives aimed at specific user groups, organizations can assess interest and gather functional data before a full-scale rollout. Take this example, if a company plans to create an AI agent for personalized learning experiences in education, partnering with a local school for a controlled implementation can provide crucial feedback from educators and students to refine the product.

And, integrating technological advancements into growth strategies is essential. As developments in areas like natural language processing (NLP) and machine learning continue to emerge, businesses must remain vigilant about incorporating the latest technologies into their offerings. A no-code platform that utilizes NLP capabilities, for example, could allow users to create workflows through simple conversational interfaces, making automation even more accessible.

Regularly assessing internal capabilities is equally important in identifying growth opportunities. Companies should evaluate their resources—both human and technological—to ensure they are positioned to innovate effectively. This includes nurturing existing talent while seeking new hires who bring diverse skills and perspectives. Embracing cross-disciplinary collaboration fosters creativity; having engineers work alongside marketing professionals often leads to solutions that are both technically sound and market-ready.

Finally, monitoring performance metrics will guide decision-making throughout this journey of discovery. By analyzing usage patterns and engagement statistics across various demographics, organizations can gain valuable insights into what resonates most with users. These metrics should inform continuous improvement efforts; adapting features based on real-world usage ensures that products remain relevant and compelling.

In summary, identifying growth opportunities within the

no-code AI landscape involves embracing change while being attuned to customer needs and market dynamics. By blending trend analysis, customer feedback, competitive research, networking, pilot programs, technological integration, resource assessment, and data-driven decision-making, organizations can successfully navigate this complex environment. Maintaining agility not only fosters innovation but positions businesses as leaders in an evolving digital economy that thrives on accessibility and user empowerment.

Infrastructure Scalability

Scalability in infrastructure is a crucial factor for businesses exploring no-code AI solutions. As organizations expand, their technological frameworks must evolve to meet growing demands without compromising performance or user experience. The ability to scale effectively often separates successful implementations from those that struggle under pressure.

To start, it's essential to grasp the core architecture of no-code platforms. Many of these platforms utilize cloud-based services, which naturally provide scalability. Take this example, leveraging Amazon Web Services (AWS) enables businesses to adjust their computational resources in real-time as user demand fluctuates. Consider a scenario where a no-code application experiences a sudden surge in traffic—perhaps due to a marketing campaign or seasonal interest. Without a cloud infrastructure capable of automatically scaling up, users may encounter slow load times or even service outages, leading to frustration and missed opportunities.

However, scaling goes beyond merely adding more resources; it also involves optimizing existing ones. Organizations should prioritize efficient data management practices that facilitate seamless integration and retrieval of information across their systems. For example, employing databases like MongoDB allows companies to handle unstructured data flexibly while ensuring quick access times. This adaptability is vital for AI applications, where user interactions can vary significantly over time.

Collaboration among various teams within an organization is another key element in building a scalable infrastructure. Engineers, product managers, and data scientists must work together to align technical capabilities with business objectives. Take the development of an AI agent designed to enhance customer service through chat functionality; close collaboration with marketing and customer support teams can provide insights on peak user times and common queries. This information helps inform decisions about how to configure the infrastructure for optimal responsiveness.

Incorporating automation into workflows further boosts scalability. Tools like Zapier or Integromat (now Make) enable organizations to connect various applications without extensive coding knowledge while ensuring smooth data flow between systems as the number of integrations increases. This not only enhances operational efficiency but also allows human resources to concentrate on more strategic tasks instead of mundane manual processes.

Another important aspect of scalability involves establishing robust monitoring systems to track performance metrics and system health in real time. Utilizing analytics tools such as Google Analytics or custom dashboards built on platforms like Tableau or Power BI provides companies with insights into how their applications perform under different loads. These metrics allow for proactive adjustments; for instance, if analysis reveals that certain features create bottlenecks during peak usage hours, teams can investigate and implement necessary optimizations before users are affected.

Building an adaptable infrastructure also requires embracing modular designs for applications. This approach involves creating components that can function independently while integrating seamlessly when necessary. For example, if a company wants to add predictive analytics capabilities to its existing AI agent, it should be able to do so without overhauling the entire system architecture. Modularity fosters rapid innovation while maintaining stability in core offerings.

Lastly, planning for future growth should be integral to any scalability strategy from the outset. Businesses need to conduct regular assessments of their technology stack and evaluate whether current solutions will continue to meet demands as they expand into new markets or introduce new products. Engaging with cloud service providers early in the planning process can offer insights into best practices for scaling and identify potential pitfalls based on industry experiences.

To wrap things up, achieving scalability in no-code AI solutions requires a combination of strategic planning, effective resource management, and continuous adaptation to evolving demands. Organizations that embrace these principles not only protect their current operations but also position themselves for sustained growth in an increasingly competitive landscape where agility is essential.

Improving Performance on a Larger Scale

Organizations exploring no-code AI solutions often face the challenge of maintaining performance as their user base grows. Achieving optimal performance at scale involves more than just increasing resources; it requires a nuanced understanding of system design, data management, and team collaboration. A comprehensive strategy is essential to ensure that applications remain responsive and effective as demand escalates.

At the heart of this strategy lies the architecture of no-code platforms, which typically leverage cloud-based services for scalability. Take this example, utilizing platforms like

Microsoft Azure or Google Cloud allows businesses to allocate resources dynamically based on real-time traffic and user behavior. Imagine launching an AI-driven marketing tool during a major sales event. If the application is designed to automatically scale with increased traffic, users will experience a seamless interaction even during peak periods. Conversely, neglecting to implement a robust infrastructure can lead to overwhelmed servers, resulting in slow response times or crashes—outcomes that can deter users and damage brand reputation.

Equally important is the optimization of existing resources. Companies must prioritize efficient data management to facilitate quick access to information across systems. Databases like PostgreSQL provide strong transactional support while enabling flexible queries and indexing strategies that enhance data retrieval speed. This efficiency is particularly crucial for AI applications where data volumes can be substantial. For example, consider an AI agent analyzing customer interactions; rapid data access significantly boosts its responsiveness and adaptability.

Collaboration among cross-functional teams also plays a pivotal role in scaling efforts. When engineers work closely with product managers and marketing specialists, they develop a deeper understanding of user needs and peak usage times. Take this example, if your no-code solution includes chat functionality for customer service inquiries, insights from the customer support team can reveal common questions or periods of increased inquiries. Such collaboration aids in configuring system resources effectively, ensuring backend processes can manage spikes in demand without compromising service quality.

Automation further streamlines workflows, enabling organizations to handle increasing complexity without sacrificing quality or speed. Tools like Airtable or Zapier automate repetitive tasks such as data entry or notifications across various platforms. By minimizing manual involvement in routine tasks, teams can concentrate on strategic initiatives that add greater value to their projects.

Implementing proactive monitoring systems is essential for staying ahead of potential performance issues at scale. Advanced analytics tools like Grafana or custom dashboards in Looker Studio allow organizations to track key performance indicators (KPIs) in real time, helping identify trends and areas needing attention before they escalate into larger problems. For example, if analytics reveal a slowdown during specific operations—such as data fetching—teams can proactively adjust configurations before users notice any impact.

In addition to monitoring, adopting modular designs in application development enhances scalability and flexibility. A modular architecture allows individual components of an AI agent to operate independently while integrating seamlessly when needed. If a business wants to incorporate machine learning models for user behavior predictions into its existing system, this modularity enables swift integration with minimal disruption—adding new capabilities without overhauling the entire platform.

Planning for future growth requires regular assessments of both technology infrastructure and market trends. Engaging with cloud service providers during these evaluations provides insights into emerging technologies and best practices tailored for scalability challenges based on real-world experiences. This foresight positions companies strategically while helping them avoid pitfalls encountered by others who may have rushed into expansion without adequate planning.

In summary, enhancing performance at scale involves interlinking various elements: efficient resource allocation through cloud solutions, agile team collaboration driven by shared objectives, automation reducing operational burdens, proactive monitoring identifying issues swiftly, modular design fostering innovation while maintaining stability—all supported by strategic foresight aimed at future growth opportunities. Organizations that embrace this comprehensive approach will not only ensure their no-code AI solutions remain effective as demands increase but also build a resilient foundation for sustained success in an ever-evolving digital landscape.

Optimizing Resource Usage

Scaling no-code AI solutions effectively depends on optimizing resource usage—not merely maximizing consumption, but ensuring that every component operates in harmony and efficiency. As organizations pursue growth, understanding how to best utilize available resources becomes essential, especially in a landscape where user expectations and demands are constantly evolving.

At the heart of effective resource management lies the architectural design of your no-code platform. Many platforms leverage cloud infrastructure for dynamic scaling. Take this example, AWS allows users to adjust resource allocation based on real-time demand. When designing an AI-driven application, incorporating features that automatically scale resources can maintain performance during unexpected surges—such as during a flash sale or a viral marketing campaign. Take, for example, a customer support chatbot deployed during peak hours; the platform can allocate additional processing power to manage an influx of inquiries without compromising service quality.

However, resource allocation alone is not enough; optimizing data management practices is equally crucial. Efficient data handling enables AI agents to retrieve and process information swiftly, directly impacting response times and user satisfaction. Utilizing database systems like MongoDB or DynamoDB can facilitate horizontal scaling and rapid data access. Consider a travel booking AI agent: when users query flight availability, quick database responses ensure they receive timely updates about their options, thereby enhancing overall engagement.

Collaboration across teams significantly shapes how resources are allocated and utilized. Close cooperation between product managers and data scientists can reveal user behavior patterns that inform resource distribution strategies. Take this example, if analytics indicate that peak usage times for an AI scheduling assistant occur during office hours, developers can prioritize enhancing server capabilities during those periods to ensure optimal performance when it matters most.

Automation tools are vital in streamlining processes that would otherwise require substantial manual effort. Platforms like Integromat or Tray.io can automate data flows between systems, reducing overhead and allowing teams to concentrate on higher-value tasks. Imagine an HR AI agent that automatically updates employee records upon completion of training sessions; this not only saves time but also minimizes errors associated with manual data entry.

Another key aspect of maintaining performance at scale is establishing robust monitoring systems that provide real-time insights into application behavior. By leveraging tools like Prometheus or New Relic, organizations can track usage metrics and identify anomalies before they impact user experience. For example, if monitoring reveals that an API call is consistently returning slower responses as traffic increases, engineers can be alerted to optimize that endpoint or adjust its caching strategies.

Incorporating modular design principles enhances flexibility within the AI architecture. This approach allows components to be developed, tested, and scaled independently. Take this example, in a customer engagement AI system where separate modules handle user interaction and data analysis, if one component requires enhancement due to increased complexity in interactions, it can be upgraded without necessitating a complete system overhaul—resulting in reduced downtime and improved adaptability.

Finally, proactive growth planning ensures that resource strategies align with anticipated market shifts. Regular engagement with cloud service providers helps businesses stay informed about innovative solutions that may offer enhanced efficiency or cost benefits as needs evolve. For example, transitioning to serverless architectures could present opportunities for significant savings while improving scalability for specific applications.

At its core, optimizing resource usage involves intertwining intelligent design choices with proactive management strategies. By leveraging cloud scalability, automating processes, fostering collaboration, and adopting modularity in development—all these elements come together to create a responsive environment capable of effectively meeting growing demands. Organizations that excel in these practices position themselves not only for immediate success but also build resilience against future challenges in an ever-changing digital landscape.

Multi-Agent Systems

Scaling your no-code AI solutions involves more than just managing resources; it requires the orchestration of multiple agents to work in harmony, forming a multi-agent system that amplifies your application's capabilities. Each agent operates as an autonomous unit, executing specific tasks while collaborating with others to achieve complex outcomes.

The advantages of multi-agent systems are particularly evident in applications that demand diverse skill sets and functionalities. Take this example, in an e-commerce platform, different AI agents can focus on various aspects of user interaction: one agent might handle product recommendations based on past purchases, another could optimize pricing strategies using real-time market analysis, and a third could respond to customer inquiries. This division of labor enhances agility and responsiveness to user needs, ultimately improving the overall shopping experience.

To effectively integrate multiple agents, it is essential to consider their interactions and communication protocols. Employing message-passing frameworks can streamline data exchange among agents. For example, an AI agent overseeing inventory management can alert a sales agent when stock levels drop below a certain threshold, ensuring that customers only see products that are available. This coordination not only boosts efficiency but also helps prevent customer dissatisfaction due to unavailable items.

When designing these systems, standardized APIs play a critical role in enabling interoperability between agents. This guarantees that each component can communicate seamlessly, regardless of the underlying technology. Imagine a travel booking assistant interacting with separate modules for flight searches, hotel bookings, and car rentals. By utilizing APIs to standardize data sharing among these modules, you create a cohesive user experience where information flows effortlessly from one agent to another without delays or errors.

Data management is also pivotal to the success of multi-agent systems. Each agent typically needs access to various datasets to function effectively. By implementing a centralized data repository, agents can quickly access relevant information without duplicating data storage. Take this example, an analytics agent could gather insights from user behavior logs, purchase history, and social media interactions to provide actionable intelligence across the system. This guarantees that all agents operate with the most current information available.

And, the adaptability of multi-agent systems shines through

their ability to scale dynamically in response to changing demands. During periods of heightened user engagement— such as promotional events or holidays—additional agents can be deployed on-demand to manage the increased interactions. For example, a holiday shopping bot could be temporarily added to assist existing customer service agents in handling queries more efficiently during peak times without requiring significant investment in permanent resources.

Successful implementation of multi-agent systems also necessitates establishing robust governance mechanisms. Clearly defined roles and responsibilities ensure that each agent understands its function within the broader system framework. In a healthcare application, for example, one agent might monitor patient vital signs while another manages appointment scheduling. Clear governance helps avoid overlaps and conflicts in responsibilities while maintaining an efficient workflow.

Continuous monitoring of agent interactions and effectiveness is crucial for maintaining performance across the system. Tools like Grafana can visualize performance metrics for different agents, enabling stakeholders to swiftly identify bottlenecks and adjust resource allocation as needed. If one agent becomes less responsive due to high query loads while others remain underutilized, timely adjustments can optimize overall system performance.

Additionally, fostering a culture of experimentation encourages innovation within multi-agent systems. Allowing developers to test new algorithms or modify existing behaviors without disrupting the entire system creates an environment conducive to continuous improvement. Take this example, a chatbot designed for customer service could experiment with different conversational strategies or personality traits based on user feedback—this iterative process not only enhances user satisfaction but also drives engagement.

As organizations look ahead in their no-code AI journey, embracing emerging technologies becomes essential for multi-agent systems. Concepts like federated learning enable decentralized model training across multiple agents while safeguarding sensitive data privacy—especially critical in industries such as finance and healthcare where data security is paramount.

multi-agent systems represent more than just a collection of independent entities; they embody a sophisticated approach to problem-solving that leverages specialized capabilities while promoting collaboration. By integrating effective communication strategies, robust data management practices, and continuous performance monitoring into your design principles, you position your organization for immediate operational efficiencies and sustained innovation in an increasingly complex digital landscape.

Cloud Platforms for Scalability

Cloud platforms are essential for scaling no-code AI solutions, serving as the backbone for the efficient deployment and management of multi-agent systems. These platforms offer the infrastructure needed not only for deploying AI agents but also for facilitating their interactions with each other and the broader ecosystem. For scalability, cloud services provide unmatched flexibility, allowing businesses to adjust resources in real-time based on demand.

A significant advantage of cloud platforms is their ability to allocate resources rapidly. Take this example, consider a marketing campaign that unexpectedly generates a surge in traffic. In traditional on-premises setups, scaling up would require considerable lead time and investment in hardware. In contrast, cloud environments enable businesses to quickly spin up additional virtual machines or containers within minutes. Platforms like AWS or Google Cloud facilitate this process through tools such as auto-scaling groups or

Kubernetes orchestration, ensuring that your AI agents can seamlessly manage increased workloads.

In addition to rapid resource allocation, cloud platforms offer robust services for data storage and processing—an essential component for no-code environments that rely on large datasets to train and operate AI models effectively. By utilizing cloud-based storage solutions like Amazon S3 or Google Cloud Storage, businesses can easily access and manage data across various agents. This guarantees that each agent operates on consistent and updated datasets without duplicating efforts, which is crucial for coordinating tasks among multiple AI agents.

And, cloud platforms often come equipped with advanced analytics capabilities that enhance decision-making within multi-agent systems. Tools such as AWS SageMaker or Azure Machine Learning allow users to train machine learning models without requiring deep technical expertise. These tools enable the development of predictive models based on user interactions or sales patterns, which in turn enhances the responsiveness of your agents to emerging trends.

Security is another critical consideration when deploying multi-agent systems on cloud infrastructures. Cloud service providers invest heavily in security measures—such as data encryption at rest and in transit, identity access management, and compliance with international regulations—to safeguard sensitive information. For organizations handling personal data or financial transactions, like healthcare apps or fintech solutions, secure cloud environments help mitigate risks while maintaining user trust.

Collaboration among teams also benefits from the use of cloud platforms. Integrated development environments (IDEs) available through these services enable multiple developers to work on different components simultaneously without conflicts. This capability is particularly advantageous when iterating on an AI agent's functionality, as team members can experiment with new features concurrently while ensuring core functionalities remain intact.

Additionally, deploying APIs through cloud services facilitates seamless integration between various agents and external applications. For example, an AI-driven customer support agent may need to retrieve information from a customer relationship management (CRM) system during a live chat session. By exposing APIs hosted in the cloud, this interaction can be streamlined effectively, allowing the customer support agent to access real-time data from the CRM without delays—thereby enhancing user experience during critical touchpoints.

Monitoring capabilities are also improved when utilizing cloud solutions for multi-agent systems. Platforms like Azure Monitor or AWS CloudWatch offer comprehensive dashboards displaying performance metrics across different agents in real time. With these insights readily available, stakeholders can quickly identify trends related to usage spikes or performance bottlenecks—enabling informed adjustments and proactive maintenance.

While the scalability offered by cloud platforms presents significant opportunities, organizations should remain cautious about potential challenges associated with dependency on external vendors. Issues such as vendor lock-in may arise if businesses become overly reliant on specific services or architectures from one provider; therefore, adopting a hybrid approach that combines both public and private clouds can help mitigate such risks.

Embracing emerging technologies provided by cloud providers further amplifies scalability prospects for multi-agent systems. Take this example, serverless computing allows functions to run without the need for direct server management—leading to cost savings by only charging for execution time rather than continuous resource allocation.

By strategically leveraging the benefits offered by cloud platforms—from resource elasticity and robust security measures to enhanced collaboration—you position your no-code AI solutions for scalable success while optimizing operational efficiencies across multiple agents working harmoniously in an increasingly digital landscape.

Budget and Cost Management

Scaling technology solutions, particularly no-code AI systems, requires diligent attention to budget and cost management. As organizations increasingly adopt no-code tools, it is crucial to harmonize the innovative capabilities of AI agents with the financial realities of their implementation. A clear understanding of the cost structures associated with these technologies can help prevent overspending and ensure that investments generate tangible returns.

To begin effective budget management, it's essential to define the project's scope clearly. What specific problems are you looking to address? By outlining your project goals and requirements, you can develop a more accurate estimate of the resources needed. For example, when building a customer service AI agent, consider factors like expected user volume, data storage requirements, and the complexity of user interactions. Each of these elements contributes to costs; grasping them early on will help you avoid unexpected expenses later.

Next, assess the pricing models offered by different no-code platforms. Many providers use tiered pricing based on usage —such as the number of active users or API calls—which can be beneficial for startups or projects in their initial stages. However, as your project gains traction, costs may escalate quickly. If your AI agent becomes popular and experiences a surge in usage, you might find yourself moving from a low-tier plan to a high-tier one with significant price increases. It's wise to analyze potential growth patterns and choose a platform that supports cost-effective scaling.

In addition to platform fees, it's important to factor in ancillary costs like data storage and processing fees. Cloud-based solutions often charge for data storage and egress (data leaving their servers), which can accumulate rapidly if your application generates substantial data traffic. Take this example, if an AI agent frequently processes user queries that require accessing large datasets, those egress costs might exceed your initial estimates. Employing strategies for efficient data management—such as batch processing or caching frequently accessed information—can significantly mitigate these expenses.

Monitoring tools are also vital for budget management as they provide insights into resource utilization. Services like AWS CloudWatch or Google Analytics can help you track spending patterns associated with your AI agents. These insights can reveal peak usage times or underutilized resources, allowing you to make adjustments that reduce unnecessary costs.

Additionally, it's crucial to anticipate hidden costs related to personnel training and maintenance. While no-code platforms aim to minimize technical barriers, some team members may still need training to use these tools effectively. Investing time and resources in comprehensive training ensures that employees maximize the potential of no-code solutions without incurring additional mistakes or inefficiencies down the line.

Establishing a contingency fund for unexpected expenses is also essential during development or deployment phases. This fund, often overlooked in initial budgeting discussions, acts as a financial buffer against unforeseen challenges such as technical setbacks or unanticipated integrations with existing systems that may require additional investments.

Finally, tracking return on investment (ROI) after deployment is critical for justifying ongoing expenditures related to your AI agents. For example, if an AI-driven chatbot reduces customer service workload by 30%, quantify the labor cost savings over time compared to its operational expenses. This approach will help you make informed decisions about whether to continue investing or pivot strategies if initial expectations aren't met.

Implementing these aspects necessitates careful planning and consideration; however, adopting best practices in budget management creates a solid foundation for sustainable scaling of your no-code AI solutions. Being proactive about both immediate costs and long-term implications allows organizations to embrace innovation while avoiding financial pitfalls.

To wrap things up, effective budget management is both an art and a science—a delicate balance between pursuing innovation through no-code AI agents and maintaining fiscal responsibility. This approach nurtures an environment where creativity thrives alongside financial prudence, ensuring that each advancement is both meaningful and economically viable for sustainable growth.

Strategic Planning for Growth

To successfully scale your AI solutions, strategic planning is essential. Growth goes beyond merely increasing capacity or output; it involves enhancing effectiveness and ensuring sustainability amidst rising demands. A key first step is to conduct a thorough analysis of your current capabilities. This entails a critical evaluation of what you have built so far— assessing the performance of your AI agents, understanding user feedback, and identifying any operational bottlenecks. By establishing clear metrics for success, you can pinpoint areas that are performing well and those that need improvement.

Once you have a grasp of your current state, the next step is to outline specific growth objectives. Whether your goals involve expanding your user base, enhancing functionality, or entering new markets, having measurable targets will help guide your efforts. For example, if you aim to increase user engagement by 30% over the next year, you can implement targeted marketing strategies alongside enhancements to your AI agents that cater specifically to user preferences. Leveraging analytics tools to gather insights on user behavior can be invaluable in tailoring features that resonate with your audience.

With objectives in place, it's important to address resource allocation. Growth often necessitates investment—be it in technology, personnel, or marketing. Evaluate whether your current resources can support these goals or if additional investment is required. Exploring partnerships can enhance your capabilities without overextending your budget; for instance, collaborating with a data analytics firm could deepen your understanding of user behavior without needing to develop those skills in-house.

As you develop plans for scaling, prioritize flexibility in your strategy. The landscape of technology and user needs can change rapidly, and strategies that are effective today may require adjustments tomorrow. This is particularly true in the field of AI, where algorithms and tools evolve quickly. Implementing agile methodologies can help you respond effectively to these changes. Regular check-ins with your team to assess progress against goals—along with a willingness to pivot when necessary—can keep your growth initiatives aligned with real-time developments.

Integrating feedback loops into your growth strategy is equally important. Establish systems for ongoing feedback from users about their experiences with your AI agents. This feedback should inform both incremental improvements and broader strategic pivots as needed. For example, if users express a desire for enhanced customization options within an AI tool, prioritizing this feature could lead to higher satisfaction and retention rates.

Additionally, consider scaling through education and community-building initiatives. Offering workshops or creating educational content on how to best utilize your AI agents can empower users while fostering loyalty. Building a community around your products not only enhances user engagement but also cultivates a network of advocates who can share their positive experiences and drive organic growth.

Finally, keep an eye on competitive positioning. Regularly evaluate what competitors are doing and how their offerings are evolving over time. Understanding industry trends will enable you to anticipate shifts in demand and adjust your strategies accordingly. By being proactive rather than reactive, you position yourself as a leader in the field.

To wrap things up, strategic planning for growth is not just about increasing size; it's about building a resilient framework that adapts to change while consistently delivering value to users. By focusing on a comprehensive approach that integrates performance analysis, clear objectives, flexible resource allocation, continuous feedback loops, educational initiatives, and competitive awareness, you'll establish a solid foundation for sustainable growth in the dynamic landscape of no-code AI solutions.

CHAPTER 14:
FUTURE OUTLOOK
OF NO-CODE AI

*Emerging Technologies
and Innovations*

E merging technologies are transforming the no-code AI landscape, offering innovative solutions that enhance functionality and broaden possibilities. A prime example is the integration of advanced machine learning models into no-code platforms. These models enable users to develop sophisticated AI agents capable of handling complex tasks, such as natural language processing and predictive analytics, all without requiring extensive technical expertise. Platforms like Bubble and Adalo have begun to incorporate machine learning capabilities, allowing users to seamlessly integrate features like chatbots and recommendation systems into their applications.

In addition to machine learning, advancements in blockchain technology are significantly influencing the evolution of no-code solutions. By integrating blockchain, these platforms enhance security and transparency in data management—

an essential feature for applications dealing with sensitive information, such as financial transactions or personal data. Take this example, the use of smart contracts within no-code environments automates processes while ensuring that all parties adhere to predetermined agreements without intermediaries.

Another promising area for innovation lies in the rise of augmented reality (AR) and virtual reality (VR) applications within no-code frameworks. These technologies create immersive experiences that greatly enhance user engagement. Platforms like ZapWorks allow creators to develop AR experiences using a visual interface, enabling marketers and educators to connect with audiences in new and engaging ways. Imagine designing an interactive training module where employees can practice skills in a simulated environment—all accomplished without writing a single line of code.

The Internet of Things (IoT) is also at the forefront of technological advancements shaping no-code AI. With IoT devices increasingly prevalent across various industries— from smart homes to industrial automation—no-code tools are emerging that enable users to automate interactions between these devices effortlessly. For example, platforms like Thunkable allow developers to create applications that communicate with diverse IoT devices, facilitating real-time monitoring and control through intuitive interfaces. This capability not only streamlines operations but also opens up vast potential for new applications in health monitoring, environmental tracking, and smart city development.

And, the integration of AI-driven analytics tools into no-code platforms is revolutionizing how users interact with their data. These tools empower individuals to derive insights without needing an extensive background in data science. By incorporating services like Google Analytics or Microsoft Power BI into no-code environments, users can visualize their data intuitively and make rapid, informed decisions. This democratization of analytics enables more organizations to leverage their data effectively, leading to improved processes and the identification of new business opportunities.

Lastly, advancements in cloud computing are facilitating the rise of serverless architectures within no-code platforms. This approach allows developers to deploy applications without the burden of server management or scaling infrastructure issues. So, users can concentrate on application logic rather than backend complexities, boosting productivity and reducing time-to-market for new solutions. A notable example is Amazon Web Services (AWS) Lambda, which supports on-demand execution of code snippets triggered by specific events —empowering users to create responsive applications with minimal overhead.

As these emerging technologies continue to evolve, they will further blur the lines between technical and non-technical roles in software development. The implications are profound: businesses will be able to harness powerful AI capabilities without being constrained by traditional barriers such as coding skills or extensive technical knowledge. This ongoing shift opens doors for a broader range of creators—from entrepreneurs launching startups to educators developing engaging learning tools—who can now utilize advanced technologies in ways previously thought impossible.

By embracing these innovations within a no-code framework, users not only gain access to powerful tools but also contribute to a rapidly changing tech landscape that prioritizes accessibility and ease of use. The future holds exciting possibilities where anyone can turn their ideas into reality through intuitive interfaces and robust integrations— regardless of their technical background.

AI Agents in the Next Decade

AI agents are on the verge of transformative changes over the next decade, poised to reshape not just industries but also the very nature of our interactions with technology. This evolution is propelled by advancements in machine learning algorithms, increased computational power, and greater data availability. As AI systems become more sophisticated, the agents we develop will improve their contextual understanding, exhibit more human-like interactions, and integrate seamlessly into our daily lives.

Take customer service as an example, where AI agents are already making significant strides. In the near future, these agents will evolve beyond merely responding to inquiries; they will predict customer needs by analyzing historical interactions and emotional cues. Imagine an AI agent that can detect a customer's tone during a conversation and adjust its responses to create a more empathetic experience. Companies like Zendesk are already exploring such capabilities through natural language processing (NLP), aiming to enhance customer satisfaction while simultaneously reducing operational costs.

The impact of AI agents extends well beyond customer service; healthcare is another sector ripe for transformation. With their ability to swiftly analyze vast amounts of patient data, AI agents can assist doctors in diagnosing conditions and recommending personalized treatments. Telehealth platforms like Teladoc are currently employing basic AI tools for preliminary assessments. However, looking ahead to a decade from now, we can anticipate fully integrated systems where AI continuously learns from new medical research and patient outcomes, providing real-time insights that significantly improve patient care.

In education, AI agents are set to become personalized learning companions for students. These virtual tutors will assess individual learning styles and adapt content delivery accordingly, ensuring each student receives support at their own pace. While platforms like Khan Academy are beginning to implement adaptive learning technologies, future iterations will delve deeper into student interactions to refine lesson plans continuously. This evolution could create a learning environment that is not only personalized but also anticipatory—able to recognize when a student is struggling before they even realize it.

The workplace will undergo a similar transformation, with AI agents emerging as collaborators rather than mere tools. These intelligent systems will streamline workflows by managing schedules, suggesting tasks based on workload analysis, and facilitating team discussions by summarizing meeting notes in real time. Tools like Microsoft Teams are already incorporating some AI features for productivity enhancement; in ten years' time, we may be working alongside fully autonomous assistants that intuitively grasp project contexts and team dynamics.

On a larger scale, smart cities will benefit from interconnected AI agents managing urban infrastructure more efficiently than ever before. Transportation systems powered by AI will optimize traffic flow in real time using live data from vehicles and sensors throughout the cityscape. Companies such as Sidewalk Labs are pioneering projects that integrate various urban systems through intelligent interfaces; soon city planners may rely heavily on these AI-driven solutions to enhance sustainability efforts and improve residents' quality of life.

Security represents another critical area where advancements in AI agent capabilities are expected to flourish. As cyber threats grow increasingly sophisticated, AI agents equipped with predictive analytics will monitor networks for unusual patterns and potential breaches before they happen. Current cybersecurity platforms like Darktrace utilize machine learning for anomaly detection; however, future developments may lead us towards fully autonomous security systems that adapt in real-time to evolving threats without human intervention.

While these advancements herald an exciting future filled with possibilities, they also prompt significant ethical considerations surrounding privacy and transparency. As AI agents become further embedded in our lives, it is crucial for developers and organizations to prioritize ethical standards in their design processes. Users must have confidence that their data is handled responsibly while benefiting from enhanced services.

Looking ahead, the next decade promises unprecedented growth in the capabilities of AI agents across various sectors. This evolution is not solely about improving efficiency or productivity; it's about redefining our relationships with technology itself. By fostering collaboration between humans and intelligent systems—whether through no-code frameworks or traditional coding methods—we stand at the threshold of a new era where innovation becomes accessible to everyone willing to embrace it.

As we envision a future where intelligent agents guide us through complex tasks while enhancing our everyday experiences, it's essential for creators to harness these innovations responsibly and inclusively—ensuring technology uplifts everyone rather than leaving anyone behind. The path forward invites all who dare to engage with this rapidly changing environment—and within it lies an expansive horizon filled with untapped potential waiting to be explored.

No-Code Impact on Workforce Dynamics

The rise of no-code platforms is fundamentally transforming workforce dynamics across various sectors. With the elimination of the need for specialized coding skills, individuals from diverse backgrounds are now empowered to contribute meaningfully to tech-driven projects. This shift democratizes access to technology and enhances collaboration among teams with varied expertise. In this evolving landscape, marketers, designers, and data analysts can unite their unique perspectives to develop sophisticated applications that tackle specific business challenges—without the bottleneck of traditional development processes.

Consider a marketing team aiming to enhance customer engagement through personalized campaigns. Armed with no-code tools, team members can create automated workflows that analyze customer behavior in real time, allowing them to tailor messaging dynamically. Take this example, platforms like Zapier or Airtable enable them to establish triggers based on user actions—such as visiting a website or clicking an email link—prompting personalized follow-ups that improve customer experience and boost conversions. This accessibility fosters an environment where creativity flourishes; team members can experiment with ideas and iterate rapidly, all without waiting for IT support.

And, this empowerment extends beyond mere productivity gains; it significantly alters job roles and expectations within organizations. As no-code solutions proliferate, employees are encouraged to take ownership of their projects, transitioning from passive consumers of technology to active creators. A project manager, for example, might start building dashboards to track project metrics or designing simple applications to streamline daily tasks. This shift cultivates a culture of innovation, where team members feel invested in their work's outcomes, leading to higher job satisfaction and retention rates.

No-code platforms also bridge the gap between technical and non-technical staff. In traditional environments, developers often worked in isolation, delivering finished products with minimal input from end-users. No-code tools dismantle these barriers by facilitating collaboration throughout the development process. Teams can engage directly in the creation and iteration phases, ensuring that solutions align closely with user needs and organizational goals. Take this example, a human resources department might use no-code solutions to design a custom onboarding portal tailored specifically to the feedback and requirements of new hires, enhancing their integration into the company culture.

However, these changes also raise important questions about job displacement and the future of technical roles. While there are concerns that automation could replace developers or technical experts, the reality is more nuanced. Rather than rendering these positions obsolete, no-code tools are likely to shift their focus toward more complex tasks requiring critical thinking and advanced problem-solving skills. Developers may find themselves overseeing no-code implementations— integrating complex systems and ensuring data security while empowering non-technical users to manage simpler tasks.

Training becomes essential in this evolving landscape. Organizations must invest in upskilling their workforce to leverage no-code tools effectively while preparing them for the future complexities of technology integration. Workshops centered on design thinking and user experience can help employees learn how to create effective solutions that address real-world needs. Equally important is fostering an environment where experimentation is encouraged; allowing employees to explore no-code platforms promotes learning through trial and error.

As companies adapt to these new dynamics, those who embrace no-code technologies will gain a competitive edge. The agility afforded by decentralized development processes enables faster responses to market changes and customer needs—traits increasingly vital in today's fast-paced business environment. Organizations leveraging these tools can pivot quickly when new opportunities arise or when unforeseen challenges emerge.

Also, this transformation enhances diversity within tech teams as individuals from non-traditional backgrounds enter the field with fresh perspectives historically overlooked in tech discussions often dominated by those with programming expertise. This diversification fosters innovation by challenging conventional ways of thinking and problem-solving—a necessary evolution for industries facing disruption.

At its core, the impact of no-code on workforce dynamics reflects a broader trend toward inclusivity and democratization in technology use. It empowers individuals not only to participate but also to lead initiatives that drive change within their organizations. As we navigate this transformative journey, embracing new roles created by these technologies will be crucial for maximizing potential across all sectors—from startups innovating rapidly in uncertain markets to established enterprises streamlining operations amid increasing competition.

The journey into a no-code future invites exploration filled with opportunities for growth—not just for businesses but for every individual willing to harness technology's power creatively and collaboratively. It's about reshaping our interactions through technology while cultivating an ecosystem where everyone has a voice in building our shared digital future.

Cross-Industry Applications Expansion

The rise of no-code AI applications across various industries marks a significant transformation in how technology addresses real-world challenges. Sectors that once adhered to traditional practices are now embracing the adaptability and potential of no-code solutions to boost efficiency, creativity, and customer engagement. From retail to healthcare, finance to education, each industry is finding innovative ways to implement no-code AI agents tailored to their specific needs.

Consider the retail sector as a prime example. No-code platforms empower businesses to craft personalized shopping experiences without the need for extensive coding expertise. A clothing retailer, for instance, might utilize a no-code AI solution to analyze customer purchase histories and online behaviors. This analysis enables the retailer to recommend products that align with individual preferences, significantly enhancing sales conversion rates by presenting customers with items they are more likely to enjoy. And, the ability to quickly update these recommendations based on real-time data further enriches the shopping experience, making it more engaging and personal.

Similarly, healthcare is poised for transformation through no-code applications. Hospitals and clinics are increasingly adopting these tools to streamline patient intake processes and enhance operational efficiencies. For example, medical practices can create custom applications that automate appointment scheduling or manage patient follow-ups without encountering IT bottlenecks. Platforms like Bubble or AppGyver enable non-technical staff to develop solutions specifically tailored to their workflows—such as automated reminders for upcoming tests or consultations. This not only allows healthcare professionals to concentrate more on patient care but also boosts overall patient satisfaction.

In the finance sector, companies are leveraging no-code AI agents for risk assessment and customer service automation. Financial analysts can use tools like Airtable or Glide to construct dashboards that monitor key performance indicators (KPIs) in real time, all without requiring deep technical knowledge. These dashboards offer a quick snapshot of market trends or internal metrics, empowering analysts to make informed decisions swiftly. Additionally, chatbots created via no-code platforms can manage routine customer inquiries, freeing human agents to tackle more complex issues.

Education is undergoing its own transformation through the adoption of no-code technologies. Institutions can design personalized learning experiences by developing applications that adapt course content based on student performance and engagement levels. Take this example, a university might create a custom app where instructors enter assignments while students receive tailored feedback based on their progress—all facilitated by intuitive interfaces offered by no-code tools. This approach not only boosts student engagement but also gives educators more time to focus on delivering impactful learning experiences rather than managing administrative tasks.

These examples illustrate a crucial point: the versatility of no-code solutions extends beyond mere efficiency improvements; it fundamentally redefines how organizations interact with their customers and operate internally. The collaborative nature of these tools encourages teams across various disciplines—such as marketing, operations, and IT—to work towards shared objectives while retaining autonomy in executing their tasks.

However, the widespread adoption of these technologies also brings forth challenges that organizations must proactively address. As reliance on no-code solutions increases, companies need to establish governance frameworks surrounding data usage and application development processes. Without proper oversight, there is a risk of fragmentation where different teams create isolated solutions that fail to integrate effectively with existing systems—potentially undermining the efficiency gains achieved through these tools.

Training initiatives will be essential for navigating this evolving landscape successfully. Organizations must equip employees not only with the technical skills needed to use these platforms but also with an understanding of best practices in application design and user experience considerations. Workshops focused on agile methodologies can facilitate effective collaboration while maximizing the benefits of no-code tools.

The expansion of no-code applications across industries reflects a broader movement toward democratizing access to technology—and this shift is just beginning. As businesses recognize the innovative potential unlocked by these platforms, we can expect an emergence of diverse applications in sectors yet untouched by this revolution.

This evolution calls for adaptability from leaders and teams alike as they rethink workflows and processes within their organizations. Embracing this change means cultivating an environment where creativity meets functionality—a space where everyone can contribute ideas that leverage technology's power regardless of their technical background.

As opportunities continue to unfold across sectors daily, one thing remains clear: the rise of no-code AI agents is not merely about enhancing operational efficiencies; it's about fundamentally reshaping industries while paving the way for future innovations yet to be imagined.

Collaboration with Other Technologies

The integration of no-code AI agents with emerging technologies marks a significant convergence that enhances their impact and broadens their utility. This collaboration not only improves the functionality of no-code solutions but also empowers organizations to leverage various technological innovations, fostering a more comprehensive approach to problem-solving.

Consider the synergy between no-code AI and the Internet of Things (IoT). Smart devices generate vast amounts of data, and when combined with no-code platforms, businesses can swiftly develop applications that transform this data into actionable insights. For example, a smart thermostat company could use a no-code solution to analyze user preferences alongside environmental data, optimizing energy consumption without requiring complex programming skills. Users would be able to create workflows that automate adjustments based on real-time feedback from IoT devices, ultimately enhancing energy efficiency and user satisfaction.

In the realm of augmented reality (AR), no-code AI agents can significantly enhance customer experiences by enabling businesses to craft interactive and immersive environments. A furniture retailer, for instance, could utilize AR technology in conjunction with no-code platforms to allow customers to visualize how a piece of furniture would fit into their homes before making a purchase. By integrating AI-powered visual recognition capabilities, customers can simply point their smartphone cameras at their living rooms to see the selected furniture overlaid in real-time. This seamless interaction not only boosts customer engagement but also reduces return rates, demonstrating how collaboration between these technologies leads to practical applications.

Blockchain also presents a promising arena for no-code solutions. By empowering users to build decentralized applications without extensive coding knowledge, organizations can effectively harness blockchain's transparency and security features. A supply chain management company might develop a no-code application that tracks product provenance through blockchain technology, allowing all stakeholders to verify product authenticity without needing deep technical expertise. This approach fosters increased trust among consumers and enhances accountability across supply chains.

The synergy between no-code AI agents and machine learning (ML) further illustrates this collaborative potential. Traditional ML applications often require data scientists to write complex algorithms; however, no-code platforms simplify this process through user-friendly interfaces for training models. A marketing team, for instance, could leverage these tools to predict customer behavior based on historical purchase data without waiting for IT support or external consultants. They can easily drag and drop components to create models that analyze trends and generate insights tailored to their campaigns, empowering teams to respond swiftly based on real-time data.

Collaboration also extends into social media analytics. Businesses can utilize no-code tools alongside sentiment analysis algorithms to effortlessly monitor brand perception across various platforms. For example, a small business owner might construct an application that gathers social media feedback in real-time, processing it through an AI agent designed to evaluate sentiment. This setup provides immediate insights into how marketing strategies resonate with customers, allowing for prompt adjustments as needed.

However, as organizations embrace these collaborations, they must navigate potential challenges. Integrating multiple technologies requires careful attention to interoperability; systems must communicate seamlessly for optimal performance. It is critical that data flows smoothly between platforms without compromising security or user experience.

Training plays a vital role in fostering effective collaborations among technologies. Employees should be equipped not only with technical skills but also with an understanding of how different tools complement each other. Workshops focused on integration strategies or cross-training among departments can be beneficial in building cohesive teams adept at leveraging these collaborations.

As businesses continue to explore partnerships between no-code AI agents and other technologies, the possibilities seem limitless. This ongoing evolution signifies a shift toward creating environments where innovation flourishes through collaboration—enabling organizations not only to adapt but also to excel in an increasingly complex landscape.

By embracing this mindset of integration and cooperation, organizations position themselves at the forefront of technological advancement, ready to seize every opportunity arising from this rich tapestry of capabilities brought together through collaborative effort. The future lies not just in deploying technology; it's about synergizing its diverse elements for unprecedented innovation and growth.

Predicting Technological Advancements

Predicting technological advancements requires a deep understanding of current trends, emerging capabilities, and societal needs. As no-code AI platforms continue to evolve, they not only mirror existing innovations but also pave the way for new developments. One promising area of exploration is the impact of machine learning on predictive analytics within these no-code environments. Given that data is the lifeblood of any AI initiative, the ability to forecast trends based on historical patterns will become increasingly sophisticated through no-code tools.

Consider a small retail business using a no-code AI platform to analyze customer purchasing behaviors. By tapping into historical sales data, the platform can uncover seasonal trends and predict demand for specific products. Take this example, if the data reveals a consistent rise in outdoor furniture purchases each spring, the system can automatically notify the retailer to adjust inventory levels accordingly. This predictive capability, accessible without any coding knowledge, empowers business owners to make informed decisions quickly, aligning their operations with market demands.

Looking forward, integrating real-time data sources will further enhance these predictive abilities. Imagine combining weather data with retail analytics; a no-code AI agent could synthesize this information with historical sales trends to predict spikes in demand for air conditioners during particularly hot months. Such applications extend beyond retail; industries like agriculture can also benefit by analyzing environmental factors against crop yields, optimizing resource allocation and increasing efficiency.

The rise of edge computing significantly influences future advancements as well. With devices becoming smarter and more interconnected through IoT technology, they generate vast amounts of real-time data that can be processed closer to its source. This development enables no-code AI agents to analyze incoming information instantaneously, delivering contextually relevant and timely predictions. For example, smart sensors in manufacturing can detect machinery performance anomalies in real-time, allowing operators to foresee failures before they occur—an invaluable advantage for minimizing downtime and reducing maintenance costs.

However, alongside these technological advancements come ethical considerations regarding data usage. As organizations strive to balance innovation with responsibility, the ability of no-code platforms to utilize sensitive personal data for predictive modeling raises important questions about privacy and consent. Companies will need to adopt transparent practices that foster user trust while maximizing the benefits of predictive analytics.

And, user-generated content is anticipated to play a significant role in future technological growth. As consumers increasingly share their experiences and preferences online, businesses can harness this wealth of information through no-code solutions designed for sentiment analysis. Take this example, social media platforms may offer APIs that enable users to create applications capable of tracking customer feedback trends over time. This allows businesses to anticipate shifts in consumer sentiment toward their products or services and proactively adapt their strategies.

This integration of user engagement with advanced analytical tools signifies a shift toward more participatory models of innovation. As end-users gain access to no-code platforms that empower them to leverage their data creatively and effectively, we may witness a new wave of grassroots technological advancements driven by those closest to market realities rather than solely by technical specialists.

At its core, predicting technological advancements involves navigating an intricate landscape where human creativity meets cutting-edge technology. By fostering collaborative environments among diverse stakeholders—businesses, developers, and consumers—we unlock possibilities that drive not just incremental improvements but transformative change across industries.

The horizon for no-code AI agents appears bright as we envision future applications intertwined with societal needs while addressing ethical implications head-on. The next phase isn't just about making predictions; it's about harnessing collective intelligence and enabling innovation in ways we have yet to fully imagine.

Potential Challenges and Solutions

Navigating the landscape of no-code AI agents presents a range of challenges, much like any transformative technology. While these hurdles can slow progress if not effectively managed, they also pave the way for innovation and growth. By understanding these potential challenges, users and organizations can better prepare themselves to mitigate risks while fully leveraging the advantages of no-code platforms.

One of the most significant challenges is ensuring data quality and accessibility. For an AI agent to function optimally, it relies on accurate and relevant data. However, many businesses face issues with data silos, where information is trapped in disparate systems or remains unstructured, making it difficult to access and analyze. Take this example, a retail company may have customer information scattered across various platforms —sales transactions stored in one system and customer feedback in another. Although a no-code tool can help facilitate integration to some degree, without a clear strategy for data management, these platforms may not deliver their full potential.

To address this issue, organizations should implement robust data governance practices. By establishing clear protocols for data collection, storage, and sharing, companies can ensure that relevant information is readily available for AI agents to process. Creating a centralized database that aggregates all necessary data will enhance the efficiency of no-code tools. Additionally, investing in staff training on best practices for data entry and maintenance can significantly improve overall data quality.

Another challenge is user resistance or a lack of understanding surrounding no-code technologies. Many employees may feel intimidated by new tools that appear complex, especially if they are accustomed to traditional methods. Education is crucial for bridging this gap. Organizations should develop training programs that demystify no-code platforms and encourage hands-on experimentation. Workshops that demonstrate how easily employees can build solutions without coding expertise will cultivate a culture of innovation and adaptability.

Case studies can also alleviate concerns about user resistance. For example, a marketing team hesitant to adopt a new no-code tool for campaign automation may find reassurance in success stories from similar companies that achieved significant efficiency gains through automated solutions built on no-code platforms. Testimonials from peers validate the technology's effectiveness and inspire confidence in its application.

Security concerns represent another substantial challenge when implementing no-code AI agents, particularly as these platforms often handle sensitive information. Organizations must navigate complex compliance requirements while ensuring robust security measures protect user data from breaches or unauthorized access. It's essential to thoroughly evaluate the security features offered by chosen no-code platforms; prioritizing features like encryption protocols and user authentication mechanisms is crucial.

To effectively address security challenges, companies can adopt a layered approach by integrating additional tools alongside their primary no-code platform. This might include deploying firewall protections or utilizing advanced threat detection systems to monitor unusual activities within applications built on these platforms. Regular audits and assessments can further strengthen security infrastructures by identifying vulnerabilities before they can be exploited.

Scalability also remains a concern as businesses grow and their needs evolve over time. Early adopters of no-code technologies may find their chosen platform limiting as operations expand or diversify into new areas. Therefore, organizations should select scalable solutions capable of accommodating increased demands without sacrificing performance.

Identifying potential future growth opportunities during the initial selection process can help mitigate scalability issues later on. Take this example, choosing a no-code platform with strong API capabilities allows for integration with other services as needs arise—ensuring flexibility in design choices and functional expansion without having to start from scratch.

Finally, ethical considerations must be prioritized amid these challenges. As organizations harness AI technologies, they must remain vigilant about inherent biases in algorithms or datasets used within their applications. Missteps in this area not only jeopardize user trust but can also lead to significant reputational damage.

To promote ethical AI usage, organizations should establish guidelines around fairness and accountability early in the development process. Including diverse perspectives throughout design stages helps minimize the risk of bias in automated solutions created via no-code tools. Continuous monitoring mechanisms should also be implemented to regularly assess AI behavior for adherence to ethical standards.

By confronting these challenges directly, organizations can transform obstacles into stepping stones toward creating more effective and responsible AI systems using no-code frameworks. Through thoughtful approaches rooted in education, tailored security measures for evolving landscapes, and ethical guidelines guiding decision-making processes along the way—businesses unlock new pathways for success while shaping a future where technology empowers rather than restricts creativity across various fields.

CHAPTER 15:
REAL-WORLD
CASE STUDIES

*Successful Implementation
across Industries*

Across a variety of industries, the successful implementation of no-code AI agents is transforming operational frameworks, enhancing efficiency, and improving user engagement. As businesses increasingly embrace the democratization of technology, the tangible benefits of these tools are becoming more apparent. Real-world examples from sectors such as healthcare, finance, retail, and education illustrate how organizations leverage no-code solutions to tackle specific challenges and forge innovative pathways.

In healthcare, for example, a hospital system integrated a no-code AI agent to streamline patient scheduling and triage processes. By deploying an intelligent chatbot within their existing systems, the hospital reduced appointment wait times by over 30%. Patients could engage with the chatbot through their preferred messaging platforms, enabling them to schedule appointments or receive medical advice without enduring long phone hold times. The bot learned from each interaction, continuously refining its responses based on user feedback. This integration not only boosted patient satisfaction but also allowed staff to focus on more complex care tasks.

Similarly, in the finance sector, a fintech startup utilized a no-code platform to create an automated customer service agent capable of addressing inquiries about account balances, transactions, and loan applications. Initially concerned that automation might weaken customer relationships, the startup's leadership closely monitored trial implementations. They discovered that clients valued quick access to information without waiting for human intervention. Within six months of deployment, customer satisfaction scores surged by 20%, enabling the company to scale operations without significantly increasing staffing costs.

Retailers are also harnessing no-code AI agents to enhance their e-commerce experiences. An online retailer implemented an AI-driven recommendation engine powered by a no-code solution that analyzed customer purchasing behavior in real-time. By providing personalized product suggestions during checkout based on past purchases and browsing history, they experienced a 15% increase in conversion rates. This success was rooted not only in technological advancement but also in a keen understanding of consumer behavior—an aspect often overlooked in traditional code-based solutions.

Educational institutions are witnessing similar advancements with no-code platforms. A university adopted an AI agent built through a no-code framework to manage student inquiries related to course registration and campus resources. Students interacted with this virtual assistant via the institution's website and mobile app. Within weeks of launch, over 60% of student questions were answered autonomously, freeing academic advisors to focus on more strategic initiatives rather than routine inquiries.

Even non-profits have recognized the value of these tools by automating donor engagement processes. A charity organization deployed a no-code AI agent to track donations and engage supporters through tailored email campaigns based on previous interactions. This personalized outreach strategy led to a significant increase in donor retention —surpassing past records—and a remarkable 25% rise in contributions.

These examples highlight not only the versatility of no-code AI agents but also their potential to drive innovation while alleviating common operational bottlenecks. What you should know is that while users may possess minimal technical know-how when adopting these tools, it is their creativity in identifying use cases that fuels effective implementations.

In each scenario discussed, organizations did more than just adopt new technology; they thoughtfully integrated it into their existing workflows. By understanding their unique pain points, they leveraged no-code solutions as enablers rather than replacements for human effort. As businesses continue to embrace this paradigm shift toward accessible technology frameworks like no-code AI agents, they are likely to uncover new dimensions of efficiency previously constrained by traditional coding practices.

Every successful implementation offers valuable insights— lessons that inform best practices across various fields and beyond. These stories illustrate how curiosity can lead organizations down previously unimagined paths after adopting such tools—a testament to the notion that innovation knows no boundaries when empowered by accessible technology.

Lessons from Failures

In the world of no-code AI agents, not every story is one of triumph; many highlight valuable lessons learned from setbacks. These experiences emphasize the critical need for strategic planning, user engagement, and adaptability. By analyzing failures in various implementations, organizations can steer clear of common pitfalls and refine their methods for effectively leveraging no-code technology.

One telling example comes from a retail company that hastily launched an AI chatbot without fully understanding its customer base. Designed to address inquiries about returns and product availability, the bot struggled to interpret colloquial language and slang used by many customers. So, frustrated users quickly abandoned their interactions, leading to a significant drop in customer satisfaction scores. This case underscores the importance of conducting thorough user research and customizing AI behavior to align with the specific needs of the audience. Recognizing customer language and preferences is crucial when developing conversational interfaces; neglecting this aspect can alienate rather than engage users.

A similar narrative unfolded at a financial services firm that sought to automate complex processes through a no-code platform but failed to provide adequate training for its staff. Management assumed that simply deploying an AI agent would lighten workloads without considering that employees required guidance on how to interact with and oversee the system. That's why, many staff members felt overwhelmed by the technology, resulting in increased frustration and declining morale. This example highlights that successful adoption relies not only on the technology itself but also on equipping personnel for effective collaboration with AI systems.

The healthcare sector has encountered its own set of challenges as well. A hospital implemented an AI-driven triage system intended to enhance patient flow during peak hours but overlooked the necessity of integrating it with existing electronic health records (EHRs). So, the AI agent provided generic responses without access to critical patient data, ultimately causing delays instead of improving efficiency. This situation illustrates that seamless integration across platforms is vital for maximizing an AI agent's effectiveness; failing to achieve this can create bottlenecks rather than resolve them.

Additionally, some organizations have faced backlash from users who felt that automation replaced essential human interaction. A non-profit organization introduced an AI chatbot for donor relations but neglected to maintain personal connections with their supporters. Many donors expressed disappointment at receiving automated messages instead of heartfelt communication from staff members they had come to trust over years of engagement. This scenario demonstrates that while automation can enhance efficiency, it should not come at the cost of meaningful relationships—especially in sectors where trust and connection are paramount.

These lessons from failure guide organizations toward successful implementations by highlighting the importance of proactive engagement with both users and employees throughout the development process. Prioritizing feedback loops allows insights from early adopters to inform ongoing improvements. Regular evaluations of performance metrics help identify weaknesses before they escalate into larger issues.

Equally vital is cultivating a culture of experimentation and adaptability within organizations adopting no-code solutions. Embracing failure as a stepping stone toward growth encourages teams to take calculated risks rather than shy away from innovation out of fear.

failures serve as valuable guideposts on the journey

toward effective no-code AI integration. Each setback offers critical insights that can lead organizations toward more thoughtful, user-centered implementations in future projects. By recognizing the significance of strategic planning, employee training, integration compatibility, and maintaining human connections, companies can confidently navigate this new technological frontier—transforming initial failures into learning experiences that drive ongoing success.

The narratives behind these failures are rich with wisdom; they remind us that technology is most impactful when designed around human experiences and needs rather than merely as a tool for automating tasks. By harnessing these lessons, organizations not only become adept at deploying no-code AI agents but also enhance their overall agility in addressing the complex challenges of modern business.

Innovative Use Cases

Innovative use cases for no-code AI agents are emerging across various sectors, showcasing their transformative potential in real-world applications. Organizations are creatively leveraging no-code platforms to address unique challenges, streamline operations, and enhance user experiences. These pioneering examples not only demonstrate the versatility of no-code AI but also highlight its ability to deliver significant value.

Consider a small e-commerce startup that integrated a no-code AI agent into its website to assist with customer inquiries. Instead of relying solely on traditional customer service methods, the company deployed an AI chatbot capable of handling common questions about order status and product information. By analyzing user interactions and feedback, the chatbot was refined over time, ultimately reducing response times by more than 50%. This improvement not only elevated customer satisfaction but also allowed human agents to focus on more complex issues, thereby enhancing overall operational efficiency.

In the healthcare sector, an innovative example arose when a local clinic developed an appointment scheduling system using a no-code platform. Traditional methods often led to long wait times and scheduling conflicts, frustrating both staff and patients. The clinic's no-code AI agent was designed to interact with patients via text or voice, enabling them to book, reschedule, or cancel appointments seamlessly. By integrating with existing patient management systems, all data was synchronized in real-time, significantly improving patient flow and satisfaction levels.

Education is another area where no-code solutions have made a notable impact. A school district employed a no-code AI tool to create personalized learning experiences for students. Leveraging data from assessments and classroom interactions, the AI agent developed tailored educational pathways for each student, adapting content based on individual progress. Teachers could monitor these pathways through a user-friendly dashboard that presented insights into student performance without requiring extensive technical knowledge. This innovative approach not only increased student engagement but also empowered educators with actionable data to enhance their teaching strategies.

Non-profit organizations have also harnessed no-code technology to enhance donor engagement through personalized outreach campaigns. One group developed an AI-driven platform that analyzed donor behavior and preferences, allowing them to create targeted communications that resonated deeply with supporters. So, donation rates surged by 30% within six months of implementation. This example underscores how even organizations with limited resources can leverage no-code solutions to foster meaningful connections and drive impact.

The logistics industry has embraced no-code AI agents for

optimizing supply chain management as well. A medium-sized logistics firm utilized an AI-driven tool to track shipments and predict delays based on historical data patterns and real-time traffic updates. The ease of setting up this system without coding expertise enabled the company to adapt quickly to changes in demand while maintaining high levels of customer service.

Real estate is yet another field where innovative use cases have flourished. A real estate agency adopted a no-code AI solution for property management tasks such as handling tenant inquiries and maintenance requests. By automating these processes through an intelligent agent capable of understanding natural language queries, the agency significantly reduced operational overhead while improving tenant satisfaction scores.

These examples illustrate how organizations are tapping into the power of no-code AI agents across diverse industries—each harnessing technology to solve specific challenges while streamlining operations and enhancing user experiences. The innovation lies not just in adopting new technology but in strategically integrating these tools into existing workflows.

By emphasizing creativity and user-centric design principles in their implementations, organizations unlock new levels of efficiency and effectiveness that traditional methods often struggle to achieve. As more businesses recognize the potential of no-code solutions in addressing unique challenges, we can expect a surge in inventive applications that redefine possibilities within their respective fields.

The ongoing emergence of innovative use cases continues to shape the landscape for no-code AI agents, paving the way for broader adoption as organizations increasingly appreciate their capabilities in driving change and delivering results. Each success story not only inspires others but reinforces a collective understanding: technology can—and should—

be leveraged in ways that prioritize human experience and operational excellence above all else.

Community Driven Projects

Community-driven projects are transforming the landscape of no-code AI agents by promoting collaboration and inclusivity. These initiatives empower individuals to share knowledge, tools, and resources, paving the way for innovative applications that might not have emerged in isolation. The spirit of community reshapes our approach to problem-solving, harnessing collective expertise to tackle challenges that span various sectors.

A prime example of this shift is the emergence of open-source platforms focused on no-code development. These projects create a communal space where users can contribute insights, enabling newcomers to learn from seasoned developers. Take this example, an online community dedicated to building chatbots without coding has established a repository of templates that anyone can utilize or adapt. This collaborative environment significantly reduces the learning curve for those who might otherwise feel daunted by technology. As members share their experiences and solutions, the diversity and quality of available tools grow rapidly.

Beyond open-source initiatives, numerous hackathons and community workshops emphasize no-code AI applications. These events bring together participants from varied backgrounds to collaborate on projects addressing real-world problems—often yielding remarkable outcomes. For example, a recent hackathon focused on healthcare innovation united data scientists, healthcare professionals, and tech enthusiasts. Their teams developed an AI-driven platform for managing patient follow-ups and reminders, enhancing communication between providers and patients. Such collaborative efforts not only produce functional prototypes but also foster lasting connections among participants who may continue their collaboration long after the event ends.

The influence of community-driven projects goes beyond technological advancements; they also nurture a culture of support and mentorship. Experienced practitioners often volunteer their time to guide newcomers through the complexities of no-code tools. This mentorship not only strengthens participants' skill sets but also boosts their confidence, particularly for those who may have previously felt excluded from tech spaces. The empowerment derived from mentorship fosters a sense of belonging that encourages further exploration into AI applications.

And, case studies highlight how community initiatives can yield scalable solutions. One such project involved a group of educators collaborating to create an AI agent for personalized student feedback in remote learning environments. By combining their insights on student engagement challenges during the pandemic, they developed an interactive tool that provided tailored resources based on individual learning styles. This project gained traction across multiple school districts, illustrating how community collaboration can extend its impact far beyond its initial intent.

Social media platforms play a crucial role in nurturing these communities by providing forums for discussion and idea exchange. Groups dedicated to no-code solutions facilitate dialogue around best practices while encouraging experimentation with new technologies. Users can post questions or share both successes and setbacks—creating a rich tapestry of shared knowledge that enhances everyone's experience with no-code AI agents.

As organizations increasingly recognize the value of collaborative efforts in developing innovative solutions, we can anticipate even more opportunities for community engagement in this realm. Each project becomes a thread woven into the broader narrative of no-code empowerment, demonstrating how inclusive practices lead not only to technological advancement but also to meaningful social change.

By prioritizing collective intelligence over individual achievement, community-driven initiatives challenge traditional ideas about ownership in innovation. This shift opens doors for diverse voices and ideas that deepen our understanding of what is possible with no-code technology —a testament to the power inherent in collaboration as we venture into uncharted territories where creativity knows no limits.

Role of Leadership in Adoption

In the fast-paced world of no-code AI, effective leadership is essential for guiding organizations through the complexities of adoption. Strong leadership goes beyond making top-down decisions; it involves creating a culture that embraces innovation, agility, and openness to new technologies. Leaders must inspire their teams to envision the possibilities of no-code solutions and actively engage them in the transformational journey ahead.

When an organization chooses to integrate no-code AI, leaders should start by fostering a shared understanding of what these tools can accomplish. Take this example, imagine a mid-sized company looking to improve its customer service through automation. A knowledgeable leader might organize workshops where team members can explore no-code platforms like Bubble or Airtable. This hands-on experience not only demystifies technology but also transforms apprehension into excitement as employees visualize potential automation opportunities.

Communication plays a vital role in this process. Leaders need to convey not only the "what" and "how" of no-code AI but also the "why." By sharing success stories from other companies—like a retail giant that optimized inventory management—leaders can illustrate tangible benefits such as increased efficiency and cost savings. This storytelling approach resonates with team members who may otherwise feel disconnected from abstract technological concepts.

Promoting cross-functional collaboration is equally important for successful adoption. Leaders should encourage diverse teams—including marketing, IT, operations, and customer service—to work together on projects utilizing no-code tools. For example, a marketing manager could collaborate with data analysts to create a dashboard that visualizes real-time customer engagement metrics using platforms like Google Data Studio or Tableau. Such collaboration maximizes input from various departments and enhances buy-in from stakeholders who see their contributions reflected in the final product.

To build confidence among team members, tailored training programs are crucial. Leaders can initiate training sessions designed for both tech-savvy employees and those less familiar with digital tools. Utilizing platforms like Udemy or Coursera allows individuals to learn at their own pace while acquiring essential skills to effectively use no-code AI. Take this example, a small bank could host regular lunch-and-learn events where employees share their experiences with no-code platforms, fostering knowledge sharing and community building.

Measuring progress through pilot projects led by enthusiastic early adopters is an effective strategy as well. These initiatives allow leaders to showcase quick wins that demonstrate the capabilities of no-code AI while generating excitement throughout the organization. When a product manager automates customer feedback collection using Typeform integrated with Zapier, it can significantly streamline operations and boost customer satisfaction scores. Sharing these successes widely reinforces the value of these initiatives and encourages broader participation.

Change often brings resistance, especially with something as transformative as no-code AI. Here, empathetic leadership is key. Leaders must actively listen to concerns from employees who may fear obsolescence or feel uncomfortable with new technologies. Creating forums for open dialogue alleviates fears and fosters trust between leadership and team members. It's important for leaders to emphasize how no-code solutions enhance roles rather than replace them; automation can relieve mundane tasks, allowing staff to focus on more strategic initiatives.

As organizations embark on the journey of no-code AI adoption, the role of leadership becomes increasingly crucial—not just in implementing technology but also in cultivating a culture that values innovation and continuous improvement. By nurturing curiosity, encouraging collaboration across departments, providing adequate training opportunities, and addressing concerns empathetically, leaders lay a strong foundation for successful integration.

At its core, leaders are not merely drivers of technology; they are visionaries who create environments where creativity flourishes and boundaries blur. This way, they empower their teams to leverage no-code solutions effectively while ensuring sustainable growth in an increasingly complex technological landscape.

Case Study Analysis Methodology

A robust case study analysis methodology is crucial for understanding the practical applications and impacts of no-code AI solutions. Instead of relying solely on theoretical concepts, examining real-world scenarios enables organizations to extract valuable insights, identify patterns, and refine their strategies based on empirical evidence. By exploring how various companies have implemented no-code AI, we can gain insights into what worked, the challenges they faced, and how these obstacles were overcome.

To begin with, it is essential to define clear objectives for each case study. Each analysis should focus on specific questions that aim to reveal insights about the use of no-code tools. Take this example, consider a company that integrated a chatbot using a no-code platform like Chatfuel. The primary objective might be to assess how the chatbot improved customer engagement and reduced response times. By centering on this particular outcome, analysts can gather relevant data that directly aligns with the project's goals.

Enhancing the depth of the analysis involves collecting data from multiple sources. This includes quantitative metrics —such as improvements in response times and user satisfaction scores—as well as qualitative feedback from team members involved in the project. Surveys and interviews with stakeholders provide context that numbers alone cannot convey. For example, testimonials from customer service representatives about their experiences with the chatbot's implementation can offer insights into employee morale and workflow changes, thereby enriching the overall understanding of the project's impact.

Once data is collected, employing a structured framework for analysis can streamline the process. A common approach is to use a SWOT analysis, which assesses strengths, weaknesses, opportunities, and threats related to the case study. This method encourages comprehensive evaluation by prompting analysts to consider internal capabilities alongside external market dynamics. In our chatbot example, strengths may include a reduced workload for staff and improved customer satisfaction, while weaknesses might highlight initial bugs or integration challenges.

After identifying key themes through analysis, synthesizing findings into actionable insights becomes crucial. This stage is where patterns across different case studies begin to emerge. Analysts should compare results from various implementations—such as marketing automation tools or data visualization platforms—to understand broader trends in no-code AI adoption. Insights may reveal that businesses experience increased customer engagement when they incorporate interactive elements in chatbots or design dashboards with user experience in mind.

Equally important is documenting lessons learned from both successes and failures within each case study. Acknowledging missteps fosters an environment where organizations can embrace continuous improvement instead of shying away from innovation due to fear of failure. For example, if a company encountered challenges integrating its no-code solution with existing systems, sharing this experience can help others anticipate potential pitfalls early in their implementation process.

Finally, effectively communicating findings is paramount for influencing future decision-making within organizations. Case study reports should present not only raw data but also compelling narratives that resonate with stakeholders at all levels. Visual aids—such as infographics illustrating before-and-after scenarios or short video clips demonstrating tool usage—can enhance engagement and comprehension among audiences who may not be familiar with technical jargon.

To wrap things up, a well-structured case study analysis methodology equips organizations with actionable insights while demystifying the complexities surrounding no-code AI implementations. By establishing clear objectives, gathering diverse data sources, utilizing analytical frameworks like SWOT, synthesizing findings into broader themes, documenting lessons learned, and communicating effectively, businesses can build a solid foundation for future innovations. As companies navigate their journeys toward adopting no-code solutions, these methodologies not only illuminate paths forward but also foster a culture of learning and adaptability essential for thriving in an evolving technological landscape.

Building a Culture of Innovation

Creating a culture of innovation within an organization requires more than just adopting new tools; it demands a fundamental shift in mindset and practices. Essentially of this transformation is the recognition that innovation flourishes when individuals feel empowered to take risks, share ideas, and collaborate across boundaries. This supportive environment not only fosters creative problem-solving but also encourages experimentation—two essential ingredients for successfully implementing no-code AI solutions.

To nurture such a culture, leadership must set the example by modeling innovative behaviors. When leaders exhibit openness to new ideas and actively engage in brainstorming sessions, they send a clear message that creativity is valued. Take this example, a marketing team might organize regular "innovation days," inviting members to pitch new campaigns or tools aimed at enhancing productivity or engagement. This approach not only ignites enthusiasm but also reinforces the notion that every employee can contribute to the organization's growth.

An equally important aspect of building this culture is providing ongoing training and development opportunities. Employees should have access to resources that enhance their skills in both no-code platforms and innovation methodologies. Workshops on design thinking or agile project management can empower teams to approach problems critically and develop user-centered solutions efficiently. By offering a variety of learning formats—such as online courses, hands-on workshops, and mentorship programs—organizations ensure that employees at all levels can engage with these concepts in ways that resonate personally.

Collaboration plays a crucial role in fostering an innovative culture as well. Breaking down silos between departments allows diverse perspectives to inform problem-solving processes. For example, a project team comprising members from IT, marketing, and customer service can leverage their varied expertise to design more effective AI-driven solutions. In one case study, a financial institution established cross-functional teams to automate customer support using no-code platforms. By involving different departments early in the process, they ensured that the resulting system not only met technical requirements but also aligned with customer expectations.

Celebrating both successes and failures further reinforces the value of innovation within the organization. Acknowledging employees who successfully implement new ideas boosts morale and encourages others to pursue their own initiatives. Conversely, treating failures as learning experiences rather than setbacks creates a safe space for experimentation. Consider a tech startup that hosts monthly "failure forums," where teams share what didn't work along with lessons learned. This practice reduces fear surrounding failure while fostering transparency and continuous improvement throughout the organization.

Feedback mechanisms are also vital in this dynamic environment. Establishing channels for employees to voice their thoughts on tools or processes ensures that innovation remains a collective effort rather than an isolated endeavor. For example, implementing suggestion boxes or digital platforms where team members can propose enhancements to existing workflows encourages engagement and demonstrates that their input is valued.

Finally, aligning innovation efforts with the organization's broader mission amplifies their impact. When teams understand how their initiatives contribute to overarching goals—whether enhancing customer satisfaction or driving operational efficiency—they become more motivated and focused on achieving tangible results. Take this example, if a company prioritizes sustainability as part of its mission, encouraging employees to develop AI solutions that optimize resource management can channel innovative energies toward meaningful challenges.

As organizations navigate the complexities of integrating no-code AI into their operations, fostering a culture of innovation becomes indispensable. By emphasizing empowerment through leadership example, offering continuous learning opportunities, promoting collaboration across functions, celebrating both wins and losses, maintaining open feedback channels, and aligning initiatives with core objectives, companies can create an ecosystem where creativity flourishes without being hindered by traditional constraints. This foundation not only enhances the successful implementation of no-code solutions but also positions organizations as adaptable leaders ready to embrace future challenges head-on.

CHAPTER 16: THE ROAD AHEAD

Recap of Key Insights

R eflecting on our journey through the world of no-code AI, several key insights emerge that capture the essence of this innovative paradigm. At the forefront of this evolution is the democratization of technology. No longer confined to those proficient in programming languages, individuals from diverse backgrounds can now leverage no-code platforms to create and deploy AI-driven solutions. This shift opens doors for entrepreneurs, small business owners, and creative thinkers who may have previously felt alienated by technical jargon.

It's essential to recognize that no-code tools are not simply substitutes for traditional coding; they are powerful enablers of creativity and efficiency. These platforms empower users to visualize their ideas and transform them into functional applications without requiring extensive training. For example, a graphic designer can now build an intelligent customer service chatbot using a no-code platform with drag-and-drop functionality, significantly reducing development time and resource demands.

Fostering a culture of innovation within organizations is equally important. Leadership plays a crucial role in creating environments where experimentation flourishes. When organizations actively encourage employees to share ideas and test new concepts, they cultivate an atmosphere rich with potential. Teams that collaborate across disciplines are often more adept at solving complex problems; for instance, a marketing team working alongside IT to develop an AI-powered tool for personalized customer engagement exemplifies this collaborative spirit.

And, ongoing education is vital in fueling this innovation ecosystem. Providing continuous learning opportunities equips employees with the skills necessary to utilize no-code platforms effectively. Workshops on user experience design or agile methodologies can spark creativity and enhance problem-solving capabilities. Investing in training not only boosts morale but also ensures that teams remain adaptable in a rapidly evolving technological landscape.

As we explored various applications of AI agents across industries, it became evident that these technologies are reshaping workflows and enhancing productivity. From automating repetitive tasks in finance to personalizing user experiences in retail, the versatility of AI agents demonstrates their potential to drive significant value. A notable example is a healthcare provider using no-code solutions to streamline patient intake processes, leading to reduced wait times and improved patient satisfaction.

It is also crucial to consider the ethical implications of deploying AI. As organizations embrace these technologies, they must stay vigilant regarding fairness, transparency, and privacy concerns. By prioritizing responsible AI use, companies can build trust with their users while ensuring compliance with regulations—an essential step toward sustainable innovation.

Lastly, reflecting on how organizations can scale their AI solutions highlights the importance of strategic planning and infrastructure alignment. As businesses grow, so too must their technology capabilities. Organizations should actively seek growth opportunities while optimizing resource usage to ensure scalability without compromising performance.

In summary, our exploration of no-code AI has revealed the transformative potential of these tools. By embracing democratization, fostering a culture of innovation, investing in education, applying AI responsibly across industries, and strategically planning for growth, organizations are well-positioned to thrive in this new landscape. The insights gained here serve as guiding principles for anyone looking to harness the power of no-code AI solutions effectively—an exciting frontier that awaits those ready to engage with it fully.

Steps to Advance Your Skills

Advancing your skills in no-code AI platforms begins with a proactive commitment to learning and experimentation. Start by familiarizing yourself with the diverse range of no-code tools available, each offering unique features, strengths, and limitations. By exploring various options, you can determine which platform aligns best with your goals. For example, Bubble provides a powerful environment for building web applications, while Airtable excels in data organization and management. Testing these tools firsthand will give you practical insights into their capabilities.

Next, immerse yourself in the vibrant community surrounding these platforms. Online forums and social media groups are rich resources where experienced users share tips, tricks, and project ideas. Platforms like Reddit and Discord facilitate lively discussions that allow you to ask questions and receive feedback on your projects. Engaging with others not only accelerates your learning curve but also sparks innovative ways to utilize the tools at your disposal.

Hands-on practice is crucial for deepening your understanding of no-code AI solutions. Begin with small projects that encourage experimentation without overwhelming you. Take this example, consider creating a simple chatbot for an imaginary business using a platform like Chatbot.com or Tars. Focus on defining the bot's purpose, understanding user queries, and crafting appropriate responses. This exercise will enhance your familiarity with design principles while providing tangible results that demonstrate your new skills.

As you grow more confident, challenge yourself with more complex projects that push your abilities further. Integrate various functionalities into a single application—perhaps developing a customer relationship management (CRM) system that automates email responses based on customer inquiries. Such a project will require combining elements like APIs for data retrieval and logic for decision-making processes. Tackling these challenges sharpens essential problem-solving skills relevant in any technology field.

Learning from existing case studies is another effective way to advance your skills. Analyze how others have successfully implemented no-code AI solutions within their organizations or projects. For example, investigate how a startup leveraged no-code tools to create an automated marketing campaign that significantly boosted customer engagement metrics. Gaining insights from real-world applications can provide valuable lessons that inform your own endeavors.

To further enhance your technical knowledge, explore online courses tailored specifically to no-code development and AI integration. Many platforms offer structured programs ranging from introductory overviews to advanced techniques in automation and machine learning within no-code environments. Engaging with these materials not only expands your technical vocabulary but also provides frameworks to help navigate the complexities of implementation.

Staying updated on industry trends and emerging technologies related to no-code development and artificial intelligence is equally important. Subscribing to relevant newsletters or following thought leaders in the field keeps you informed about new tools or features that could streamline your work processes or expand your capabilities. This ongoing awareness positions you at the forefront of innovation rather than merely reacting to changes as they occur.

Lastly, consider the pivotal role of mentorship in skill advancement. Seek out individuals experienced in implementing AI agents or effectively using no-code platforms; their personalized insights can illuminate challenges they faced along their journey. Establishing a mentor-mentee relationship fosters an exchange of ideas and support that greatly enriches your learning experience.

At its core, advancing your skills requires a multifaceted approach that includes exploration, community engagement, hands-on practice, case study analysis, structured learning, staying informed about industry developments, and seeking mentorship opportunities. Embrace this holistic strategy as it prepares you not only to use no-code AI tools effectively but also to confidently innovate within this exciting realm of technology.

Building a Community Around AI

Building a community around AI involves more than just technical skills; it's about fostering connections, sharing knowledge, and inspiring collaboration. Such communities act as fertile ground for innovation, where diverse ideas can thrive through collective effort. The foundation of a successful community lies in openness and inclusivity, inviting individuals from various backgrounds to contribute their unique perspectives and talents.

To cultivate this environment, start by engaging with existing online platforms that focus on AI and no-code solutions. Websites like Meetup.com can help you discover local gatherings or virtual events centered on AI topics. These events often feature workshops, panel discussions, and networking opportunities that encourage participants to share their experiences and insights. Take this example, at a recent meetup I attended, a group of entrepreneurs discussed their successful integration of no-code tools into their business models. Their stories not only educated the audience but also sparked conversations about potential collaborations and shared projects.

Social media also plays a crucial role in community building. Platforms like Twitter and LinkedIn host vibrant discussions among AI enthusiasts, developers, and innovators. By joining relevant groups or following influential thought leaders, you can enhance your learning and stay updated on the latest industry trends. Engaging with these communities through comments and shares fosters connections and positions you as an active contributor rather than just an observer.

Creating your own community can be equally rewarding. Consider organizing regular meetups or online forums focused on specific AI applications or challenges faced by no-code tool users. For example, hosting a series of webinars where experts walk through case studies of successful AI implementations can provide significant value while encouraging attendees to share their insights as well. Organizing such events not only establishes you as a leader within the community but also deepens your understanding of the subject as you prepare content and facilitate discussions.

Collaboration is at the heart of any thriving community. Once you've established connections with fellow enthusiasts or professionals, consider embarking on joint projects that leverage no-code AI solutions to address real-world problems.

Whether it's building an application for local businesses or developing educational resources for newcomers, these initiatives strengthen relationships while yielding tangible outcomes that benefit everyone involved. A memorable project I participated in involved creating an automated system to track local environmental changes using data from open sources—an effort that required pooling together diverse skill sets and perspectives.

Encouraging mentorship within your community can significantly enhance its effectiveness. Pairing seasoned practitioners with newcomers allows for organic knowledge transfer while fostering growth for both parties. Many individuals are eager to share their experiences; leveraging these relationships enriches individual learning and strengthens the overall fabric of the community. The shared victories—and even failures—become collective learning moments that bind members together.

As you nurture this ecosystem, remember the importance of celebrating achievements—no matter how small they may seem. Highlighting member contributions through newsletters or social media shoutouts reinforces a culture of recognition and appreciation. This way, you create an environment where individuals feel valued for their contributions, motivating them to remain engaged and invested in communal goals.

building a community around AI requires ongoing effort to maintain connections, promote collaboration, encourage mentorship, and celebrate achievements. Each action taken strengthens ties among members while fostering an atmosphere ripe for innovation. With shared experiences and collective intelligence at play, individuals are empowered not only to learn but also to push the boundaries of what's possible with no-code AI solutions. The journey ahead is filled with opportunities, waiting for those ready to take bold steps together into uncharted territories of technology and creativity.

Opportunities for Continued Learning

Opportunities for continued learning in the realm of no-code AI are both abundant and diverse, catering to a wide range of interests and skill levels. As this landscape continually evolves, staying updated and enhancing one's knowledge becomes essential. One of the most effective pathways for ongoing education is through online courses. Platforms like Coursera, Udemy, and edX offer numerous courses specifically focused on no-code tools and AI concepts. For example, courses on Zapier or Airtable provide practical insights into automation without requiring programming skills.

Engaging in these courses not only builds foundational knowledge but also paves the way for exploring more advanced topics such as machine learning and natural language processing. A notable example is the "AI for Everyone" course by Andrew Ng on Coursera, which demystifies AI concepts and makes them accessible to non-technical audiences. Many participants find themselves inspired to delve into specialized subjects once they grasp the basics.

Conferences and workshops offer another valuable avenue for growth, allowing individuals to connect directly with industry experts and peers. Events like the No-Code Summit or AI Expo provide hands-on experience with cutting-edge tools while also shedding light on emerging trends. Networking at these events can lead to collaborative projects or mentorship opportunities that further enrich your learning journey. A friend of mine attended an AI-focused conference where he not only learned about the latest technologies but also connected with mentors who helped him implement a no-code solution for his startup.

To complement online learning efforts, reading books and subscribing to newsletters can be incredibly beneficial.

Many authors are publishing insightful materials on no-code solutions and AI applications. Take this example, "No-Code: The Complete Guide" offers practical advice alongside case studies from successful entrepreneurs who have effectively harnessed no-code platforms. Staying informed through newsletters like TechCrunch or NoCode Journal helps individuals keep up with the latest innovations and best practices in the field.

Participating in online communities and forums dedicated to no-code AI also fosters continuous learning. Platforms such as Reddit's r/NoCode or the Makerpad community create spaces where members share tips, project ideas, and resources. Actively engaging in these communities allows you to learn from others' experiences while sharing your own insights. This exchange of knowledge can lead to unexpected solutions and ideas that you may not have considered otherwise.

And, experimenting with personal projects can be one of the most rewarding ways to learn. Taking an idea from conception to implementation using no-code tools offers practical experience that solidifies theoretical knowledge. Take this example, if you're interested in improving local community services, try building a simple application with Glide or Adalo that addresses a specific need, like tracking volunteer hours or managing donations. Each iteration provides valuable lessons about user experience, design principles, and functionality.

Finally, consider leveraging mentorship opportunities within your network or community. Finding a mentor who has navigated similar paths can provide tailored guidance that accelerates your learning process. These relationships foster deeper insights into challenges faced during implementation and strategies for overcoming them, benefiting both parties involved.

At its core, the journey of continued learning in no-code AI is characterized by exploration, experimentation, and collaboration. By embracing diverse educational resources—from online courses to networking events—you can remain at the forefront of innovation while adapting to ever-changing technologies. Each step taken not only enhances individual capabilities but also contributes to a collective understanding of how we can creatively leverage these tools for meaningful impact in our personal lives and broader communities.

Encouraging Experimentation

Encouraging experimentation is fundamental to driving innovation in the no-code AI landscape. When individuals and organizations cultivate a culture of trial and error, they unlock the potential for groundbreaking solutions. The appeal of no-code tools lies in their accessibility, enabling users to quickly prototype and iterate without the fear of breaking complex code. This democratization of technology fosters creative thinking and problem-solving in ways that traditional development environments often cannot match.

Take, for example, an entrepreneur aiming to create a platform for local artists to showcase their work. With limited technical skills, they turned to no-code tools like Bubble. By sketching their ideas and utilizing drag-and-drop functionalities, they built a functional prototype in just a few days. Although the initial version was rough around the edges, it allowed them to gather valuable feedback from potential users early on. Each piece of feedback informed subsequent iterations, helping to refine the platform's features based on real-world experiences. This case exemplifies how rapid experimentation can lead to significant learning; by iterating quickly, creators can effectively adapt to meet user needs.

To nurture a mindset that values experimentation, it's essential to foster an environment where failure is viewed as an opportunity rather than a setback. A well-known tech leader once said, "Fail fast and learn faster." This philosophy encourages teams to tackle challenges with curiosity, pushing boundaries while acknowledging that not every idea will succeed on the first attempt. Take this example, a marketing team might experiment with various messaging strategies using no-code automation platforms like Zapier to identify what resonates most with their audience. By analyzing engagement metrics after each campaign, they can dynamically refine their approach.

Integrating regular brainstorming sessions into your workflow can further promote experimentation. Inviting team members from diverse backgrounds to share ideas without fear of judgment creates a space ripe for innovation. These sessions can serve as incubators for concepts that might otherwise be overlooked. Utilizing tools like Miro or Trello during discussions allows participants to visualize ideas collaboratively, sparking creativity while nurturing a sense of ownership among team members—empowering them to explore new possibilities.

Encouraging individual exploration can also yield significant benefits. Allow team members to dedicate part of their workweek to personal projects aligned with company goals or their interests. This freedom often leads to unexpected breakthroughs as individuals test hypotheses or develop new skills through hands-on experience. Take this example, a data analyst experimenting with AI-driven data visualization tools might discover more efficient ways to present insights, ultimately enhancing decision-making across departments.

As you promote experimentation within your organization or personal projects, it's crucial to document the process thoroughly. Keeping track of what works and what doesn't helps build a knowledge base that others can reference in future endeavors. Creating internal wikis or shared folders to store lessons learned enables teams to avoid repeating mistakes while capitalizing on successful strategies.

Finally, celebrate successes—no matter how small—and

acknowledge lessons learned from failures alike. Recognition reinforces positive behavior and encourages others to take risks without fear of repercussions. Whether through shout-outs in team meetings or rewards for innovative projects, highlighting these moments significantly contributes to cultivating an experimental culture.

experimentation is not just about trying new things; it's about embracing the entire discovery process that leads to innovative solutions and improved workflow efficiency. By fostering an environment where testing hypotheses is encouraged and supported by resources, you empower yourself and those around you to harness the full potential of no-code AI tools—driving progress both individually and collectively within your organization or community.

Joining No-Code AI Conversations

Engaging in the dynamic conversations around no-code AI is crucial for anyone eager to leverage these tools effectively. Becoming part of a community not only deepens your understanding but also cultivates collaboration and innovation. Picture stepping into an environment where ideas flow freely, and your questions can spark insights that elevate your projects.

Online forums, social media groups, and local meetups serve as excellent entry points into this vibrant landscape. Platforms like Reddit and LinkedIn host dedicated communities centered on no-code development and AI. By participating in discussions, you can access a wealth of knowledge and experiences from others facing similar challenges. For example, when someone poses a question about integrating an AI agent into their workflow, the ensuing dialogue often yields diverse perspectives and solutions, significantly shortening your learning curve.

And, attending webinars or workshops can provide a substantial boost to your skills. Many organizations offer free or low-cost sessions that explore specific tools or concepts within the no-code AI realm. These interactive formats allow you to learn directly from experts while having the chance to ask questions in real time, facilitating a deeper understanding of the material. A recent webinar on using Zapier for automating customer service interactions exemplified this, as participants engaged in live demonstrations and interacted with presenters, enhancing their comprehension far beyond what reading alone could achieve.

Collaboration can also spark creativity, so look for opportunities to partner with others on projects. If you're developing an AI agent for customer support but lack expertise in user experience design, seek out someone whose strengths complement yours. Working together can yield a more robust solution that meets user needs more effectively than if you tackled it alone. Tools like Figma for design and Airtable for project management facilitate this process, enabling seamless communication and iterative work.

Don't overlook the importance of sharing your journey as well. Documenting your experiences—whether they are successes or setbacks—through blogs or social media posts contributes to the broader conversation and assists others facing similar challenges. By sharing an early prototype of your project and detailing how you gathered feedback, you not only showcase your process but also invite constructive criticism that can lead to meaningful improvements.

Mentorship can be another powerful avenue for growth in this landscape. Connecting with a mentor who has navigated the no-code AI terrain can provide tailored insights specific to your context. Their guidance can help you avoid common pitfalls and offer strategic advice on scaling your projects effectively. Whether through formal arrangements or casual connections made at meetups, these relationships often yield benefits that extend beyond mere technical knowledge.

As you immerse yourself in these discussions and communities, remain open to diverse perspectives. Different industries present unique challenges and solutions that may resonate with your own work in unexpected ways. Take this example, insights from someone in healthcare regarding patient engagement might inspire innovative features for a retail customer service bot.

To keep pace with emerging trends and best practices, consider subscribing to newsletters or following thought leaders in the no-code AI field on social media. Their content often highlights new tools, case studies, and industry shifts that could be pivotal for your projects. Engaging with their posts can also spark fruitful discussions that deepen your understanding.

participating in no-code AI conversations is about forging connections—both with individuals and ideas—that propel you forward in this ever-evolving landscape. Each interaction is an opportunity to learn something new or refine your existing knowledge. The true power of community lies in its ability to transform individual journeys into collective advancements; by actively engaging, you not only contribute to your own growth but also to the broader dialogue shaping the future of no-code AI solutions.

Long-Term Vision for No-Code AI Agents

The long-term vision for no-code AI agents extends far beyond simplifying development processes; it represents a transformative shift in our perception of technology and its accessibility. Imagine a world where anyone, regardless of their technical background, can leverage AI to tackle the unique challenges they face in their lives and businesses. This democratization of technology fosters an environment ripe for innovation, allowing a diverse array of voices to contribute solutions that were once limited to specialized experts.

Looking ahead, the integration of no-code AI agents across

various sectors will be crucial. Businesses will increasingly turn to these tools to streamline operations and enhance customer experiences. For example, small retailers could use no-code platforms to create personalized shopping experiences through chatbots that understand customer preferences and offer tailored recommendations. Such advancements will not only elevate service standards but also empower smaller enterprises to compete effectively against larger corporations.

Education stands to benefit significantly as well. No-code AI can facilitate personalized learning experiences, enabling educators to develop customized curricula that cater to individual student needs. By employing AI agents capable of assessing learning styles and adapting content accordingly, educational institutions can create environments where every student can thrive. This innovation will redefine traditional teaching methods, making learning more engaging and accessible.

In healthcare, the promise of no-code AI agents is equally compelling. The ability to create patient engagement systems without extensive technical expertise allows healthcare providers to focus on what truly matters: patient care. Take this example, a hospital might implement an AI-driven chatbot that assists patients with appointment scheduling, medication reminders, and post-discharge follow-ups—all built on no-code platforms. This approach not only enhances operational efficiency but also improves patient satisfaction and outcomes.

However, as the adoption of no-code AI agents becomes more widespread, security concerns will inevitably arise. As more organizations utilize these tools, prioritizing data privacy and compliance with regulations like GDPR will be essential. Developers of no-code platforms must embed robust security features and transparent data handling practices to foster trust among users. Establishing strong ethical frameworks for AI use will help mitigate risks associated with automated systems making decisions based on sensitive information.

And, as these tools gain traction, we can expect a flourishing ecosystem of complementary services and products. From data analytics solutions that integrate seamlessly with no-code platforms to marketplaces offering pre-built templates for various applications, the support structure surrounding no-code AI will expand dramatically. This growth will enhance user experiences by providing resources that simplify the journey from idea conception to deployment.

Another vital aspect of this vision is the continuous evolution of user interfaces for no-code platforms. As technology advances, we can anticipate increasingly intuitive interfaces that leverage natural language processing (NLP) and visual programming techniques. Users may soon be able to describe their desired outcomes in plain language —similar to conversing with a colleague—and the platform would automatically generate the corresponding workflows or functionalities. This sophistication will significantly lower barriers to entry and encourage broader participation across diverse demographics.

Community-driven development models also hold immense potential for the future of no-code AI agents. Imagine vibrant communities where users share innovations and collaborate on projects; such ecosystems not only foster creativity but also provide support structures that enhance learning and problem-solving capabilities. Open-source initiatives could play a crucial role here, enabling users to contribute to existing platforms while benefiting from shared knowledge and resources.

While this exciting future beckons, we must remain cognizant of the challenges that may accompany rapid advancements. Addressing issues such as accessibility for underrepresented communities and ensuring equitable distribution of technology benefits will require concerted efforts from industry leaders, policymakers, and advocates alike. The responsibility lies in creating a balanced ecosystem where innovation leaves no one behind.

In this dynamic landscape where creativity meets technology, fostering open dialogue about best practices and ethical considerations becomes essential. By promoting transparency in decision-making processes within organizations using no-code AI agents, stakeholders can build trust both internally among teams and externally with clients or customers.

As we consider the trajectory of no-code AI agents in the coming years, it's clear they will profoundly reshape our interactions with technology. The potential for unprecedented creativity and problem-solving capacity invites us all to participate in building solutions that address real-world needs without requiring advanced technical skills.

By wholeheartedly embracing this vision, we can collectively shape a future defined not just by what technology can do but by how it empowers individuals from all walks of life—transforming dreams into tangible realities through intelligent systems designed by those who dare to imagine a better tomorrow.

Call to Action for Readers

Engaging with no-code AI agents is more than just a technical pursuit; it invites you to join a transformative movement that is redefining how we tackle problems, streamline operations, and enrich our daily experiences. These tools hold immense potential for anyone who has faced challenges that seem overwhelming. Imagine being able to create solutions that once felt exclusive to tech experts—now, they are accessible to you, regardless of your coding background.

To effectively harness the power of no-code AI, start by pinpointing specific pain points in your environment. Whether you're a small business owner aiming to enhance customer service or an educator seeking to personalize learning experiences, recognizing your unique needs is the first step toward meaningful innovation. Take some time to list recurring challenges or processes that could benefit from simplification; these observations will form the foundation of your AI journey. For example, if managing customer inquiries consumes too much of your time, you might consider developing a chatbot using no-code tools to automate responses, allowing you to focus on more strategic initiatives.

Once you've identified your use case, explore the various no-code platforms available today. Each platform boasts distinct features tailored to different needs and industries. Some excel in automating workflows, while others may specialize in data visualization or user interface design. Take advantage of free trials and community forums; these resources can offer valuable insights into each tool's strengths and weaknesses. As you experiment with different platforms, pay attention to their user-friendliness and how well they integrate with your existing systems. Take this example, connecting a no-code platform with popular CRM systems can significantly boost your operational efficiency.

Learning by doing is one of the most effective strategies for mastering no-code AI development. Start small by building simple applications or automation scripts that address immediate needs. Platforms like Zapier or Airtable allow you to create workflows connecting various services without any coding knowledge. These initial projects will not only build your confidence but also provide practical experience that will be invaluable as you tackle more complex challenges.

Don't overlook the importance of community involvement on this journey. Connecting with others who share your interests can spark creativity and offer support as you navigate obstacles. Online forums, social media groups, and local meetups present opportunities to exchange ideas, seek advice, and collaborate on projects. Take this example, joining a community focused on no-code development could lead to innovative partnerships or even mentorship from seasoned practitioners.

As you grow more comfortable with these tools, consider how you might give back to the community or create templates for others to use. Sharing your successes and lessons learned not only reinforces your own understanding but also helps foster an ecosystem where collective knowledge thrives. Documenting your processes through blog posts or tutorials can solidify your expertise while empowering others on their journeys.

Lastly, let a commitment to continuous improvement guide your efforts in building no-code AI agents. Regularly seek feedback from users interacting with your solutions and remain open to iterating based on their insights. This dedication to enhancement will ensure that the systems you create remain relevant and effective over time. Implementing user feedback loops will refine functionalities and deepen engagement by making users feel heard and valued.

Engaging with no-code AI is about more than simply adopting new technology; it's about reimagining our approach to problem-solving in both personal and professional contexts. Embrace this opportunity wholeheartedly—by using these tools creatively and collaboratively, you're not just building solutions; you're actively shaping a future where technology serves everyone and unlocks endless possibilities.

So take that first step today—explore the available platforms, connect with like-minded individuals, and start crafting solutions that align with your vision for tomorrow's challenges transformed into opportunities for growth and innovation. The landscape is wide open; all it takes is curiosity coupled with action to embark on this rewarding journey into no-code AI development.

CONCLUSION

Reflecting on our journey through the world of no-code AI agents, we arrive at an exciting intersection of technology and creativity. This exploration has shed light not only on the technical capabilities of these tools but also on their potential to empower individuals and organizations. No-code platforms dismantle the barriers that once kept innovative solutions hidden behind complex lines of code, inviting people from diverse backgrounds— entrepreneurs, educators, non-profit leaders—to engage with artificial intelligence in meaningful ways.

The applications of no-code AI agents are nearly limitless. By enabling users to automate tasks and streamline processes without requiring extensive programming knowledge, we unlock a new realm of possibilities. From developing intelligent chatbots that enhance customer interaction to implementing automated workflows that boost productivity, the impact is both immediate and profound. Take this example, a small business could leverage a no-code tool to create an inventory management system, saving time and allowing owners to focus on growth strategies instead of mundane tasks.

Throughout our discussions, we've highlighted essential strategies for successfully navigating the landscape of no-code development. Identifying specific pain points is crucial;

it's about pinpointing areas where technology can make a significant difference. This targeted approach ensures that your solutions are effective from the outset. Additionally, experimenting with various platforms provides users with valuable hands-on experience, empowering them to choose the right tools for their unique needs—there's real power in learning by doing.

Community involvement has emerged as another vital aspect of this journey. Engaging with others who share a passion for innovation fosters collaboration and support. By connecting with like-minded individuals or participating in forums dedicated to no-code development, creators can tap into collective wisdom that accelerates learning and inspires creative solutions.

As you contemplate your next steps in this evolving landscape, keep in mind that continuous improvement is key. Gathering feedback from end-users not only refines your projects but also fosters a sense of ownership among those interacting with your AI agents. This transforms technology from being merely functional into something truly responsive and user-centered.

embracing no-code AI development is about more than mastering a new skill; it's about joining a movement that democratizes technology. This shift enables diverse voices to contribute ideas and innovations reflective of their unique perspectives and experiences. The future is indeed bright for those willing to explore this space.

As you embark on your own journey within this realm, take comfort in knowing that every step contributes to a larger narrative—a narrative where technology serves humanity's needs and aspirations rather than the other way around. You are equipped not just to build solutions but also to shape outcomes that matter, catalyzing change within your community or organization.

Engage fully with this transformative opportunity ahead of

you. Dive deep into experimentation, connect with others, and commit to ongoing learning. The potential for innovation is vast; all it requires is your curiosity paired with action. Together, let's redefine what's possible as we craft intelligent systems that are accessible and impactful across all sectors of society.

The canvas is yours—embrace it boldly and watch as your vision comes to life through the power of no-code AI agents.

Reflections on the Journey

The journey through the realm of no-code AI agents has been one of empowerment and discovery. Each concept we've explored has unveiled layers of complexity that often obscured the field of artificial intelligence, making it seem intimidating and accessible only to a select few. Now, as we reflect on our experiences, it's important to consider the lessons learned and the profound implications for individuals and businesses alike.

Throughout our exploration, we have seen how no-code platforms democratize technology, allowing people from diverse backgrounds—entrepreneurs, educators, and non-technical professionals—to harness the potential of AI without requiring extensive coding skills. This shift represents more than a passing trend; it marks a transformative wave in our approach to problem-solving. Solutions are no longer limited to those with technical expertise; instead, creativity and insight can thrive in any environment where ideas are nurtured.

Consider the stories shared along the way: a small business owner automating customer service with chatbots or a non-profit organization utilizing data analytics for community outreach. These examples demonstrate that innovation is not confined to large corporations; it can emerge from grassroots initiatives addressing specific community needs. By equipping individuals with tools that require no programming knowledge, we foster diversity in thought and creativity in solutions.

Yet, reflecting on this journey also brings to light the challenges encountered along the way. Navigating this new landscape is not without its hurdles. Initial apprehension about adopting new technologies is common; many fear losing control over processes or becoming overly reliant on automated systems. However, as we've discovered, the key lies in viewing these tools as allies rather than replacements. Embracing no-code AI agents enables users to maintain oversight while enjoying enhanced efficiency—striking an important balance that fosters trust and engagement.

Ethical considerations also play a critical role in our technological advancements. With great power comes great responsibility; understanding how AI impacts privacy, fairness, and transparency is essential for sustainable innovation. As we move forward in this field, adhering to ethical standards will be crucial—not only for compliance but also for building trust with users.

Scalability is another vital topic as we delve deeper into this new era. The ability to adapt solutions as needs evolve is paramount for both startups and established enterprises. Systems that start as simple automations can develop into robust frameworks capable of tackling more complex challenges. This adaptability lies at the heart of effective deployment strategies.

At this stage in our exploration, it's clear that the road ahead is filled with opportunities waiting to be uncovered. Each of us has the potential to make meaningful contributions— whether by developing innovative applications or advocating for responsible technology use within our networks. The insights gained serve not just as theoretical knowledge but also as actionable steps toward harnessing technology for the greater good.

As you reflect on your own journey through this material, think about what you can create or change in your environment with no-code AI agents at your fingertips. The invitation stands: embrace your power as a creator and innovator, free from the traditional barriers imposed by coding languages or technical jargon. Every small action contributes to a larger movement toward inclusivity and accessibility in technology.

By engaging with these tools creatively and ethically, we can redefine innovation within our respective fields. Together, let's continue cultivating environments where ideas flourish unencumbered by limitations—transforming aspirations into tangible solutions that enhance our lives and communities alike. While many paths lie ahead, every step we take today brings us closer to a future where technology is not just a tool but an extension of human ingenuity itself.

The Role of AI in the Future

The role of AI in our future is not just a topic for speculation; it is an emerging reality that is already transforming industries, enhancing everyday experiences, and reshaping our interactions with technology. Today's advancements in artificial intelligence are laying the groundwork for significant societal shifts, influencing areas such as healthcare, education, finance, and transportation. Understanding how AI will impact our lives and the decisions we make is essential as we navigate this evolving landscape.

One of AI's most transformative features is its ability to deliver personalized experiences. Take platforms like Spotify and Netflix, for instance; they utilize algorithms to analyze user behavior and preferences, curating content tailored to individual tastes. This level of personalization extends beyond entertainment; in education, adaptive learning technologies assess student progress and customize lessons accordingly. By fostering an environment where learners can thrive at their own pace, AI enhances educational outcomes and makes learning more engaging.

In the business realm, companies are increasingly harnessing AI-driven analytics to glean insights from vast amounts of data. Retailers, for example, use predictive analytics to forecast demand patterns, ensuring they stock products appropriately while minimizing waste. The implications are profound: businesses that effectively leverage data can improve operational efficiencies and enhance customer satisfaction through targeted marketing strategies. A local bakery could predict peak customer times by analyzing past purchase data, allowing for strategic adjustments in staffing and inventory that ultimately bolster revenue.

In healthcare, the potential of AI is particularly remarkable. Machine learning algorithms can analyze medical images with impressive accuracy—sometimes even surpassing human doctors—when detecting conditions like cancer or heart disease. These advancements not only expedite diagnoses but also improve treatment outcomes by enabling earlier interventions. Imagine an AI system alerting medical professionals to unusual patterns in patient data; such early detection could lead to life-saving treatments that were once out of reach for many patients.

As we delve deeper into this technological landscape, collaboration between human intelligence and artificial intelligence becomes increasingly vital. The rise of "augmented intelligence" highlights this partnership—AI tools enhance human capabilities rather than replace them. Take this example, lawyers using AI-powered legal research tools can access vast databases much more efficiently than traditional methods allow. This efficiency frees up time for strategic thinking and client engagement instead of routine tasks.

Navigating this new terrain also requires vigilance regarding ethical considerations surrounding AI deployment. Issues like algorithmic bias have gained significant attention; if left unchecked, they risk perpetuating inequalities across various domains—from hiring practices to loan approvals. Addressing these challenges involves advocating for diverse teams in AI development who can proactively identify potential pitfalls. A comprehensive approach ensures that as AI systems evolve, they promote fairness and inclusivity rather than exclusionary practices.

The conversation around sustainability is gaining momentum within the context of AI's role in shaping the future. As organizations seek greener solutions—whether through optimizing energy use or reducing waste—AI emerges as a powerful ally. Smart grids powered by AI can manage energy distribution efficiently based on real-time demand feedback; consider how homes equipped with intelligent devices adjust energy consumption dynamically based on usage patterns.

Looking ahead, we cannot overlook the rapid pace at which technology evolves; the future promises even more extraordinary innovations driven by artificial intelligence. Fields such as quantum computing may provide breakthroughs that render today's sophisticated systems rudimentary by comparison. We stand at the threshold of an era where tasks currently perceived as complex could be simplified dramatically through smarter algorithms and enhanced computing power.

By weaving together these threads—personalization in user experience, efficiency in business processes, advancements in healthcare outcomes—we reveal a clear overarching theme: artificial intelligence will continue to integrate seamlessly into our daily lives and professional practices. Those who embrace these changes today are likely to emerge as pioneers tomorrow.

As we collectively embark on this journey into an increasingly automated future powered by no-code solutions alongside advanced AI capabilities, the call for proactive engagement resonates louder than ever. It's not just about adapting; it's about actively participating in crafting solutions that reflect our shared values while propelling innovation forward responsibly and ethically.

Embracing this future presents boundless opportunities —a canvas awaiting your creative strokes as you envision applications and interventions previously deemed unattainable or impractical. The stage is set for creators across all sectors: now is the time to seize the moment!

Thanking the Community and Supporters

In our journey of exploration and innovation, the significance of community cannot be overstated. The development of no-code AI solutions has been enriched by countless individuals who have generously shared their insights, experiences, and encouragement. This vibrant ecosystem fosters creativity and collaboration, with the collective wisdom emerging from the community acting as both a beacon and a foundation for aspiring creators. It guides them through the complexities of building intelligent systems without relying on traditional coding.

One particularly inspiring aspect of this community is its diversity. Voices from seasoned developers to enthusiastic beginners come together to share their stories and challenges. Take this example, an educator might illustrate how they used a no-code platform to create an interactive learning tool that enhances student engagement, while an entrepreneur could recount how they streamlined their business processes with AI agents, significantly reducing operational overhead. These narratives serve not only as case studies but also as motivational examples, showcasing the possibilities that arise when we harness the power of no-code technologies.

Support networks further enrich this landscape. Online forums and local meetups have become essential hubs for exchanging ideas, troubleshooting problems, and celebrating successes. The camaraderie within these groups is palpable; during a recent virtual summit dedicated to no-code innovations, participants shared breakthroughs in integrating AI with everyday applications. One developer even showcased a chatbot designed to assist elderly users with daily tasks. This spirit of sharing reinforces the notion that collaboration accelerates progress—it's about lifting one another up rather than competing.

Educational resources have also played a critical role in democratizing access to knowledge about no-code AI solutions. Organizations dedicated to open-source projects and community-driven tutorials ensure that information is readily available for anyone eager to learn. Platforms like YouTube and specialized blogs feature creators who share step-by-step guides on utilizing specific tools for building AI agents. These resources empower individuals to embark on their journeys equipped with both knowledge and practical skills.

Acknowledgment extends beyond those who create tools; it encompasses advocates for ethical practices in AI deployment. Community members who prioritize responsible AI usage contribute significantly to discussions about fairness and transparency in technology. Their work highlights the importance of diverse voices—those who can identify potential biases or ethical dilemmas before they arise. By promoting inclusive practices within the community, they enhance technological development and foster trust among users.

Looking ahead at the evolving landscape shaped by no-code AI solutions, it's clear that the collaborative spirit inherent in this community will continue to drive innovation. Many members actively seek opportunities for mentorship or partnerships with newcomers, recognizing that sharing knowledge is vital for sustaining growth in this rapidly changing field. Such interactions often lead to unexpected collaborations—imagine two creators combining their expertise to develop an app that addresses a specific market need or solves a social challenge.

We must also express gratitude to those working behind the scenes—the educators, mentors, and thought leaders who share their experiences through webinars and workshops. Their dedication transforms abstract concepts into actionable insights for practitioners at all levels, ensuring that learning evolves alongside technological advancements.

the success we see in building no-code AI systems reflects not only individual achievements but also the collective efforts of a supportive network driven by shared goals and aspirations. As you embark on your own journey within this dynamic ecosystem, remember that you stand on the shoulders of many innovators fueled by curiosity and ambition.

Final Thoughts and Inspirations

Embarking on the journey into the realm of no-code AI is more than just a technical endeavor; it's a transformative experience that redefines our understanding of what we can achieve. Each project—whether it involves creating an intelligent chatbot or automating everyday tasks—holds the potential to inspire and innovate. These initiatives transcend simple automation; they enhance human creativity and empower individuals across various sectors to realize their visions without being constrained by technical barriers.

Take, for example, a small non-profit organization seeking to improve community engagement but lacking the resources for extensive software development. By utilizing no-code platforms, they built an interactive space where community members could share ideas, volunteer opportunities, and local events—all without needing a dedicated tech team. This initiative not only strengthened community connections but also illustrated how accessibility can catalyze significant societal change. It shows that when tools are democratized, everyone can contribute creatively, enriching their communities in ways previously thought impossible.

As you delve into this landscape, let yourself be inspired by the possibilities offered by no-code solutions. Picture artists merging technology with creativity or educators crafting unique learning experiences tailored to their students' needs. This intersection of creativity and technology is a fertile ground for innovation, fostering a mindset that embraces experimentation rather than fearing it. Each attempt—successful or otherwise—provides valuable lessons that deepen our understanding and guide us toward effective solutions.

In this rapidly evolving field, cultivating a mindset open to learning and adaptation is crucial. While the pace of technological change can feel overwhelming, it also presents incredible opportunities for growth and discovery. Engaging with others who share your passion can lead to breakthroughs as diverse perspectives come together around a common goal. Participating in online forums or local meetups creates an environment rich in knowledge-sharing and offers support for navigating challenges.

Reflection is another essential component of your journey. Take time to assess what you've learned from each project or interaction within the no-code community. What strategies worked well? What might you approach differently next time? These reflections serve as stepping stones for continuous improvement and innovation in your future endeavors. The more you engage in this cycle of action, reflection, and adaptation, the more proficient you will become at leveraging these tools effectively.

As you step into this new era of no-code AI development, remember that your contributions are valuable. Whether you're developing a simple application for personal use or tackling complex issues within your industry, every effort adds to the collective progress. You are part of a broader movement toward inclusivity in technology—a movement fueled by curiosity and collaboration that seeks to break down traditional barriers.

Embrace your role in shaping the future through no-code AI solutions. Allow your ideas to flourish as you harness these innovative tools, knowing that they offer not only practical benefits but also foster meaningful connections among people striving toward shared goals. Each project you undertake reflects your unique perspective while expanding the boundaries of what's possible—encouraging others on their own journeys.

In every action lies potential; let yours inspire not only yourself but also those around you who dare to dream big alongside you in this exciting adventure ahead.

APPENDIX

A t the forefront is a glossary of terms that provides clear definitions for the jargon and technical language encountered throughout the book. Take this example, terms like "machine learning," "natural language processing," and "API" can be daunting for newcomers. By offering straightforward explanations, this glossary demystifies these concepts, ensuring that readers from all backgrounds can grasp fundamental ideas without feeling overwhelmed.

Complementing the glossary is a curated list of resources for further learning. This includes online courses, webinars, and community forums dedicated to no-code development and AI technologies. Platforms such as Coursera and Udemy offer specialized courses that allow you to deepen your knowledge at your own pace. Additionally, forums like Stack Overflow or Reddit's r/nocode community provide spaces for real-time discussion and problem-solving among peers with similar interests. Engaging with these communities fosters a sense of belonging and opens doors to new collaborative opportunities.

Following this, templates and checklists emerge as practical tools for your projects. For example, a project planning template outlines steps from ideation to execution while considering audience needs and resource allocation. This roadmap simplifies project management by breaking tasks into manageable segments—an ideal approach for anyone embarking on their first no-code AI project.

Incorporating best practices into your workflow can significantly enhance productivity. Checklists outlining common pitfalls to avoid when using no-code platforms help you stay focused on quality while developing your systems. They maintain clarity in your processes by reminding you to consider critical factors such as user experience design and data privacy regulations—elements often overlooked in the rush to deploy solutions.

Additionally, community support forums are highlighted as crucial touchpoints for engagement and shared learning experiences. Participating in discussions where others share their challenges or successes can inspire innovative ideas or solutions you may not have previously considered. The collective wisdom of users—from novices to seasoned professionals—can guide you through complex scenarios.

the appendix is more than just supplementary material; it reflects a commitment to fostering growth among readers eager to expand their horizons in no-code AI development. By equipping you with accessible knowledge and practical tools, it empowers you not only to take action but also encourages ongoing curiosity—a vital trait for navigating this rapidly evolving technological landscape successfully.

This resource-rich appendix complements your journey through no-code AI by ensuring you are well-equipped with both foundational knowledge and actionable insights as you continue exploring this exciting domain. Embrace these tools; they are designed to support your growth every step of the way.

Glossary of Terms

Artificial Intelligence (AI)** refers to a branch of computer science dedicated to developing systems capable of performing tasks typically requiring human intelligence. This encompasses problem-solving, natural language understanding, pattern recognition, and data-driven decision-making.

Machine Learning (ML)** is a subset of AI that employs algorithms and statistical models to allow systems to improve their performance on tasks through experience. Rather than being explicitly programmed for every possible scenario, these systems learn from data over time.

No-Code Development** is a methodology that empowers individuals to create applications or automation without writing any code. By utilizing visual interfaces and drag-and-drop features, it makes technology accessible to non-technical users.

An API (Application Programming Interface) consists of a set of rules and protocols for building and interacting with software applications. APIs facilitate communication between different software systems, allowing for integration across various services.

Workflow Automation** involves automating repetitive tasks within business processes through technology. No-code platforms typically provide tools that streamline workflows by connecting different applications and reducing manual effort.

A Data Pipeline is a sequence of data processing steps that includes collecting, transforming, and storing data for analysis or use in applications. Effective data pipelines ensure that clean, structured data flows seamlessly through various stages.

Natural Language Processing (NLP)** is an area of AI focused on enabling machines to interact with humans using natural language. NLP allows computers to understand, interpret, and respond to human language meaningfully.

A Chatbot is an AI-driven application designed to simulate conversations with human users through text or voice interactions. These bots can be integrated into websites or messaging apps to enhance customer service experiences.

The User Interface (UI) is the space where interactions between humans and machines take place. UI design prioritizes usability by creating intuitive layouts and visually appealing components that enhance the user experience.

User Experience (UX)** encompasses the overall experience a user has while interacting with a product or service. It considers every aspect of the user's interaction with a company's offerings and aims to boost satisfaction by improving usability and accessibility.

Data Annotation** involves labeling data so machine learning algorithms can learn from it more effectively. This practice is crucial for training models in supervised learning tasks, which require labeled input-output pairs.

Predictive Analytics** employs techniques to analyze current and historical data to make predictions about future events. In AI contexts, this often involves using algorithms to identify trends within large datasets for forecasting purposes.

Sentiment Analysis** uses NLP techniques to determine the emotional tone behind words. This analysis enables businesses to gauge public sentiment toward products or services by interpreting user feedback effectively.

Cross-Platform Compatibility** refers to the ability of software applications or tools to function seamlessly across different operating systems or environments without modification. This capability is essential in today's diverse tech landscape as users operate on multiple devices.

Ethical AI** focuses on developing artificial intelligence systems responsibly. It addresses concerns such as bias, privacy violations, transparency issues, and fairness in automated decisions made by AI agents.

Finally, Scalability describes a system's ability to manage increasing amounts of work or its potential for efficient growth. Scalable solutions adapt smoothly as demand increases without compromising performance.

Resource List for Further Learning

To gain a comprehensive understanding of no-code AI agents, it's essential to continue exploring beyond the pages of this book. Here, you'll find a carefully curated list of resources designed to enhance your knowledge, featuring a blend of online courses, books, communities, and tools. This selection provides pathways for ongoing learning and practical application, ensuring you remain engaged with the latest advancements in the field.

Begin your journey with online courses focused on no-code and AI concepts. Platforms such as Coursera and Udemy offer a variety of courses that delve into relevant subjects. Take this example, the "No-Code AI Development" course on Coursera equips learners with essential skills for building intelligent applications without coding. Another great option is Udacity's "Introduction to Artificial Intelligence," which offers foundational insights into AI technologies.

Books are invaluable companions on your quest for knowledge. Titles like "The Pragmatic Programmer" by Andrew Hunt and David Thomas foster a mindset beneficial for anyone interested in technology, extending beyond just coding. Meanwhile, "AI Superpowers" by Kai-Fu Lee provides crucial perspectives on how AI is reshaping industries worldwide—insights particularly relevant for those exploring no-code solutions.

Engaging with community forums can significantly enhance your learning experience. Platforms like Reddit's r/NoCode or the no-code section on Stack Overflow serve as rich repositories of information where you can ask questions and explore discussions with peers. Joining dedicated Discord servers for no-code development allows for real-time interactions, enabling you to share experiences, challenges, and tips with fellow enthusiasts.

Additionally, toolkits and resources designed specifically for no-code development can facilitate hands-on practice. Websites like Bubble or Adalo offer intuitive interfaces where users can drag and drop components to create applications without prior programming knowledge. Both platforms also provide tutorials to help you get started and deepen your understanding of building functional systems. Incorporating these tools into your routine will help solidify the concepts you've learned through theory.

Podcasts have also emerged as accessible educational formats worth exploring. Shows like "No Code No Problem" feature interviews with industry leaders who share insights on project development without traditional coding practices. These discussions provide real-world context and often introduce innovative use cases that may inspire your own projects.

Participating in webinars hosted by thought leaders in the field adds another dimension to your learning journey. Companies like Airtable frequently conduct sessions focused on maximizing their platforms' potential while seamlessly integrating AI capabilities into workflows.

Lastly, staying updated on industry trends is crucial for anyone looking to excel in no-code AI applications. Websites such as TechCrunch and Wired often feature articles highlighting innovations within the tech landscape. Subscribing to newsletters from organizations like The AI Alignment Forum keeps you informed about ethical considerations and emerging best practices.

By immersing yourself in this diverse array of resources, you'll not only reinforce what you've learned but also expand your perspective on how no-code solutions can evolve within the broader context of artificial intelligence technology. Engaging consistently with these materials will ensure you remain at the forefront of this dynamic field, ready to transform new insights into actionable projects that drive innovation forward.

Template and Checklists

Templates and checklists are invaluable tools for navigating the world of no-code AI agents. They provide a structured framework that streamlines processes, ensuring essential steps aren't overlooked while still allowing for flexibility and creativity in your projects. For those new to building AI solutions, templates can significantly enhance efficiency by offering a reliable starting point.

When starting a project, it's beneficial to use a project template specifically designed for AI agent development. A well-structured template typically includes sections for defining objectives, outlining key functionalities, and identifying target users. For example, a basic project template might have headings such as "Project Title," "Objective," "Key Features," and "Target Audience." Completing these sections clarifies your vision from the beginning, reducing ambiguity as you progress.

Once you have a solid foundation, shift your focus to a checklist tailored for the development process of your AI agent. This checklist can cover all stages, from initial brainstorming to deployment. Take this example, during the brainstorming phase, you might include items like "Define user pain points," "Research existing solutions," and "Identify key performance indicators." This careful approach ensures that every aspect of your project is considered, promoting thoroughness throughout the development lifecycle.

As you move from planning to execution, leverage templates for specific components of your AI agent's functionality. If you're designing workflows or interactions within your application, templates that outline common user scenarios can be particularly helpful. Consider creating a workflow template with sections dedicated to triggers (what initiates an action), actions (what the agent does), and outcomes (the expected results). This visual representation of interactions not only clarifies processes but also simplifies the refinement of complex tasks into manageable steps.

Quality assurance is crucial when launching an AI agent, making a dedicated testing checklist an essential component of your toolkit. Your testing checklist might include items such as "Test all user interactions," "Check API integrations," and "Validate data processing accuracy." This meticulous attention to detail helps mitigate potential errors that could arise post-launch.

Additionally, it's important to incorporate feedback loops within your templates and checklists. Including a section for feedback collection can guide ongoing improvements after deployment. Take this example, you might include questions in your feedback form that address usability issues or additional features users would like to see. Gathering this information systematically allows for effective iterations on your designs.

Integrating performance metrics into your checklists is another way to evaluate the success of your AI agent after launch. Create sections that outline key performance indicators related to user engagement or efficiency gains— metrics like response time or user satisfaction ratings will provide valuable data for informing future iterations.

Lastly, maintain flexibility in how you utilize these templates and checklists. While they serve as excellent foundations, adapting them to meet specific project requirements is essential for fostering creativity and innovation. The ability to tweak standard templates allows you to align them closely with unique project demands while retaining their foundational structure.

By incorporating these tools into your workflow for developing no-code AI agents, you'll establish an organized approach that enhances both productivity and creativity. With each new project, you'll find yourself relying on this rich repository of resources not only for consistency but also as springboards into new realms of exploration and capability within the expansive landscape of no-code solutions.

Community and Support Forums

Community and support forums have become essential resources in the realm of no-code AI agents. These platforms foster collaboration among users and serve as valuable repositories of shared knowledge, experiences, and solutions. As you embark on your journey into no-code AI, engaging with these communities can significantly accelerate your learning curve and improve your project outcomes.

Participating in community discussions provides real-time insights into common challenges and innovative solutions. Platforms like Stack Overflow and specialized groups such as the No-Code Founders community allow users to ask questions, celebrate their successes, and seek advice on technical hurdles. By connecting with experienced developers and fellow enthusiasts, you can discover pathways you may not have considered, turning seemingly insurmountable problems into manageable tasks. Hearing firsthand accounts from others who have faced similar obstacles can boost your confidence as you tackle your own projects.

Support forums often feature user-generated tutorials that break down complex topics related to no-code platforms and AI functionalities. This peer-to-peer learning is especially valuable when you're trying to grasp new tools or methodologies. Imagine discovering a detailed post where a user outlines their entire process for creating an AI-driven chatbot—from initial concept to deployment—complete with screenshots and snippets of workflows. Such resources not only clarify the steps involved but also showcase best practices that you can apply directly to your own work.

Beyond troubleshooting technical issues, these communities emphasize the importance of feedback loops—an essential concept for the iterative improvement of your AI agents. After launching a new feature, sharing it in a forum can generate valuable feedback that you might otherwise overlook. Other users may offer insights into usability that could enhance how your agent interacts with end-users or suggest improvements that elevate its functionality beyond your initial vision.

Networking within these forums is another critical aspect of community involvement. Building relationships can connect you with potential collaborators or mentors who share similar interests or expertise. You may encounter someone skilled in integrating APIs who can help you overcome a specific challenge or a peer eager to co-develop a project. These connections often lead to fruitful partnerships that amplify the impact of your work.

Engaging with community-driven projects can also ignite ideas for unique applications of no-code AI agents. Many forums highlight challenges or hackathons where users collaboratively innovate around themes such as enhancing educational tools with AI or improving customer service experiences through automation. Participating in these initiatives encourages creative thinking and keeps you at the forefront of emerging trends within the field.

As you immerse yourself in these support networks, remember to give back by sharing your insights and experiences as you gain knowledge. Writing a post about a breakthrough you've had with a particular tool reinforces your understanding while helping others who may face similar challenges in the future. This cycle of knowledge exchange strengthens the entire ecosystem.

Regular engagement with community forums enriches your journey through no-code AI development. The collaborative spirit not only empowers individuals but fosters an inclusive environment where learning flourishes amidst diverse perspectives. As you navigate this vibrant tapestry of ideas and solutions, you'll realize that innovation transcends technology; it thrives on the collective effort of people coming together to push boundaries and explore new frontiers.

Harnessing this collective wisdom transforms challenges into opportunities, enabling participants—regardless of their coding background—to create impactful AI agents that effectively address real-world needs. Through community engagement, you're not just building technology; you're contributing to an evolving narrative where everyone plays a role in shaping the future of no-code solutions together.

References and Bibliography

In the world of no-code AI, referencing credible sources is essential. A well-curated bibliography not only supports your work but also deepens your understanding of the subject. Insights gleaned from reputable texts, articles, and studies create a solid foundation that enhances your projects and bolsters your credibility within the community.

A key resource for those venturing into no-code development is "No-Code: The Future of Software Development" by Thomas E. Fuchs. This book offers a thorough overview of no-code platforms, complete with practical examples and case studies demonstrating their effectiveness across various industries. Fuchs underscores the significance of accessibility in technology and illustrates how no-code solutions are transforming traditional workflows.

For artificial intelligence, "Artificial Intelligence: A Guide to Intelligent Systems" by Michael Negnevitsky provides essential knowledge for integrating AI into no-code frameworks. Negnevitsky presents foundational concepts such as machine learning, neural networks, and data mining in an accessible manner, making it an excellent primer for newcomers to the field. Understanding these principles is crucial for developing effective AI agents.

Online platforms also serve as invaluable resources. Take this example, websites like Towards Data Science on Medium host a rich array of articles discussing current trends in AI and no-code development. Contributors often share personal experiences with various tools and methodologies, offering insights that may not be found in traditional literature. Engaging with these articles can inspire innovative ideas and strategies for your own projects.

Additionally, academic journals such as the Journal of Artificial Intelligence Research publish peer-reviewed articles that explore cutting-edge developments in AI technologies. These articles delve into both theoretical aspects and practical applications, providing a deeper understanding and encouraging critical thinking about the ethical implications of AI deployment.

To further broaden your knowledge, communities dedicated to no-code solutions often compile lists of recommended readings. For example, NoCode.tech features a curated selection of books, articles, and tutorials tailored for aspiring no-code developers. Engaging with these resources keeps you informed about industry standards and best practices.

And, online courses can complement your learning by providing both foundational knowledge and skill enhancement. Platforms like Coursera and Udacity offer courses specifically focused on no-code development and AI applications. Participating in these courses allows you to engage in structured learning environments where interaction with instructors and peers fosters deeper discussions about the material.

When compiling your references, it's important to consider both depth and breadth. Include seminal works that lay the groundwork for your understanding alongside contemporary studies that reflect the latest innovations in the field. Striking a balance between theoretical texts and practical guides ensures a holistic approach to your research.

Finally, remember that references are not merely a checklist at the end of a project; they represent an ongoing conversation within the community. Regularly updating your bibliography with new findings keeps your work relevant and connects you with others who share similar interests or goals. As you navigate the evolving landscape of no-code AI development, leveraging these resources will not only enhance your projects but also contribute meaningfully to the broader discourse surrounding technology's future.

Building a robust references section establishes credibility for both you and your projects while fostering a culture of continuous learning and collaboration in the rapidly growing field of no-code AI agents. Embrace this journey— every citation is a step toward greater understanding and innovation in this exciting domain.

INDEX

C reating a comprehensive index is essential for any book, especially one as multifaceted as this one on no-code AI agents. An index serves as a navigational tool, guiding readers to specific topics and insights they seek. It goes beyond being a mere list of keywords; it is an organized collection of concepts that captures the depth and breadth of the content covered.

To begin compiling your index, carefully consider the key terms and themes that emerge throughout the book. Foundational concepts such as "AI Agents," "No-Code Platforms," and "Data Management" should be readily accessible. Each term should link to relevant pages or sections where readers can explore discussions or examples. This facilitates quick reference, enhancing the reader's experience and allowing them to dive into specific topics without having to sift through entire chapters.

As you create your entries, consider incorporating various formats—such as sub-entries—that provide clarity and context. Take this example, under "AI Agents," you might include subdivisions like "Types," "Applications," and "Success Stories." This hierarchical structure not only organizes information but also serves as a roadmap for readers seeking to deepen their understanding in specific areas.

It's equally important that your index reflects the real-world applications discussed in the text. If you've explored case studies showcasing successful implementations across different industries, be sure to include those industry names in the index. This approach reinforces the practical relevance of your content and connects theoretical insights with tangible outcomes.

Don't overlook common terminologies associated with no-code platforms and AI technologies. Including terms like "API Integrations," "User Experience," and broader categories such as "Ethics in AI" will help facilitate navigation through complex discussions surrounding responsible AI usage and technological advancements.

As you finalize your index, keep accessibility in mind for diverse audiences—those familiar with technology and those just beginning their journey into no-code solutions. Using clear language and avoiding overly technical jargon ensures that everyone can benefit from this resource.

Regularly updating the index as new sections are added or revised during the editing process is crucial for maintaining its accuracy. A robust index is not static; it evolves alongside your text, adapting to reflect any enhancements or changes made along the way.

an effective index enriches your book by transforming it into a user-friendly resource that empowers readers to engage deeply with the material. It acts as a bridge connecting them to invaluable insights while encouraging exploration beyond what they may initially set out to discover. By investing time into crafting a thoughtful and comprehensive index, you enhance both the usability of your book and its overall impact within the no-code AI community.

The structure above uses non-uniform chapters to give readers a paced learning journey through the process of building no-code AI agents, incorporating various aspects from setup to scaling and future development.

This book is organized to take you on a progressive journey, enabling you to understand the concepts of no-code AI agents in a structured yet flexible way. Each chapter builds on the previous one, seamlessly integrating insights and practical applications that empower you to create intelligent systems without writing a single line of code.

We begin with foundational chapters that introduce the core principles behind no-code platforms and AI agents. Here, you'll explore their evolution, how they democratize technology, and the various types of AI agents available. This groundwork is essential, as it establishes a shared language and understanding of both the capabilities and limitations of these systems.

As we move forward, the focus shifts to practical applications and real-world examples that highlight how no-code solutions are being utilized across different industries. These case studies not only provide inspiration but also serve as concrete evidence of how organizations have successfully implemented no-code AI solutions to drive efficiency, enhance customer experiences, and foster innovation. The stories of these implementations create a rich backdrop against which you can evaluate your own ideas for potential use cases.

The structure of the book is intentionally diverse; some chapters concentrate on specific tools while others explore broader themes such as data management or user experience enhancement. This variety keeps you engaged, allowing for smooth transitions between high-level strategic thinking and detailed, hands-on technical guidance. Take this example, when you reach the chapter on data preparation, you will learn techniques for cleaning and preprocessing your datasets —essential skills for ensuring optimal performance of your AI agents.

Each section not only details practical steps but also reflects on lessons learned from both successes and setbacks. By examining what went wrong in certain projects alongside what thrived, you'll gain valuable insights into best practices as well as pitfalls to avoid. This dual perspective enriches your understanding and equips you to tackle real-world challenges effectively.

A recurring theme throughout the book is the emphasis on user-centric design principles. You'll discover how to create interfaces that not only meet functional requirements but also enhance user satisfaction and engagement. This approach reinforces the idea that technology should serve people, making intelligent systems more accessible and enjoyable to use.

As we delve into advanced topics such as automated decision-making and integrating AI agents with existing systems, the discussions will focus on scalability and adaptability. These insights will prepare you for future-proofing your projects as technology continues to evolve and new challenges emerge.

this structured yet flexible journey culminates in a comprehensive toolkit for creating no-code AI agents tailored to your specific needs. By interweaving theoretical concepts with practical applications throughout the chapters, this book aims not just to inform but also to inspire action —empowering you to embark on your own projects with confidence and creativity.

In this dynamic landscape of no-code solutions and AI, effectively leveraging these technologies is crucial. By guiding you through each step—from conceptualization to implementation—you'll be well-equipped to navigate this exciting domain without any prior coding experience. This guarantees that anyone with curiosity can actively participate in shaping the future of technology.

www.ingramcontent.com/pod-product-compliance
Lightning Source LLC
LaVergne TN
LVHW051221050326
832903LV00028B/2189